THE HO
MODEL RAILROADING
HANDBOOK

REVISED EDITION

THE HO
MODEL RAILROADING
HANDBOOK

Robert Schleicher

CHILTON BOOK COMPANY
Radnor, Pennsylvania

Copyright © 1992, 1983, 1979 by Robert Schleicher
Revised Edition   All Rights Reserved
Published in Radnor, Pennsylvania 19089, by Chilton Book Company
First edition published under the title Tyco® Model Railroad Manual

No part of this book may be reproduced, transmitted or stored
in any form or by any means, electronic or mechanical,
without prior written permission from the publisher

The owner of this book may make photocopies of illustrations as an aid
to modelmaking, but may not distribute or sell copies to others

Front cover: A pair of Atlas diesels, with added details
and new paint and decals, on Dick Trotter's Coyote Pass Railroad

Manufactured in the United States of America

Library of Congress Cataloging in Publication Data
Schleicher, Robert H.
    The HO model railroading handbook/Robert Schleicher.—Rev. ed.
        p.   cm.
    Includes index.
    ISBN 0-8019-8346-0 (pbk.)
    1. Railroads—Models. I. Title.
TF197.S337   1992
625.1′9—dc20   92-53147
                                                              CIP

1 2 3 4 5 6 7 8 9 0   1 0 9 8 7 6 5 4 3 2

Contents

PART III Tools and Techniques

PART IV Scenery and Buildings

PART V Miniature Empires in Action

PART I

Getting Started

CHAPTER 1

Model Railroading

THE ONLY DIFFERENCE between a set of toy trains and a real railroad in miniature is your own state of mind. If that surprises you, you are not alone. If you thought the difference between the two might be the scenery, the number of track switches, or the size of the layout, you are right, because that's the way it appears to the eye. When you look at the illustrations on these pages and in model railroading catalogs and magazines, you will see all the things that can make a model railroad. Even the most realistic layout can still be seen as a toy train set if those who built it and operate it think of it as only an adult toy or a grownup plaything. That is why your state of mind is important. If you become totally involved, if you can convince yourself that you are creating and operating a real railroad in miniature, then you really are doing just that. Of course your particular railroad will not have many of the problems that a real one has, so in a sense it's still a model. But keep in mind that it can be a "perfect" model, or replica, of the real thing.

Creating a real railroad in miniature is an art. Just like any other art form, such as painting or sculpture, it requires skill and imagination. In effect, you become an artist because your technique and style combine to establish your own personal signature. In this book you will find explanations, descriptions, and advice on how to apply exactly the art of model railroading to your toy trains and how to create a layout that is fine enough to be classified as art.

A Brief History of the Hobby

Model railroading has been a hobby for at least as long as toy trains have been made, and that's more than one hundred years! Tens of thousands of true railroads in miniature have been built during that time, and the men and women who built them have learned some very cunning tricks. Many of those tricks are collected and described for you on these pages.

The pioneer model railroaders had a difficult time because they had to go through the painstaking process of building every piece of their railroads. Imagine how few part-time artists there would be if they had to make their own paints and stretch their own canvases.

The Early Model Railroaders

Although the greatest advances in the art of model railroading have occurred during the last fifty years, lessons have been made

Fig. 1–1. The romance of real railroading. A great Western Railroad train struggles upgrade on the frontal range of the Rockies, circa 1955. (Photo from the collection of H. K. Vollrath.)

available to almost anyone only during the last twenty years or so. The early model railroaders had no publications to turn to for advice except those books and magazines that described the real railroads of the time. Most of the clever adaptations of real railroading to our miniature railroads were first used and perfected in the 1930s. That aspect of the "art" of model railroading, then, is not really new; but it is new in that it is finally being rediscovered by hobbyists and craftspeople. The few really clever model railroaders of the 1930s devised most of the methods of operating their miniature trains like real ones because there was no other source of "advice" except that offered to and about the real railroads. The concept of using insulating gaps to allow two-rail track like the real railroads, rather than the toy trains' three rails, was also developed then, as were switching

operations and timetables and a host of other model railroading methods and concepts.

Much of the realism we take for granted today was developed by several modelers who used museum dioramas as their inspiration. The museum models were among the few that were built with everything to the same scale. In other words, the people were matched in proportion to the size of the trees and the doors in the buildings and in the passenger cars. The proportions of a "scale" model are virtually identical to those of the real thing. These early modelers were the first ones to make a model railroad appear to be realistic to the eye.

"Model" Versus Real

Very few model railroads in the 1930s either looked or operated like real railroads. It was so difficult to build a scale model with the right proportions that most of those modelers didn't have enough time, energy, or inspiration left to operate their models like the real thing. However, a number of other modelers were operating their three-rail toy train sets almost exactly like they were real railroads. Men like the late Watson House, John Page, Minton Cronkite, Al Kalmbach, Harry Bondurant, and Linn Westcott ran trains over their three-rail layouts with switching and timetable operations that were almost identical to the real thing. It was the late Frank Ellison, however, who was one of the first model railroaders to combine the art of running a model railroad as though it were real and the art of true scale miniatures into one system. Mr. Ellison was also the first to describe it in the model railroad books and magazines published just before and after World War II. And it was he who made model railroaders aware that they were indeed practicing the art of railroading in miniature; but even he was not willing to share with his readers the true significance of the painting or sculpturelike quality of the hobby that can make it a true art form as well.

Plastic Trains

The real breakthrough in technology, which allowed almost anyone to enjoy the art of railroading in miniature, came with the much maligned plastic models in the late 1950s. In the preplastic age, it took about a week's worth of evenings to build every car or every structure, and it often took a month to assemble a locomotive. The alternatives were relatively expensive brass models or the ready-to-run "toy" trains. Plastics allowed the manufacturer to include even more detail than the many wood and metal model kits that were sold ready-to-run or the kits that could be assembled in two or three evenings. The use of plastic also allowed the manufacturers to produce more of their products in

less time, so the selling price was lower. These lower prices resulted in even more sales, and that, in turn, resulted in even lower prices. Even at today's inflation-boosted prices, you can buy a complete ready-to-run train set for less than the price of a single locomotive in the 1950s, and the locomotive and cars in that set look more like the real thing, run more like the real thing, and are more reliable than most hand-assembled kits.

Kits and Ready-Built Models

The availability of inexpensive kits and ready-built model railroad products allowed almost every model railroader the time to construct a truly artistic setting for his realistic models and time to operate his layout in miniature like a real railroad. Space, rather than time or skill, became more of a limiting factor to the creation of a miniature railroad empire. Fortunately, the experience of other model railroaders, together with the reliability of small-scale models, such as HO-scale miniatures, has even solved the space problem. The compact "shelf" layout designs, larger layouts that can be disassembled for moving, and the efficient use of space to allow the creation of a true "empire" in an area as small as 4 × 8 feet have made model railroading a hobby that is accessible to everyone.

Keep It Simple

Today, anyone can practice the art of model railroading. The incredible array of inexpensive products and easy-to-learn techniques give you a freedom to concentrate on whatever aspect of the hobby you find most pleasing. You can, for example, assemble just a few simple building kits and use ready-built structures in order to have more time to enjoy the actual operation of the set or for adding more details to the scenery.

Please do *not* feel that you must master

Fig. 1–2. What was once only a Christmastime toy can become a real railroad in miniature.

Fig. 1–3. The Burlington Northern layout (Chapter 16) is just one example of what a "complete" model railroad might look like.

every technique in this book in order to build a model railroad. Most chapters include enough information so you can "specialize" in that area of the hobby with just a touch of the techniques from the other chapters applied to those areas of your miniature railroad. The locomotives, rolling stock, trackwork, wiring, structures, and scenery on the 9 × 9-foot layout in Chapter 16 appear throughout the book, but they are included only as examples, with the layout itself as an example that combines all the elements of the hobby into a balanced whole. It should take an experienced model railroader at least two years to build a layout to the state of completion you see in the illustrations; however, most of us would want to take even more time for such a project. The goal of any model railroader is to have fun first and foremost; and the "old-timers" are those who are wise enough to know that their layouts will really never be finished.

Tackling the Project

Don't be appalled at the thought that a model railroad is a project with no end; in fact, this aspect is what makes this hobby so exciting and rewarding. A model railroad is

Fig. 1–4. Constructed from Life-Like's expanded-foam layouts, this scene has additional trees and ground foam texture for realism. (Courtesy, Life-Like Products.)

truly a growing and living thing. When it stops growing, most model railroaders tear the layout apart and start another, building on the lessons and experience they collected from that first creation. Every genuine model railroader has built at least two layouts for whatever reason or excuse he or she cares to offer. One of the most valuable lessons this book can provide, then, is that your first model railroad be for "practice." The practice layout is the one you can use to try, at the very least, some of the techniques and tips from every chapter of this book. Then you'll know which ones you like and which ones you would rather touch on lightly.

A Good Eye View

It's difficult, indeed, to convince even yourself that you're not playing with trains when you're crawling around on your hands and knees chasing little trains around the floor. It's also very hard on the equipment, because the floor is the final resting place for every bit of dust, lint, and debris in the room, and those oil-coated gears can pick up and absorb every particle. Dust and lint also land on the track itself and form an insulation layer that not only stops the flow of electricity but also the progress of the "noon freight."

You can purchase a $\frac{1}{2}$-inch-thick piece of "C-C grade" 4 × 8-foot plywood, a $\frac{1}{2}$-inch 4 × 8-foot piece of Homosote, and four screw-on legs or 2 × 4s and sawhorse brackets for about the price of a train set. I recommend the sawhorse brackets and 2 × 4s because they'll allow you to raise the layout all the way to your chest, which is where it belongs. Most of the screw-on table legs are

Fig. 1–5. You can duplicate the realism of car-loading with the Tyco "action" cars or with the "Loads-In Empties-Out" track arrangement in Chapter 15.

Fig. 1–6. The boom and hook are operated by cranks, while the searchlight actually lights and swivels on Bachmann's models.

Fig. 1–7. The "Waybill System" of operation (Chapter 15) allows every car to carry a load just like the real railroads' cars.

so short that they'll only lift a 4 × 8 piece of plywood to your waist, and that's really only half the way "up" from toy train to miniature railroad. Chest-height is close enough to the eye level for viewing real trains to make that viewing angle possible with just a slight bend at your knees. The layout is still low enough, however, so you can see it all and, of more importance, reach at least half-way across the table. Position the 4 × 8 layout so you can reach at least three sides. Any attempts to reach across a four-foot miniature railroad will only result in a very sore back or some very flattened models. The plywood and the 2 × 4s can be used (recycled) on your next layout too, so nothing will be wasted.

Building an Empire

This "practice model railroad" empire in 4 × 8 feet will also need at least two turnouts (switches) and a few pieces of track in addition to the circle or oval supplied with most sets. Bargain packs of track that often include a pair of turnouts and some extra track section make that purchase a simple one. You can use the plans that come with the pack of track and turnouts or you can use one of those described in Chapter 3 if you want something more complex than an oval with a couple of stub-end sidings. It's your model railroad; if a simple track plan suits your fancy, then stick to it and spend some extra time on the trains themselves, on structures, on scenery, or just in perfecting your knowledge of operations. The advice of a half-century's worth of model railroaders' mistakes is valuable, so try everything in every chapter of this book on your 4 × 8-foot layout.

For instance, don't assume that you dislike real railroad operation until you've tried it, and don't think fashioning scenery is "too hard" until you spend an afternoon with plaster and paper towels. You might want to skip the steps needed for two-train operation, particu-

Fig. 1–8. Modern Railroads are romantic; a GP–20 leads a string of locomotives at the head of this freight near Chicago. (Burlington Northern photograph.)

Fig. 1–9. All locomotives and passenger cars shown are Great Northern Railroad replicas from most of the r-t-r brands.

larly if you've decided on a simple track plan with two or three turnouts. Do try the "walk-around" control system, though, so you can see what it feels like to stay with your train rather than just watching it come and go. Try it all and you'll have the confidence to build that second model railroad to the "perfect-ion" level you'd promised yourself for the first layout.

Model railroading is one hobby where you can only learn by doing; all I can do for you is to show you the easiest possible methods and some typical results to serve as "models" for you to use when judging how good a modeler you are becoming and will become over the months and years ahead.

Do's and Don'ts for New Model Railroaders

Do mount all track on a tabletop, even if the tabletop rests on the floor.

Don't try to operate HO scale trains on track resting on bare floors or carpets; there's just too much dust, dirt and lint to allow reliable operation of the trains.

Do try to imagine that the trains are real and operate them at the relatively slow speeds of real trains. This will increase both the realism of the scene and the illusion of having a larger layout.

Don't try to operate trains—even passenger trains—as though they were racing cars.

Do try to limit your purchases of locomotives to 8-wheeled or smaller diesels and 40-scale-foot or shorter freight cars if you have only 4 × 8 feet or less of layout space. The shorter equipment looks more realistic on the tight curves.

Don't purchase 12-wheeled or larger diesels, 50-scale-foot-long freight cars, or 80-scale-foot passenger cars for a 4 × 8-foot layout. Save them for the time when you can have an around-the-wall layout with 30-inch or larger radius curves.

Do lay the track directly onto the tabletop or roadbed, with no up or down grades for the first layout you build.

Don't use the over-and-under trestle sets on any model railroad. The steep up- and downhill grades cause derailments, and the track is both unstable and toylike.

Do create your own world or copy a real one— duplicate reality or create a fantasy, or combine fantasy and reality. Remind yourself, if you must, that *this is fun!*

Don't take model railroading so seriously that it becomes a task or chore with unreasonably high standards of fidelity to prototype or detail.

Do keep that first layout simple, with no more than six turnouts and no reversing loops or other track configurations that can cause wiring complications.

Don't try to build the more complex layouts on your first try. Consider that first layout a practice run and just enjoy trying anything.

Do build any layout with strong enough benchwork or tables so you can add or delete entire sections of track without destroying the remainder of the layout.

Don't ever consider a layout to be finished or so perfect that you are not willing to change it. Even the real railroads change track alignments and locations as their equipment and traffic change.

CHAPTER 2

Inspiration

AMERICA LOVES TRAINS. They are a large and romantic part of the American heritage, and they remain in our history books—if not completely in contemporary American life—to remind us how our nation grew and expanded westward in years past. Trains were the key that opened the great American West. The sight of mountainsize, monolithic cubicles zigging and zagging down a twisting and turning stretch of track, guided by only those tiny flanges, is awe inspiring. A train is so tall, so wide, and so infinitely long that it almost seems to be more a part of nature than a man-made contrivance. The train is truly more of a symbol than the eagle of everything that is America. If you stand a few feet from a passing train, you cannot help but have an emotional experience. A train can carry you a few miles or it can take you across the country, but time and distance are merely relative. Many Americans' fondest memories are of spending nights in berths of trains while the country clickety-clacked its way beneath them, or of having meals in the dining car while watching the panorama of America—the cities and wheatfields, small towns or huge mountain ranges—or of just stand-

ing in the protection of dad's huge hand while the earth shook under the might of a passing locomotive. It doesn't even matter whether or not you have taken a trip on a train, for no doubt almost every person feels some trace of nostalgia about trains.

Toy Trains

Toy trains also can evoke a feeling of love from a person, particularly a young person. There's something very exciting about a string of brightly colored cars following that engine wherever those two shiny steel rails might lead it. And it's thrilling in a way that's completely different from the experience of watching a real train. A toy train is one of the few toys that duplicates real life with the fairyland of action and color and the fantasies of adventure. A toy train is the dream of real railroading brought to life, and it can be as lovable as a bear cub, even if the real thing may be as frightening as a grizzly bear. Because toy trains are a kind of living magic, it is almost impossible not to love them.

Romance and Adventure

Model railroading combines the "lovable" aspects of real-life railroading with all the charm of the toy train. No wonder it's one of the most popular hobbies today. What else can make dreams come alive in three dimen-

Fig. 2–1. Compare this view of stock trains with the weathered rolling stock on the following pages.

Fig. 2–2. Weathered equipment, bridges, roads, and rivers add to the reality—and romance—of real railroading in miniature.

Fig. 2–3. The real railroads powered old trolleys with gasoline engines for one-car, branch-line passenger-train service.

sions, and in living color and action? The hard work of real railroading can be ignored to include the movements and environment that are the rewards of that work. Model railroading, in the best sense of any art, captures only the romance of real railroading. The model railroad world is that absolutely perfect environment we can only dream of in our day-to-day lives. As a world, it's a wondrous place to escape to, and it offers what television and books can only promise. The model railroad world, however, is one that demands the involvement of the builder. This is a participatory pastime. In modern terms, model railroading is similar to watching three-dimensional television, where the sets, the actors, and the scripts are created by the viewer.

In some ways, you really can bring dreams to life.

The Magic World of Model Railroading

A magician is one who makes dreams of the impossible appear to be not just possible, but probable. He creates the illusion through the power of suggestion that you are, indeed, seeing what you would like to see. The model railroader needs a very similar bag of tricks to make his or her toy trains appear so realistic that they invoke the feelings we have for both real railroads and for toy trains. Many of the illustrations on these pages, and particularly

Fig. 2–4. The "magic" of a mirror doubles the apparent size of the town of "Alliance" on the Burlington Northern layout in Chapter 16.

Fig. 2–5. Most freights begin their trips in the "Alliance" yard. Our diesel-powered pedlar is scheduled out ahead of the steam-powered freight.

those in the color section, are supposed to do just that: to give the impression of real railroading without losing the hint, at least, that the models began as toys. The effect that should be achieved on a model railroad is the same one that is created at Disneyland or Disney World, where you imagine you are boating through real caverns at the same time you know you are surrounded by only toy figures.

It is very easy to get carried away with the idea that you are running a real railroad, because you are using real railroad freight bills and order forms and much of the stuff that makes running a real railroad a job. Model railroading should be more than a job, it should be fun (and it is, even for me). The experienced model railroader often gets caught up in his own act, so to speak, and will build a few cars or structures that literally have every board and bolt and rivet that was on the real thing. This "expert," caught in the whirlpool of realism, finds he cannot make his entire model railroad totally realistic and still find time to run it. Model railroading is fun when you can achieve a balance between realism and operation. You may like one more than the other, but don't let yourself get so involved in building that you don't have time to operate, or, conversely, don't get so caught up in its operation that you don't have

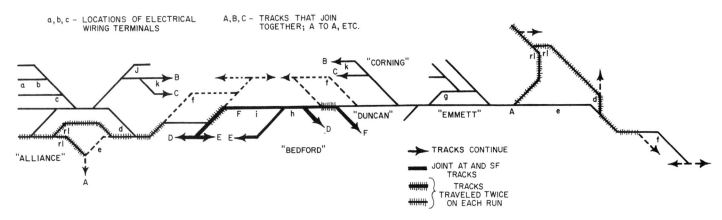

Fig. 2–6. The trackage on the Burlington Northern can be traveled in a point-to-point route that duplicates the stops made by a real railroad.

time to create a reasonably realistic "world" for those operations.

This book is similar to magic books in that it reveals the "secrets" you need to create the illusion that your toy trains really are real ones. If you follow the examples you see here, you'll find you can capture that romantic thrill of real railroading, and it's no more "magical" than the stage magician's magic.

I have included the methods for making miniatures of real railroads and their surroundings that use easy-to-find and inexpensive materials. More complicated and more expensive ways of making locomotives, cars, buildings, scenery, and wiring are included in *The Model Railroading Handbook,* Volume I (published by Chilton Book Co.), as well as a dozen or so other examples of model railroads. If you like to build scenery so much that you want every possible alternative to the methods in Chapter 13, then you might want to purchase this volume from your book store, toy store, or hobby dealer.

The Apprentice Model Railroader

You cannot learn to build or to operate a model railroad by just reading one, two, three, or even a dozen books; you can learn only by applying the basic lessons to your own model railroad. Everything about model railroading falls into the learn-by-doing category. I have tried to show the simplest possible ways of doing everything you'll want to do to create a real railroad in miniature. I have also been particularly careful to select materials that are both inexpensive and readily obtainable in toy, lumber, hardware, and craft stores or departments. You can obtain those materials for yourself and use them in the ways you see on these pages. Nobody was ever a "born" model railroader; each of us has to practice the simple techniques for painting, weather-

ing, track laying, wiring, and the like to teach ourselves how to do it.

All the photographs in the book, with the exception of those of real railroads, were taken in my own workshop. The model railroad photos with scenery were taken on the 9 × 9-foot Burlington Northern layout illustrated in Chapter 16 and on other home layouts. There are no contest winners here, just "average" models that have been assembled and painted by "average" model railroaders especially for this book. Frankly, the layout in Chapter 16 is far too complex for a beginner or even for a group or "club" of beginners; rather it is one you should consider as a "dream" layout that you could try for your second or third model railroad. Any of the buildings on that layout and all the scenery and wiring and operation ideas can be applied to the simpler 4 × 8-foot layouts in Chapter 3. The technique of running trains around one or two ovals or a figure eight connecting one siding with the next, via rail, is another that can be used on any layout. Real railroads connect one town with another; a model railroad can "connect" one siding with another and each of them can be called a "town" to effectively match the function of a real railroad.

Think Small

A completely finished and detailed layout like the one in Chapter 16 is the dream or goal of most model railroaders. Before I discuss "how" to create a layout like that, it would be helpful to see just what a railroad in miniature might be like.

HO Scale

Imagine that you're an HO-scale person, which means you're only 1/87 of your own size. You might wonder, at this point, *Why HO scale?* HO scale is by far the most popular scale for model railroading; more than 80

Fig. 2–7. The train stops at "Bedford" to find out if any trains are scheduled on the Santa Fe interchange track into the tunnel.

percent of the hobbyists build in that scale. The only other scales that have more than five percent of the 300,000 or so model railroaders' attention are N scale (1/160 the size of the real thing), O scale (1/45 to 1/48 the size of the real thing) and G scale (also called Gauge 1, approximately 1/24 scale).

N Scale

The tiny N-scale locomotives and cars are fine if you want to run very long trains, because they do allow you to capture the "train" aspect of real railroading in a relatively small space. It is difficult to keep the track and wheels clean enough for stall-free operation in N scale, and the price of cars and locomo- tives may be as much as double those you see on these pages. The proportions of N-scale equipment are not as close a match for the real thing either; the rails and wheel flanges are several times too large, and the distance between coupled cars is far too great. The size of N-scale models, relative to your size, makes it advisable to build layouts large enough for long trains; an N-scale version of the Burlington Northern "empire" should be at least the same size as the 9 × 9-foot HO-scale version.

O Scale

O scale is primarily for experienced model- ers who like to build much of their equipment

Fig. 2–8. The train enroute from "Alliance" to "Points East" travels past the "Duncan Grain Elevator" twice, but not on the same tracks.

from small parts and from "scratch" (raw wood, metal, and plastic). There are very few O-scale ready-to-run items, so the O-scale model railroader is virtually forced to spend a large proportion of his or her time just assembling models. O scale is only twice the linear size of HO, but it takes up four times the surface area and eight times the volume. An O-scale version of the Burlington Northern layout would completely fill a two-car garage. The cost of the wood, plaster, track, and rolling stock could easily be eight times that of the HO-scale layout, and the construction time might well be proportionally longer. HO-scale models generally have as much visible detail to the naked eye as O-scale models,

and HO models are small enough to allow an "empire" in a space about equal to that needed for an N-scale layout. If you're cramped for space, then build a small shelf-style layout, such as those in Chapter 16, rather than going into N scale. If you like the bulk of O scale, then raise your layout to eye level and you'll find HO-scale equipment looks quite large enough.

"Alliance" to "Emmett," All Aboard

You can follow our trip by train from "Alliance" to "Emmett" over an imaginary branch of the Burlington Northern by looking at the illustrations in the color section. A "satellite" view of the layout and a track plan is illustrated in Figure 16–4 in Chapter 16, and a schematic diagram of the route is included in this chapter. Both should provide more than enough "reality" to allow your imagination to "see" what real railroading in miniature is all about. Use the schematic diagram in conjunction with the track plan in Chapter 16 (make a photocopy if you need to) and you will be able to see which direction our train must take at each switch in order to travel over a two-loop layout as though it were stretched out like a string connecting towns imaginary miles apart. Our train will travel very briefly over the crossed lines on the schematic diagram twice in its journey over the "road"; with the exception of those few feet of track, our flanged wheels will pass over the same rails only once as we travel from "Alliance" to "Emmett" on the Burlington Northern.

An Imaginary Journey

Imagine the town of "Alliance" as a place that might have a population of 30,000 people. It could be located in any state. Imagine it in southern Illinois if you wish, but it could be anywhere, with a simple change of railroad names and colors on the locomotives. "Alliance" is a center of small manufacturing plants and feed mills. It is also a collection point for towns from miles around to load and unload trailers from "piggyback" flat cars and other lcl (less than carload) freight at the "American Express Co." plant or at the "Alliance Freight Station" and its "team track." Concrete pipe and other construction materials, fuel, seed, and lumber for the furniture factory are just a few of the commodities that arrive in "Alliance" by rail.

An endless string of coal-filled hopper cars are emptied at the electrical power-gen-

Fig. 2–9. The second trip past the "Duncan Grain Elevator" routes the train toward the switch back to the "Corning Mine."

Fig. 2–10. The green Burlington Northern boxcar will have to be pushed ahead of our locomotive so that we can take the siding to let the Amtrak local onto the main line out of "Emmett."

erating "Alliance Company" plant on the outside of the town. The Burlington Northern has a connection or interchange with the Union Pacific just far enough away (track "j") from town to keep the Union Pacific from serving local industry. There is also an engine house, fuel-oil facility, water tower (left over from the days of steam), and sand house at "Alliance" to service the locomotives used on the line. The few remaining steam locomotives receive their tender loads of coal by hand-shoveling at the "Alliance Fuel" trestle or directly from the coal mine at "Corning." There is also a wye at "Alliance" to turn locomotives, cabooses, or passenger cars.

"Points East"

Trains are scheduled out of "Alliance" as rapidly as the line can handle them (see Chapter 15 for Sequence-Timetable operations) for "Bedford," "Corning," "Duncan," "Emmett," and "Points East." The first stop will be the "Santa Fe Interchange" at "Bedford," so our train rolls right past "Duncan" and its tiny grain elevator as though it didn't exist (Figure 2–8). There's a Santa Fe freight train waiting on our right for us to clear the joint main line (actually the layout's inner oval) between "Bedford" and "Duncan" and Train 9 (from "Points East"—the holding siding "f" at "Duncan") waiting to enter "Em-

Fig. 2–11. The three empty hopper cars are swapped for three loaded ones at the "Corning Mine" and the train heads for "Emmett."

mett" on our left. "Bedford" has no interchange traffic, so our train will continue east through a short tunnel and back past the "Duncan Feed & Fuel" grain elevator (Figure 2–9). The mine at "Corning" is always switched before dropping off or picking up any cars for "Duncan" on that "Points East" holding track "f". Our train has three loaded hopper cars for the "Corning Mine" and three empties are waiting there for us to pick them up. While we're switching, the steam-powered Train 5 for "Emmett" has left "Alliance" and is following our path to "Bedford" and beyond.

"Emmett" is our next stop, and we're scheduled to arrive there in time to meet the Amtrak streamliner. There's a passing siding at "Emmett," but a car at the "Trailer Train" freight dock must be pushed away ahead of our locomotive to clear the main line for the Amtrak passenger train (Figure 2–10). Our "waybills" tell us that the stock car in our train is supposed to be dropped off at the cattle pen outside of "Emmett." There a loaded hopper of coke is to be picked up at the coke ovens in "Emmett." The series of train movements needed to perform those operations are illustrated, step by step, in Chapter 14. The load of coke won't be ready until our return trip from "Points East," so we can proceed on through "Emmett" after the Amtrak train leaves and after we spot that boxcar back at the "Emmett Trailer Train" platform.

Meeting the Schedule

The series of "meets" with other trains, the switching operations with cars that really are loaded with coal (and with other cars), and the use of "waybills" to tell our train crew what cars are to be switched are just part of the real railroad action that has been condensed for model railroading. The "work" of meeting the deadlines of a real railroad timetable has been eliminated by simply "scheduling" trains as quickly and as often as you can operate them, and the "work" of making

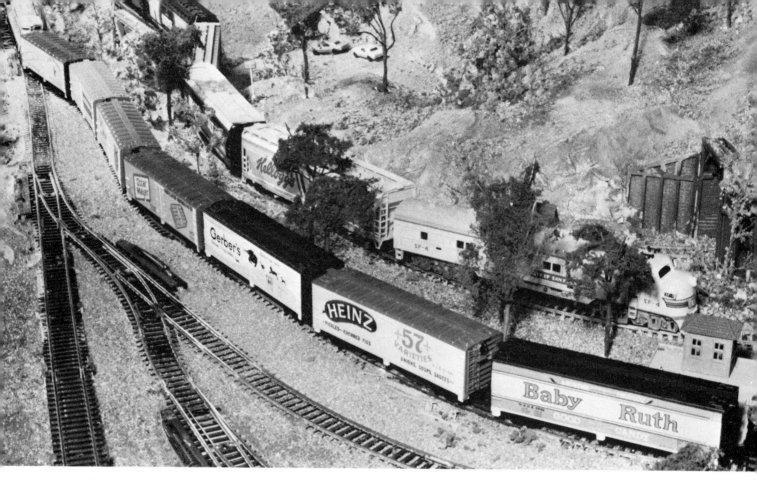

Fig. 2–12. The bright "private-owner" freight cars from the 1930s (foreground) contrast with longer modern equivalents (background).

Fig. 2–13. Solid trains of trailers on flatcars duplicate the most modern "hot shot" freights of real railroading.

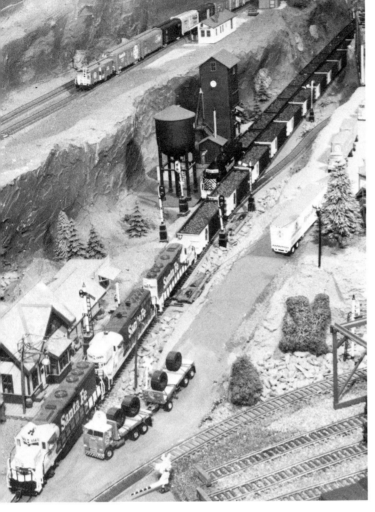

out paperwork for waybills and switch lists has been reduced to just handling some "playing cards" and plastic envelopes, which is discussed in Chapter 15. The "magic" ways to have "loaded" freight cars are described in the "Loads-In Empties-Out" section of Chapter 15. All these ideas will help to make even a simple oval with two sidings as much fun to operate as our Burlington Northern 9 × 9-foot "branch-line empire."

Fig. 2–14. Both trains of gondolas are "unit train" cars, made from Model Die Casting kits by the late Leonard Frere.

PART II

Planning, Benchwork, Trackwork and Wiring

CHAPTER 3

Track Planning

THE PURPOSE of a model railroad is to simulate as many of the movements of a real railroad as is possible with the limitations of available space. The only difference you might notice between the track plans in this book and the layouts you might see in toy or department stores at Christmastime is that these layouts seem to have more than their share of stub-end sidings. The locations of the other switches have been selected because they can be used to route trains over a track system that is like the real railroads. Each of these layouts is designed to be used with point-to-point operation. The model trains that move over these tracks, like the real trains, will be bound for some distant town, rather than just running in circles. These miniatures will be running from one point to another; hence the term point-to-point. The two 4 × 8-foot layouts in this chapter may look like only a double-track oval and a figure-eight with a few extra switches and sidings. These layouts, however, have a purpose like the prototype's, thanks to careful track planning.

A Matter of Space

Two conflicting desires are present in most model railroaders' minds. Each of us wants to build our railroad as much like the real ones as possible—and to operate it that way. Each of us also wants to see trains run and run and run. It's okay to watch a switch engine or a pedlar freight move cars in and out of sidings, but at least half the trains should still be running, or at least appear to be. You'll have to balance your list of priorities with the amount of space you have available. Most of the ready-to-run track sections and turnouts (switches) are inexpensive enough, so it will be space, rather than money, that will probably be the limiting factor. Remember, you can often select a rather complex track plan that can be started with just a simple oval or figure eight and extended with switches and track as quickly as your budget allows. If you happen to have the almost limitless space of an empty basement, a complete spare room, or a garage, you'll have to restrain yourself and build a smaller first-time layout before attempting to fill the larger space with benchwork, track, and scenery.

I suggest that you consider the following priorities before you create or select the track plan for your first layout.

1. Try to have at least four turnouts so you can include a passing siding as well as a

"facing-point" and a "trailing-point" stub-end siding, such as those described in Chapter 15.

2. Do not feel you have to have enough length of storage tracks to hold every one of your cars and locomotives. Only 40 percent of the length of all the passing sidings and stub-end sidings should be "filled" with cars and locomotives. You need the "empty" factor in order to give the trains enough room to maneuver so they can switch. Keep any extra cars or locomotives on shelves beneath the layout.

3. Try to include at least one stub-end siding near the edge of the table. This can serve as a "fiddle" yard so that you can maintain a 40-percent "full" rate by hand-carrying cars and locomotives from storage shelves or drawers (rather than from storage tracks) to and from the layout. You may want to include a two, three, or four-track "fiddle" yard (such as the one in Figure 16–5 in Chapter 16) inside an existing or specially built cabinet. The extensive "fiddle"-yard trackage will allow you to have complete trains that appear and disappear from the scene during operating sessions (as they leave and arrive at those hidden "fiddle"-yard tracks). The consists of those trains can be "fiddled" by hand before each operating session in order to arrange whatever variety of freight or passenger trains you might want to "schedule" on the layout.

4. I recommend that you arrange the layout so that there will be at least one possible route that is an oval or a figure-eight. This will allow continuous operation of the trains. Obviously, real railroads don't run around in circles; they have hundreds of miles of space.

5. You should arrange some of the sidings

to allow point-to-point operation like the real railroads.

The 4 × 8-Foot Main Line

The layout plan in Figure 3–1 appears to be nothing more than a double-track mainline oval, but it has far greater possibilities. The plan could be shortened to as little as 4 × 6 feet, but you would have to eliminate the switch to "H." The trackage is angled, relative to the sides of the table, to improve the effect of trains running along a table edge. By angling the track, the train is moving toward or away from the edge, and this lends a far greater sense of reality to your operation.

A Point-to-Point Run

This plan is designed so either one or two trains can be operated at the same time. One train can be circulating on the outer oval while the second runs on the inner oval and switches the sidings. For realistic operation, however, the layout can be used as a point-to-point run for a single train: beginning at siding "A" and traveling through the crossover from "B" to "C," around the outer oval through "D" and "E," and over the crossover to "F," for a trip halfway around the inner oval to "G" and "B," and the final destination siding "H." The train's path would then be reversed, but not before the locomotive used the "run-around" switching maneuvers at the two crossovers, thus placing the caboose at the rear of the train and the locomotive at the front for the trip back to siding "A."

Additional curved turnouts in at least two of the corners could provide other "towns" and industrial-switching possibilities along the way. Several turnouts could be added at "A" and "H" for locomotive "holding" tracks and additional industries. There's even room for a passing siding at "A" (such as that at "A" on Figure 3–2), which could make it more of an independent town. A mountain ridge down

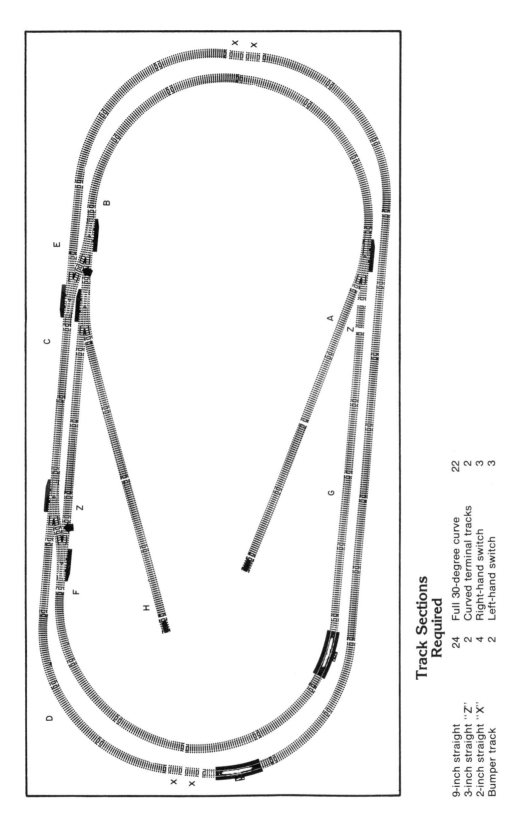

Track Sections
Required

9-inch straight	24	Full 30-degree curve	22
3-inch straight "Z"	2	Curved terminal tracks	2
2-inch straight "X"		Right-hand switch	3
Bumper track	2	Left-hand switch	3

Fig. 3–1. The 4 × 8-foot main-line layout plan.

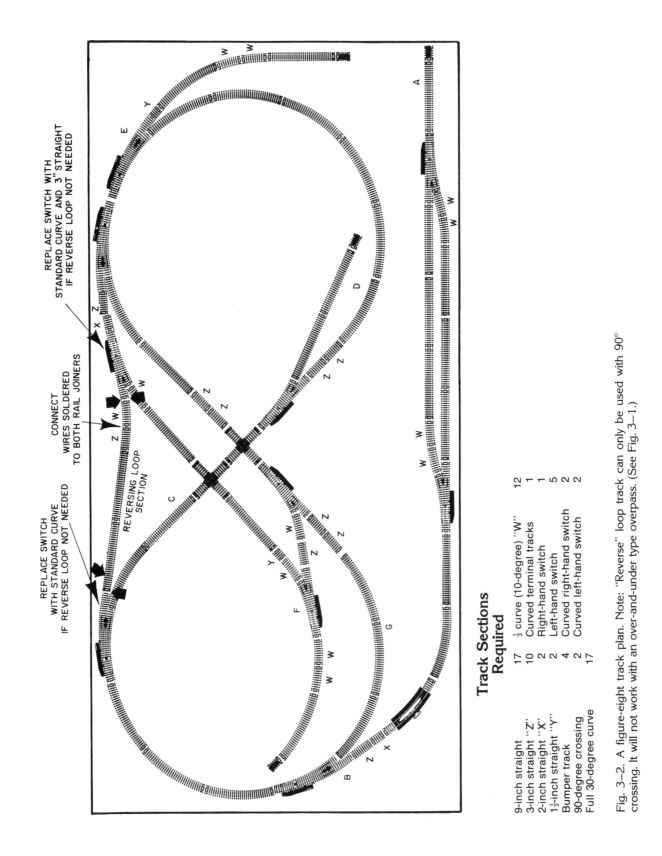

REPLACE SWITCH WITH
STANDARD CURVE AND 3" STRAIGHT
IF REVERSE LOOP NOT NEEDED

CONNECT
WIRES SOLDERED
TO BOTH RAIL JOINERS

REVERSING LOOP
SECTION

REPLACE SWITCH
WITH STANDARD CURVE
IF REVERSE LOOP NOT NEEDED

Track Sections Required

9-inch straight	17	$\frac{1}{3}$ curve (10-degree) "W"	12
3-inch straight "Z"	10	Curved terminal tracks	1
2-inch straight "X"	2	Right-hand switch	1
$1\frac{1}{2}$-inch straight "Y"	2	Left-hand switch	5
Bumper track	4	Curved right-hand switch	2
90-degree crossing	2	Curved left-hand switch	2
Full 30-degree curve	17		

Fig. 3–2. A figure-eight track plan. Note: "Reverse" loop track can only be used with 90° crossing. It will not work with an over-and-under type overpass. (See Fig. 3–1.)

the middle of the layout would separate "A" and "H" visually.

The Figure-Eight Plan

The figure eight is one of the most interesting of all the possible model-railroad track plans because it gives the effect of "many" trains crossing at a single point. The effect is somewhat more credible and more realistic than watching a train work its way around and around an oval. This layout plan is just about the best one I have seen for the popular and practical 4 × 8-foot space, which is the site for most first-time layouts. The only drawback to this layout, however, is that you cannot see two trains in motion and sit back and watch them like you can with the layout in Figure 3–2. The layout is drawn with just enough terminal tracks and gaps for operating one train (the gaps on the reversing section are there just for that feature, as described in Chapter 7). The long siding "A" to "B," as well as the siding "F," could become a separate "block," so you could operate one train switching in either of those areas while a second train circulated around the figure eight.

"Out and Back"

This layout (Figure 3–2) is also designed for point-to-point operation from "A" through "B," "C," "D," and "E" (in that order) to "F." A run-around or passing siding at both "A" and "F" allows the train to operate engine-first on the return trip to "A," and to be rearranged or switched for an engine-first trip back to "F." If you want to add some "mileage" on the route from "A" to "F," circulate the train around the figure eight (just as you would circulate around either or both ovals in Figure 16–2) until you're "scheduled" to have it arrive at "A" or "F." The advantage of this layout, as compared to many others, is that it includes a reversing-loop section so

that you can turn complete trains around "hands-off." The reversing loop would allow you to operate to *and* from "A," with "F" as a town along the way. The route would begin at "A" and proceed through "B," "C," "D," and "E" to "G," and from "G" on back to "B," around into the reversing-loop section through "E," "D," and "C," before going back to "B" and into "A." This type of operation is called "out and back," and its advantage is that most of the switching operations, including placing the locomotive at the front of the train, are only done in one "large" yard (at "A," on this layout).

Do-It-Yourself Track Planning

You can create your own track plans by taking advantage of the simple snap-together feature of most brands of HO scale sectional track. Each section of track is part of a geometric system based on nine-inch pieces of straight track (or fractions thereof) and on 10- and 30-degree segments or sections of a 360-degree circle of track. If you use a 30–60–90-degree plastic triangle to help plan your trackwork, you'll be far more likely to get those critical track alignments right.

Reduce to Scale

All the plans in this book are reduced to a scale of 1 inch to the foot, which means that each foot on the layout is just 1 inch on the plan, and each inch on the layout is but $\frac{1}{16}$ inch on the plan. A draftsman's triangular ruler has one side marked in one-inch scale, or you can use the $\frac{1}{4}$-inch marks on any rulers for 3 inches. Use the drafting triangle or ruler to pencil in the outline of the available area you have for your layout. If you're looking for something for a 4 × 8 board, just trace the outline of the table in Figure 16–1 or 16–2; the track plan in Figure 16–2, in Chapter 16, is the 5 × 9-foot size of a pingpong table, so

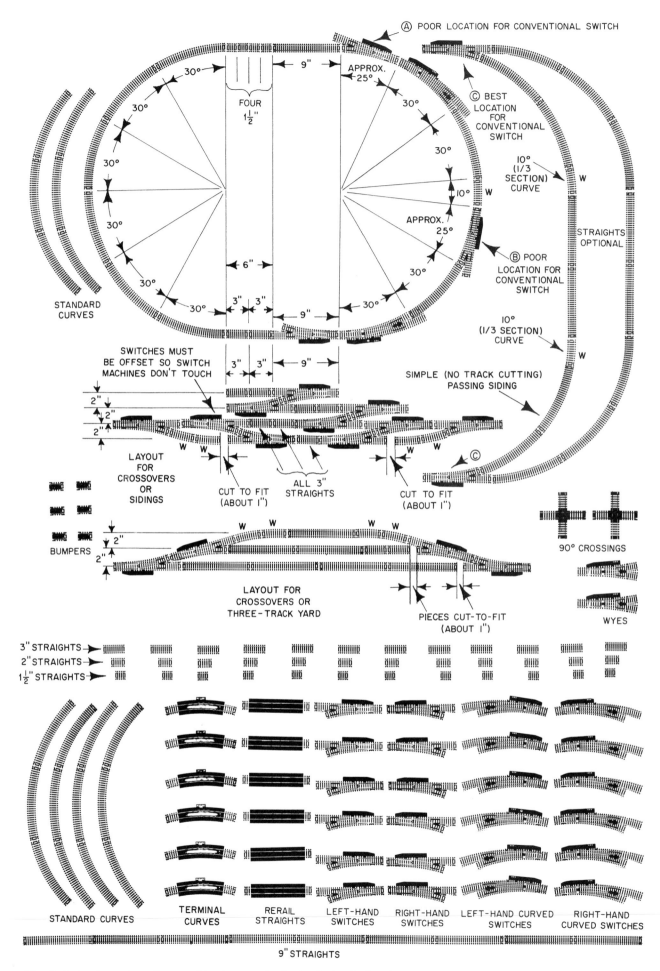

Fig. 3–3. Scale track sections and track geometry basics for track planning.

you can trace it to provide an outline if you have that size table available.

Track Sections

The track sections in Figure 3–3 can be photocopied, then cut out with scissors and glued down with rubber cement. This means that you can plan what track you need *before* you buy it. When you cut the track sections apart, keep the ends (where the rail joiners would be) perfectly even with the ties, but don't worry about how close you trim on the sides of the ties. The object is to get an idea of how well the track will fit together. Use the 30–60–90-degree triangle to align the ends of the curves. The paper track plan may not be a perfect replica of what you will actually build because there may be some areas where small filler pieces of track might have

to be used (such as the "½W" and "½Y" sections in Figure 16–3). You can avoid having to cut these fillers and have a more accurate track alignment if you pay attention to the geometry of the system.

Aligning Track Sections

The oval, the passing siding on the left, and the yard-style tracks in the center of Figure 3–3 are there to show you how the track sections must be fitted for perfect alignment and where slight misalignments might have to occur. The standard turnouts (either remote controlled or manual) are best placed in areas where a 9-inch straight section would normally go. The curved portion of these turnouts is a perfect match for the 18-inch-radius standard curved tracks, *but* the curve begins about 1½ inches from the single-

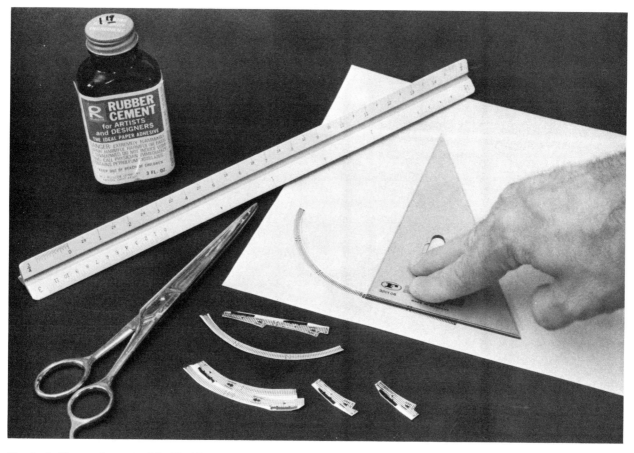

Fig. 3–4. Use a ruler and a 30–60–90-degree triangle to obtain accurate track plans with the copy-and-cutout scale-track sections in Figure 3–3.

track end of each turnout. Two standard turn-outs on the right end of the oval show you how this can create a misalignment when the standard turnout is used in place of a curved track. Each standard turnout is supplied with a single piece of $\frac{1}{3}$-curved track (10 degrees of a circle). The curved sides of those stan-dard turnouts are indeed $\frac{2}{3}$ of a curve (about 20 degrees), but there is still that $1\frac{1}{2}$ inch of straight track to be accounted for.

If you can use two turnouts in a half-circle curve, such as the one on the right of the oval, then just *one* of the $\frac{1}{3}$ curves will almost com-pensate for the portions of the circle that those short pieces of straight track fill. A slight misalignment in a curve will be made that way because you are actually lacking about 10 degrees worth of curved track. Follow the rule that if you must use a turnout to "re-place" a piece of curved track in the middle of a curve (where there are curved tracks on both ends of the turnout), use one of the curved turnouts. Another rule is to use the standard turnouts only to "replace" a piece of straight track. The turnouts at either end of the passing siding to the far right will allow perfect track alignment. Any of the curved pieces of track on the left of the oval could be replaced with a curved turnout without af-fecting the geometry or the alignment of the track in any way.

When you add a piece of straight track (or a turnout or 90-degree crossing) to one side of an oval, you must add exactly that length of straight track to the opposite side in order to maintain track alignment. Many track config-urations have the 180 degrees of track that create an oval (including any figure-eight plan), so you'll have to watch for them when you're working out a track plan and when you are actually laying track.

Parallel Sidings

You may find it helpful for both track plan-ning and actual track-laying to draw the cen-ter line of the track with a pencil. Each of the r-t-r curves is an 18-inch radius to the *center* of the track, with the exception of the 22-inch-radius curves on the outside of the curved turnouts. Curved track sections with a 22-inch radius are available from most man-ufacturers of HO scale track, but they are not shown in any of the plans in this book. You can squeeze a large number of sidings into a small space if you align the switches and/or the two $\frac{1}{3}$ curves ("W" on all the plans for layouts) as shown on Figure 3–3.

Parallel straight tracks can be spaced two inches center-to-center. The three-inch straight-track sections will often fill in the gaps, but some places will need little one-inch pieces of filler track. *Note:* I do *not* rec-ommend that you try to cut a piece of filler track that short. In most cases, you can add the length of the adjacent track to the re-quired cut-to-fit filler in order to increase the length. You may have to make a short piece of flexible track, using the techniques shown in Chapter 5. The filler tracks shorter than $1\frac{1}{2}$ inches just aren't strong enough, and, since you have to cut one to fit in any case, you might as well make it long enough so that it will have plenty of strength.

Clearance

It's best to check very tight track-planning situations with actual pieces of track and, if necessary, with structures you might want to include. You don't need to build the entire layout, just the area where you expect to have tight clearance problems. Always try to leave room at the end of any passing siding for at least one locomotive, and, if switching must be done on switches with "facing points" toward that end, allow room for a locomotive and your longest car. The far upper corner in the town of "Alliance" on the track plan in Figure 16–3 is an example of a confined area where a minimum car-and-locomotive length is needed. You can often gain a few extra inches in such tight areas by using con-ventional track rather than bumper tracks at

Fig. 3–5. The actual track sections, structures, and a locomotive and car must be used to double-check track plans for tight areas.

the end of the stub-end siding. You can just glue on some plastic ties cut from old track sections. The real railroads often use a method to stop cars from rolling off the ends of tracks.

Planning Uphill and Downhill Grades

Uphill and downhill grades are more trouble than they're worth in terms of realism. You can make the edge of the table slope up or down (like it does for the river-crossing on the 9 × 9-foot Burlington Northern layout in Chapter 16) in order to give the effect of uphill or downhill railroading. It's hard enough to keep the tracks level without trying to build in a slope. The most difficult problems to overcome are those that result from too sudden a change at the top or the bottom

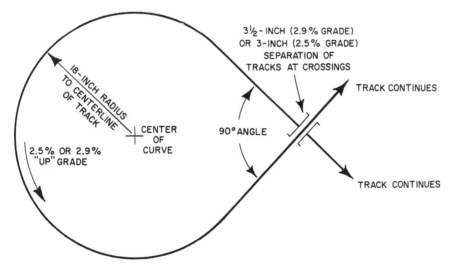

Fig. 3–6. The shortest route to create an overpass for HO-scale layouts.

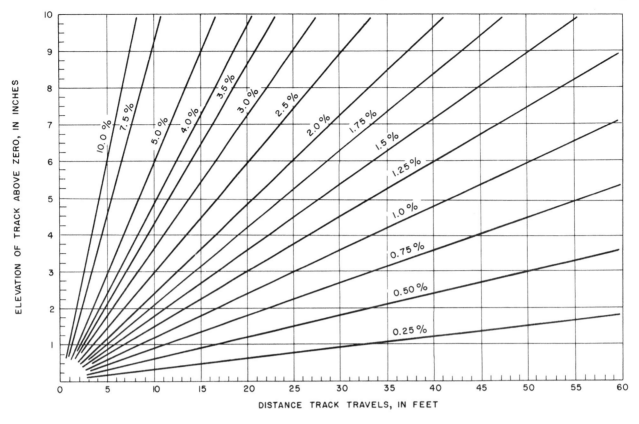

Fig. 3–7. Chart of grade percentages.

of any hill. The diagram in Figure 3–6 shows the percentage of grade that is needed for the bridge and trestle kits in the train sets to elevate the tracks about three inches above one another at the crossing. If you are using a plywood and Homosote roadbed (see Chapter 4) for a bridge inside a tunnel, you will need to have at least $3\frac{1}{2}$ inches of clearance below the Homosote at the bridge. That 2.5- to 2.9-percent grade is as steep as you'd want on your model railroad. The real trains seldom exceed 1 percent on their climbs. That grade "percentage" is figured on so many "units" per hundred, so a 2.5-percent grade would be a rise of 2.5 "units" for every 100 "units" of track.

It is extremely difficult to apply scenery to the simple plastic trestle supports, except on a short industrial trestle. If you do use grades on your layout, then you should be capable of doing the carpentry work to build the open-grid type of benchwork shown in Chapter 4. Use the chart in Figure 3–7 to detemine how steep any of the grades on your layout must be. The figures above 3.0 percent are there only for interest. You would be lucky to get just a locomotive alone up a hill as steep as 10.0 percent.

Do's and Don'ts for Track Planning

Do design a trackplan, even if you use actual track sections, before nailing the track in place.

Don't attempt to squeeze in tracks that don't match the track geometry, they'll create sudden lurches in the smooth path of the rails that will cause derailments.

Do build any layout on a shelf no wider than about 30 inches or on peninsulas no wider than 60 inches so you can reach the track and scenery at the rear of the layout.

Don't try to fill a 4 × 8-foot piece of plywood with a layout and shove the layout into a corner— you won't be able to reach anything along the back 18 inches of the layout.

Do position yards, tracks and industrial sidings, where you will want to couple and uncouple cars and operate turnouts, near the forward edges of the table for better accessibility and easier viewing.

Don't place complicated trackage at the rear of the layout, even if it is only 30 inches away from the front of the table.

Do try to find space for an around-the-wall layout, built on a shelf 12 to 30 inches wide. The trains will really seem to be going someplace.

Don't build a 4 × 8-foot layout as your "final" layout unless you really are limited to that small an area.

Do keep most of the tracks at least 6 inches away from the forward edge of the table to leave room for some foreground scenery on at least half of the layout.

Don't try to cram track into every square inch of tabletop. There won't be room for credible scenery or structures.

CHAPTER 4

Bridges and Benchwork

THE VARIOUS BRIDGES on a real railroad serve a purpose that is somewhat similar to the benchwork on a model railroad. Both support the tracks that carry the trains. The benchwork has to come before the bridges on a model railroad, but the two "supports" should be planned together for the best effect. A model of a bridge cannot look even remotely realistic unless the track that bridge carries is elevated above the surrounding terrain. The over-and-under type of bridge and trestle sets are fine for toy trains, but they add very little to the realism of a miniature of a real railroad. You can certainly use those well-detailed parts from the over-and-under sets as they have been on the Burlington Northern layout in Chapter 16. The concept of using only trestle bents to elevate a track is best limited to industrial sidings, such as the "Alliance Coal & Fuel" and the "Coke Ovens" at "Emmett" on the Burlington Northern layout. You must do some planning in order to build benchwork that allows the scenery to "fall away" from beneath the tracks, which makes a bridge just as necessary as it is on a real railroad.

Benchwork Elevations

The benchwork for your model railroad is in about the same construction category as the framework for your house, and it's made of many of the same materials. The benchwork will eventually be hidden by scenery on the top side and by Masonite or plywood panels along the sides so that only the legs will show. Many modelers even hide the benchwork's legs and the other under-the-table debris with drapes made from inexpensive materials. If you do decide on drapes, avoid the mistake of selecting those bright railroad-style patterns; they are a major distraction from what is on *top* of the table. A nice dark green or blue or brown, which will make the underside of the benchwork seem to disappear, is the shade to select.

Use only the best grades of 1 × 3 fir or pine with no knots for your benchwork. You don't want warped wood and other track-distorting problems, and quality wood will help to avoid them. Use 2 × 4s for the legs. I strongly suggest that you raise the top of the track to at least the level of your chest so you will have a more true-to-life (model-size life) view of the railroad. If you want to feel like Gulliver, then stand on a stool (the stool can also be used to reach more easily during some of the construction stages).

Fig. 4–1. An electric drill, a number 8 × 1½-inch screw-pilot bit, a power saw, and a Yankee screwdriver will make bench-work construction easy.

Open-Grid Benchwork

Divide your layout into subassemblies or modules that are no more than 30 × 60 inches. A 4 × 8-foot area can, for example, be divided conveniently into four 2 × 4-foot subassemblies. A pattern for dividing a 5 × 9-foot area is shown in Figure 16–1 in Chap-

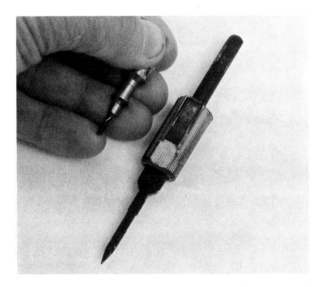

Fig. 4–2. Two styles of Number 8 pilot bits. Either one will make assembling benchwork with screws as easy as using nails.

ter 16. Make a box with overall dimensions to match each of these subassemblies, with the 1 × 3s placed on edge. Add enough cross-braces so there is no open area wider than 15 inches (three crossbraces are needed for each of the 2 × 4-foot subassemblies). Secure each of the joints with two No. 8 × 1½-inch wood screws. Drill a pilot hole for each of these screws with an electric drill and a No. 8 × 1½-inch pilot bit, which you can buy in any hardware store.

You can make quick work of driving the screws by buying or renting either a Yankee screwdriver (see Figures 4–1 and 4–3), where you just push the handle down to drive the screw, or a screwdriver attachment for an electric drill with variable speed. Touch each of the screws with a dab of soap to make it even easier. Bolt the subassemblies together with ¼ × 2-inch stove bolts, washers, and nuts. Attach the legs with 2½-inch-long × ¼-inch stove bolts or hex-head bolts with flat washers and nuts. Attach one leg to the table with a single screw, and clamp the others with C-clamps or vise-grip clamps while you adjust the legs to see that the benchwork top surface is level. Don't trust the floor to be level: Use one of the carpenter's spirit or "bubble" levels. When the legs are in the correct position, drill them and attach each leg with two of the 2½-inch stove bolts. This completes the "open-grid" portion of the benchwork.

Fig. 4–3. The Yankee screwdriver drives screws with pressure on the handle.

Fig. 4–4. Temporarily lay the plywood and Homosote tabletop on the floor in order to locate the positions of the track and switches. Mark their locations with a felt-tip pen.

Fig. 4–5. Five separate "open-grid" units are used to make the L-shaped Burlington Northern layout.

Fig. 4–6. Vise-grip clamping pliers, such as these, or conventional C-clamps can be used to hold the "open-grid" units together while the attaching bolt holes are drilled and the bolts installed.

The top of the benchwork should be ½-inch plywood (inexpensive C-C grade is fine) with ½-inch Homosote wallboard between the plywood and the track. There is no known substitute for the Homosote, so call the lumber yards until you find one willing to order as many 4 × 8-foot sheets as you'll need. I suggest a simple flat tabletop for your first model railroad. If you're working on your second layout and you're certain the track plan you are using is perfect, then you can cut both the plywood and the Homosote about an inch on each side of the track's center line. The plywood and Homosote can then be elevated about three inches above the top of the 1 × 3 benchwork, with short lengths of 1 × 3s placed vertically and attached to the plywood and the benchwork with the 8 × 1½-inch wood screws. You can add a stream at a later date using the technique in the Burlington Northern layout. Most of the scenery was to be above the track, so the plywood was just attached directly to the edges of the benchwork with screws.

Fig. 4–7. Five "open-grid" benchwork subassemblies were clamped and bolted together to build the Burlington Northern layout in Chapter 16.

Bridges

Small streams or lakes can be created by slicing through the Homosote with a hardware knife to lower the earth to the level of the plywood's surface. That's how the lake near the "Lumber Supply Co." was formed. The complete subassembly in the river section of the Burlington Northern, between the towns of "Alliance" and "Emmett," was dropped about six inches below the benchwork (Figs. 4–9, 4–10, and 4–11). Two-inch wide strips of the ½-inch plywood and ½-inch Homosote were placed beneath the track and supported by additional 1 × 3 scraps. The plastic trestle bents from the Tyco Number 909 Bridge and Trestle set were spaced about two inches apart for the approach to one bridge. The steel-girder bridge was cut from the span of the Tyco Number 7792 Rolling Bridge with abutments (vertical-end supports) from the

Fig. 4–8. A hardware knife, guided by a steel ruler, is all that's needed to cut ½-inch Homosote. Make four or five or more heavy passes with the knife in order to slice clear through the Homosote.

Fig. 4–9. This 18 × 48-inch open-grid benchwork subassembly was lowered 6 inches below the rest of the Burlington Northern layout in order to create space for a river.

Fig. 4–10. The 2 × 4 is one of the bolted-on legs. The river section is also attached by bolts so the layout can be disassembled for any later relocations.

Number 909 set. White glue—and lots of it— was used to attach the plastic to the benchwork and tube-type plastic cement holds the track to the bridges. Notice that an "earth fill" leads all the way to the abutment on the steel-girder bridge, while the Number 909 Steel Truss is approached by track supported on a trestle. The earth fill is far more common on modern railroads, and, in fact, some of the earth fills you'll see are actually wood trestles that were buried with dirt to become fills as soon as the railroad could find the time.

The benchwork for the center subassembly on the Burlington Northern was not built, because the plan indicated that that area would be nothing more than the interior of a mountain. You may be able to find similar areas of many large layouts where no benchwork at all is required. The 1 × 2 wood supports for the center of the mountain were

Fig. 4–11. An under-the-table view of the opposite end of the lowered river section. The small triangle is part of the 2 × 4½-foot leg of the L-shaped layout.

Fig. 4–12. Real railroads often use combinations of both wood and steel bridges in one span. This steel deck-girder bridge is supported by a central steel trestle bent with concrete end piers and a wood trestle on either end.

Fig. 4–13. This through-girder bridge was made from the Tyco Number 7792 Rolling Bridge kit. The steel truss on the back track and all of the trestle bents are from Tyco's Number 909 Bridge and Trestle set.

Fig. 4–14. The tracks across the river area are supported on narrow strips of ½-inch plywood and ½-inch Homosote by vertical 1 × 3 boards.

cantilevered from the other portions of the benchwork.

You can finish off the edges of the benchwork with profile boards of $\frac{1}{8}$-inch tempered Masonite or plywood cut to match the proposed hills and valleys. I suggest you delay cutting those supports until you have mocked up the shape of the hills with wadded newspapers, as described in Chapter 12. A lot of construction time is needed between the completion of the benchwork and the initial scenery work; all the track-laying and wiring should be completed and the structure sites selected (even if the structures themselves have not been purchased) before scenery is started.

Do's and Don'ts for Benchwork

Do consider building the benchwork so the track is at about the level of your chest or shoulders so you can view the model trains from the same angle you view the real trains.

Don't build a layout at waist or hip level unless you want it to be visible or accessible for very small children—from that high viewing angle even the most realistic models look like toys.

Do use screws to assemble every joint in the benchwork and install those screws from below the table so they will be accessible even when the layout is completed. You will be able, then, to alter or move the track without destroying the entire layout.

Don't use nails or glue to assemble the benchwork. If you do want to make any changes, later, the terrific force needed to separate the joints will destroy most of the layout.

Do use only well seasoned or aged wood that has been stored in the same area as the layout for a year, if possible, to avoid any radical changes in the benchwork caused by the lumber warping and bending. For this same reason, it's also wise to seal all wood with at least one coat of paint.

Don't use green, freshly-cut wood for benchwork. It's better, in most cases, to find old used wood that has already warped or bent as much as it is likely to before it becomes part of your model railroad.

Do build the benchwork in modules or sections no larger than 30 × 60 inches and bolt the sections together so you can unbolt them if you ever need to move the layout. The 30 × 60-inch sections will fit through most standard doorways.

Don't build a room-filling layout with 8-foot or longer boards that can only be moved by tearing the layout completely apart.

Do raise the roadbed and track (or lower some of those segments of the benchwork) so the track can be elevated above the earth on embankments or fills and to provide spaces, below track level, for rivers and streams.

Don't build the entire layout on a flat piece of plywood or Homosote unless you are creating just an industrial yard or city scene.

CHAPTER 5

Trackwork

LAYING MODEL RAILROAD TRACK is one of the easiest aspects of creating a real railroad in miniature. In fact, it's almost too easy; the snap-together feature of the individual track sections makes it seem that that's all there is to laying track. But if you've operated a train set on the floor before, you know that it's not quite that simple. The tracks do snap together easily, but they snap apart almost as easily. And sharp dips and bends in the track are the rule rather than exception. The primary method—and in fact the only way—of ending the battle with track joints is to attach the track to a roadbed or ballast board with nails. In this way, the track will be secure and won't move about. In the various pieces of track are holes that fit a Number 19 × $\frac{1}{2}$-inch nail just fine. The trap here, however, is that you won't solve all the track-caused derailments and train stallings by simply nailing it down, particularly if you haven't been extremely careful. With some care and the application of the experience of other model railroaders, though, you can virtually eliminate derailments and other track problems.

The Surveyor's Task

No brand of model railroad track is truly self-aligning. Even if you manage to get every single rail joint to fit tightly, other problems can occur. Slight variations in the length of the individual pieces of rail, slight warpage in a few plastic ties, and a few other minor misalignment problems can add to one another to create a major problem.

Track Alignment

I suggest that you purchase a three-foot-long steel or aluminum ruler or, at least, a

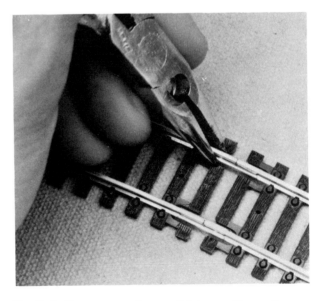

Fig. 5–1. Squeeze any loose rail joiners with needlenose pliers to ensure a tight track joint.

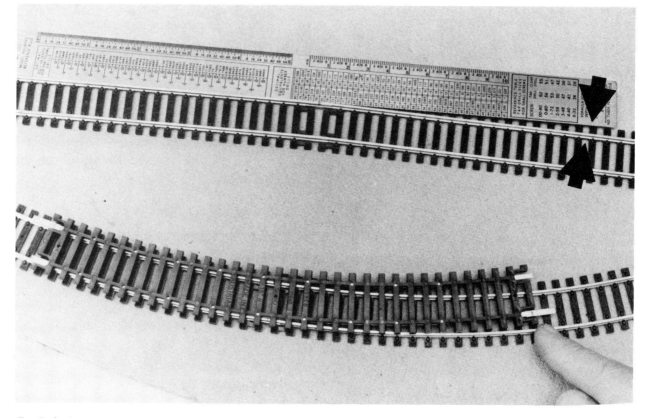

Fig. 5–2. Use a straightedge to help locate out-of-alignment straight track (arrows) and a spare piece of curved track for curve alignment.

perfectly straight two- or three-foot 1 × 4 board. The board will keep the straight track sections truly straight when two or more of them are snapped together. An extra piece of curved track can be used as an alignment gauge for curve-to-curve joints, as shown in Figure 5–2. That leaves only one problem— the places where a curved section joins a straight section must be aligned so the geometry will be almost perfect. Any sudden lurch to the left or right at the beginning of a curve is too toylike, and, worse, it can be the cause of unpredictable derailments. Use a pair of right and left conventional turnouts to help you eyeball that curve-to-straight alignment. The r-t-r turnouts are "perfect" combinations of straights and curves. By placing the turnout upside down over the curve-to-straight transition, you can see that the rails are all in alignment.

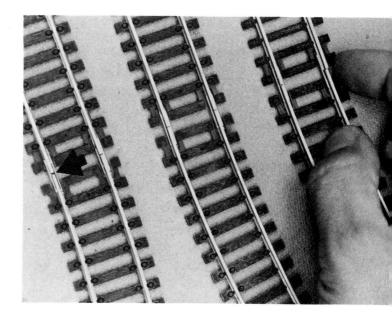

Fig. 5–3. The track may be slightly out of line even when the rails touch (center). However, the tracks at left are fine despite the slight rail gap (arrow).

Railroad Grades

I cannot recommend upgrades or down-grades for anything but industrial sidings. If you're an experienced carpenter and like to build benchwork, you may not have too much trouble. The plastic supports for "over-and-under" figure-eight-shaped layouts are nice toys, but they are neither substantial enough nor realistic enough for a model rail-road. The transitions between the level and the bottom and the tops of any grade are very difficult to make. An abrupt change isn't that much of a problem when you're just pushing a single car or two into a siding on a hill. Pulling or pushing long trains up or down-grade, however, will cause derailments, and that can take a lot of the pleasure out of the hobby.

Try it this way: When you've built a layout as complete as the 9 × 9-foot or 10 × 10-foot empires in Chapter 16 and you have a smooth operation with few derailments, then you can advance to your "third" layout and experiment with all kinds of up and down-grades. (The charts for figuring grades appear in Chapter 16 for advanced modelers.) Spend your track-laying time on that first layout or two, and get the track to align properly

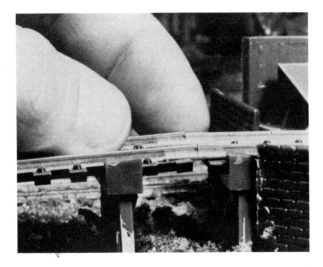

Fig. 5–4. The track must be bent slightly at the tops and bottoms of grades to eliminate sudden changes like this one.

in the two dimensions of a level layout before complicating things with the third dimension of up or downgrades.

Track-Laying Simplicity

The real railroads and even a few model railroads have a spiked track, with four spikes per tie. You will be able to lay hundreds of spikes at a time thanks to the prefabrication of sectional track. You will discover, however, that most layouts require the use of short $1\frac{1}{2}$-, 2-, or 3-inch sections of track. And some sidings will require pieces even smaller than that. Dealers usually carry an assortment of $1\frac{1}{2}$-, 2-, and 3-inch straight track sections, or you can cut your own to fit. A razor saw and hobby knife are the only tools you will need. Just be sure to follow all of the steps shown in the photographs so the custom-cut track pieces will fit as well as the other track sections.

Flexible Track

You may want to consider using the three-foot sections of flexible track in place of several shorter pieces of sectional track. The flexible track can make the transition from curve to straight even gentler because the transition point can extend for an inch or two into the curve.

Flexible track is also useful when there are three-foot and longer stretches of just straight track because the flexible track comes in straight pieces. You must bend the flexible track into a curve by carefully working apart ties on the outside of the curve. First, though, be sure to keep a section of sectional curved track to use as a guide for any curves you may bend with flexible track. This way you're sure to have a smooth radius all the way through the curve. You'll find that one of the rails will windup being longer than the other with any flexible track curve. Cut that rail with a razor saw and trim away any burrs with a hobby knife. The sections of flexible

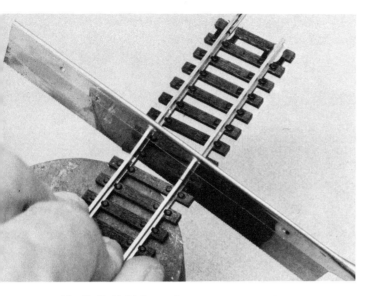

Fig. 5–5. Hold the track against a vise or other sturdy object while you cut through it with a razor saw. Be sure the cut is perfectly straight.

Fig. 5–7. The flush-cut diagonal cutters make a cut with a flush surface (top) on one side and a severe angle on the other (bottom).

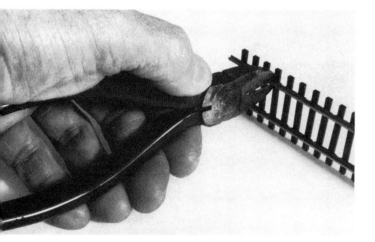

Fig. 5–6. Special flush-cut diagonal cutters are available from hobby shops to cut track and rail.

track must be prefitted, just like any other piece of track, before nailing the track in place.

The secret to perfect trackwork with flexible track is to see that the entire portion of your layout is in perfect alignment before you drive any nails to secure the track. Try to work with a complete oval or the entire passing siding so you can align every inch of the track with every other inch. When you're sure that portion of the layout is perfect, mark the edges and each track joint with a pencil. Then you'll know if any section shifts while you're nailing down the rest. Be very patient and pull as many nails as you must to realign any of the track that has shifted out of alignment.

The Roadbed

Remember, there is no equally useful substitute for Homosote-brand cardboard wall panels as a roadbed for a model railroad. Ordinary plywood is too hard; you'll snap plastic ties (and your temper) trying to get the track laid and the trains will sound like toys when you're done. Other types of wall board, such as Celotex, are too soft, and plaster board is too brittle and crumbly. The Homosote can be cut with a hardware store's carton-cutting knife, and then you can shape the

Fig. 5–8. Shave the plastic beneath the rails with the razor saw to make room for the rail joiners on tops of the ties.

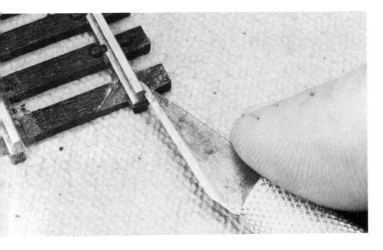

Fig. 5–9. Scrape the corners of the cut rails with a hobby knife to remove any burrs before installing the rail joiners.

edges into ballast shoulders with any hobby knife. The Homosote is just hard enough to hold the track nails securely, but it's soft enough so you can drive the nails into place with a pair of needlenose pliers. Be sure to support the Homosote with at least $\frac{1}{2}$-inch-thick plywood. (The benchwork to support the plywood is described in Chapter 4.)

Nailing the Track

Use number 19 × $\frac{1}{2}$-inch common nails to hold the track sections. Push the nails through the holes in the center of some of the ties in each piece of sectional track with the needlenose pliers. The head of the nail should *not* actually touch the top of the tie or it will likely pull the tie downward to distort the tie and alter the track gauge (rail spacing). I cut a v-shaped notch in the end of a plain index card. I hold the index card next to the shank of the nail and push the nail head down with the tip of the pliers until I can just feel it touch the index card. I then remove the index card. That leaves just the right amount of clearance between the head of the nail and the top of the plastic tie.

Fig. 5–10. Cut through every other tie, on opposite sides of the bottom of the track section, to make your own flexible track.

Fig. 5–11. The ½-inch-thick Homosote can be cut with heavy pressure on a hardware or box knife. Trim the edges to simulate ballast shoulders.

Fig. 5–12. Cut an index card to use as a gauge so you won't push the track nails too far into the Homosote.

Ballasting the Track

Before you apply simulated ballast to the area between and beside the ties of your track, I suggest that you wait until the scenery is almost complete. You may find that you want to relocate the track or add additional turnouts during the interim, and those changes are a lot easier if you don't have to worry about the ballast and the track at the same time.

The very first step when applying ballast is to seal the area beneath the track with a coat of latex paint. This is a job that's really best done when you first glue and nail the Homosote to the plywood, but it can also be done by using a small paint brush (Number 1- or 2-size) to apply the paint between the ties. It won't hurt if you get some of the paint on the ties; the ballast and the weathering you add later will disguise the paint smears. The paint seals the Homosote, so the glue or matte medium won't soak into the Homosote before it has a chance to glue the ballast.

I suggest that you use common dirt or sand for ballast. Pick a color that corresponds to the type of ballast used on your favorite real railroad. You can even pulverize chunks of real ballast by putting them in a thick cloth bag and hitting it with a hammer. Sift the "ballast" through a kitchen strainer. The mesh in the strainer should be the same size as door screen, or use a scrap piece of door screen for the sieve. Use only the finer portion of the material that passes through the screen for your ballast. For extra realism, use a gray or brown color for the "main-line" tracks' ballast and a beige color for the sidings. Later, in the weathering phase of track-laying, you can spray on a "wash" of black acrylic paint and water to give the ballast the "dirty" look it has on the real railroads. Always check for iron particles in any dirt you use by passing a small magnet over the loose dirt. If any particles cling to the magnet, find another source of dirt.

Fig. 5–13. Spread the glue and water mix between the rails with a plastic ketchup bottle.

Fig. 5–14. Sprinkle on the ballast and wet the area with a spray bottle to spread the glue through the ballast.

Buy a plastic mustard or ketchup dispenser with a pointed tip and use this to apply the artist's matte medium or white glue to bond the ballast. Apply a bead of the ballast cement right down the center of the ties and another along the edges of the ties. Next, spray the track and the ballast cement with mist from a plastic pump-type spray bottle or a plant atomizer. Cover the turnout's moving switch points with small strips of masking tape so the spray cannot reach them to carry the cement into the working parts of the switch. You can spread the cement around a bit with a paint brush if the water spray didn't do the job well enough. The ballast can now be sprinkled over the track. Apply more than you feel you might need and spread it around with another brush. Finally, spray the ballasted track with water. This will allow the cement to work its way around each grain of ballast through a general diluting action. Let the ballast dry for at least a day and vacuum away the excess. Remove the masking tape from the turnout's moving switch points.

Ready-to-run Amcoach-type low-level cars are Bachmann models (ConCor offers simple kits for the newer Amtrak Superliners). The other diesels are Athearn models, repainted by Leonard Frere.

A pair of converted Burlington Northern diesels are shown in action, double-heading out of Emmett. Even a "new" diesel will show some signs of weathering.

Larry Larson holds the tethered walk-around controller as he watches his freight pass another, which is operated by Bill Wright from the control panel at the town of Duncan.

An Atlas Alco RS-1 diesel with new paint and decals sits next to some cars from the mines built from Evergreen styrene sheet and Grandt Line windows on Lee Nicholas's Utah-Colorado Western Railroad.

Two ConCor GP38 diesels with added details, new paint and decals on the Rennselaer Polytechnic Institute layout in Troy, New York.

Three Athearn GP38-2 diesels that were detailed, repainted and decaled by Steve Kley.

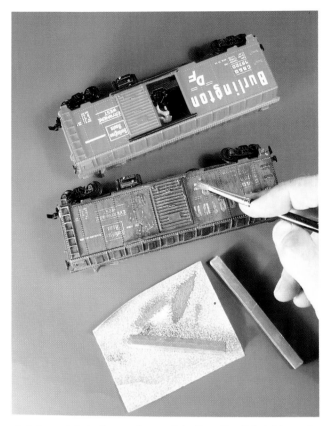

Artist's pastel chalks can be used to "weather" freight cars by powdering the chalk on sandpaper and dusting it onto the cars with a paintbrush.

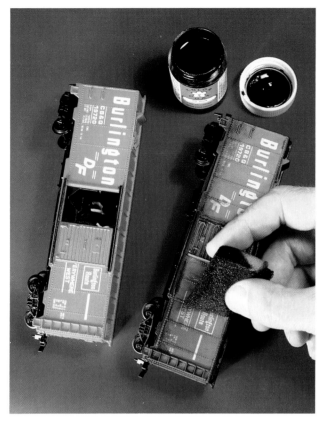

For a different weathering effect, try artist's acrylic colors from a jar or tube. Apply by dabbing a very wet sponge in the color, then onto the car.

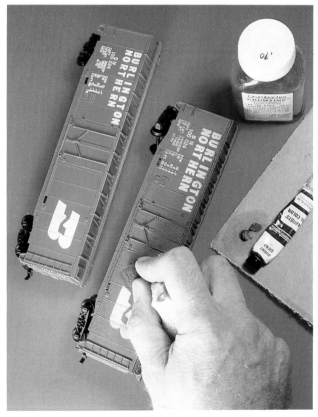

Artist's oil colors, thinned with turpentine, can also be used to "weather" cars and locomotives. This technique works well on trucks and other slick plastic surfaces.

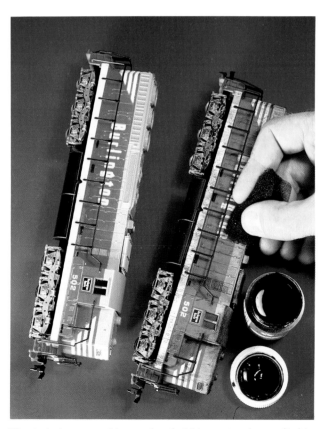

The techniques used to weather freight cars can be applied to both steam and diesel locomotives. Most of the dirt collects on the roof and is washed down the sides in streaks.

George Booth's Great Western Railway sugar plant was featured in the February, April, and June 1991 issues of *Railmodel Journal* magazine. The locomotive is a modified Athearn SW7 (SW1500).

A tree made from clothesline and wire is dipped in ground foam rubber, which has been dyed green. The ground foam will effectively simulate individual clusters of leaves.

Carefully selected weeds and twigs can be used to simulate tree trunks, using ground foam rubber, dyed green, for the leaves.

Form the stream bed with plaster and ground cover and seal it with a thick spray of water and Artist's Matte Medium. Cover the bed with a layer of 1/8-inch rocks, followed by some finer sand.

Pour a 1/8-inch-thick layer of Artist's Gloss Medium over the rocks and let it dry overnight. Pour additional 1/8-inch layers (and let them dry) until the water is as "deep" as you wish.

For rapids, dab on some Artist's Gel Medium as lumps below the larger rocks (add some 1/4-inch rocks for rougher water). When it dries, touch the tops with gloss white paint to simulate foam.

Add some more rocks along the edge of the water and pour on one final thin layer of Artist's Gloss Medium to retain the rocks and finish the surface of the stream.

This mountain stream was created with several layers of Artist's Gloss Medium and some lumps of Artist's Gel Medium for the "white" water areas.

Use tweezers to position both the decal and its paper, then hold the decal with a knife tip while you slide the paper from beneath it with tweezers.

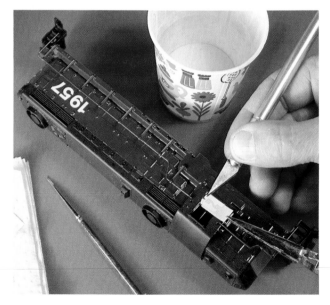

Decal application (from bottom to top): The car is painted with gloss paint; decals are applied; the surface is sprayed with Testors "Dullcote"; "weathering" is brushed on.

Fig. 5–15. Use an old paint brush to brush away any excess ballast; then vacuum it up into a clean vacuum bag.

Fig. 5–16. Paint both sides of each rail with dark brown paint to simulate rust; then scrape the tops and edges to allow electrical contact.

One note of warning: Keep both the ballast and the glue well away from the working parts of all the track turnouts, that is, the moving switch points. Simply paint the area around the switch points in a color to match the ballast. (No one will ever notice that there aren't any of those "loose-looking" rocks in that area.) The ballast itself can jam the switch points, and the glue will obviously render the switch worthless. I cannot provide a suitable method of removing glue-stuck switch points, whether you use white glue or the artist's "matte medium" I prefer. The matte medium is used for mixing acrylic paints and it's available at any good artists supply store. It looks and feels almost exactly like plain white glue. However, it's just enough more flexible to keep the trackwork from amplifying sounds, and it's a bit easier to pry the trackwork loose when you want to relocate it or add a switch to it.

No doubt some granules of the ballast will have been glued to the sides and the tops of the rails. Go over the track with an old hobby-knife blade to scrape away both glue and ballast from the tops and the inside edges of the rails. Push a gondola or flat car over the track with a bit of downward pressure so you can feel if the wheels encounter any glue or ballast on the running surfaces of the rails that you might have missed. If you decide to weather the track (a step I feel is as important as the ballast itself), then you might as well save this track-cleaning until that step is completed.

Weathering the Track

The track on a real railroad is constantly exposed to weather, and that is why the cars and locomotives look so well used. Few modelers realize that their layouts have this major "flaw." Clean track simply doesn't look like the real thing.

In weathering track, first spray all the trackwork with a wash of 95 parts water to 5 parts black acrylic paint. The sides of the rails can then be painted with reddish brown (burnt umber mixed with burnt sienna is about right)

Fig. 5–17. The varying colors of the ties and the rust on the sides of the rails can be simulated with shades of brown/gray and reddish-brown paint on model railroad track.

artists' oil paints thinned about fifty-fifty with turpentine. A few dribbles of paint on the simulated plastic spikes or on the ties will probably look just like rusted ties or tie plates, so don't worry about them. Then, spray the entire area with a wash that matches the color of the "dirt" on the surrounding hills. This means everything, including the buildings. The entire layout should have that "earth" tint. Now you can scrape the rail tops and check for any paint or ballast that might stop the flow of electricity between the rails and wheels or cause a derailment.

Do's and Don'ts for Track and Turnouts

Do cut track sections to fit precisely into any odd-length gaps so the track and rails flow smoothly with no kinks.

Don't try to bend the track to fill any gaps.

Do squeeze each rail joiner with pliers, along the base or web of the rail, to be certain it fits tightly.

Don't rely on the fit of rail joiners as they are furnished by the factory.

Do be certain the track is in perfect alignment across each rail joint, then nail or glue the track in place.

Don't rely on the rail joiners to hold or push the track into alignment.

Do place at least one 9-inch section of straight track between any S-bend so the trains will not lurch from left to right as they travel through the S-bend. The lurch is not realistic and it can cause derailments.

Don't connect any radius right curve to a left curve without that "transition" section of straight track.

Do try to place a larger-radius "transition" curve at the beginning and end of every curve. Use, for example, one length of 22-inch radius track at each extreme end of every 18-inch radius curve.

Don't join tight curves (18 or 15-inch radius) directly to straight track sections except in yards or industrial areas.

Do use only a hard rubber eraser like those sold by Life-Like, Model Power and Bright Boy to clean the tops of all rails.

Don't use a file, emery paper or sandpaper to clean the rails. The surface of the rail will be scratched and the scratches will make it easier for dirt to collect and oxides to re-form.

CHAPTER 6

Remote-Control Turnouts

FEW MODEL RAILROADERS will admit it, but the sight of a miniature train following a path they have selected for it by remote control is one of the most exciting aspects of the hobby. The movement of the turnout's moving points, which change the direction of the train, is so slight compared to the bulk of the train that the whole process almost seems miraculous. The track turnouts allow two trains to pass, cars to be switched in and out of trains, trains to be made-up, reversing movements of complete trains or locomotives, and for the multiple routes that make the track plans in Chapters 3 and 16 so versatile. If you have to choose between buying another locomotive and buying another pair of turnouts, pick the turnouts. Through them, you'll get a hundred times more enjoyment out of all the model railroad equipment you already have.

Turnout Positioning

There are good and bad places to put turnouts. In some places, you should use remote-controlled turnouts, and in other places it's better to use manual turnouts.

The diagrams and data in Chapter 3 will explain where curves and turnouts can and cannot be mixed in order to minimize the chances for track misalignment and the resulting derailments. In brief, the standard straight/curve turnouts should be used only in place of straight track sections or at the beginning of curves. The curved/curved switches should be used only in place of a piece of curved track. Wye turnouts should be used only in stub-ended wyes, such as those in Chapter 7.

If a turnout is placed more than two feet from the edge of the table or in a tunnel, it should definitely be a remote-control turnout. Try to avoid placing turnouts in tunnels, and, if you must, make a portion of the mountain above the turnout removable so you can work on the turnout or rerail any wrecks. Turnouts that are within two feet of your control panels might just as well be the manual type, which are thrown by moving the pin directly at the turnout. The remote-control turnouts add three more wires for each turnout to what is already complicated wiring. The fewer turnouts you can use, the easier your layout will be to maintain. If you have to walk up to the control panel to work a remote-control button or turnout lever for a turnout that's as easy to reach as the panel itself, you are adding unnecessary complication to the layout. You might notice, by the way, that every turnout on the "project" Bur-

Fig. 6–1. Drill a $\frac{1}{4}$-inch hole for any triple wires and a $\frac{1}{16}$-inch hole for single wires.

lington Northern 9 × 9-foot layout in Chapter 16 is a remote-control type. This was done so we would have complete freedom in locating the control panels. The remote-control turnouts can still be operated by moving the pin beside the turnout, however.

Wiring Fundamentals

Working with the wires from a remote-control turnout may very well be the first bit of "complicated" wiring you will have to do on your layout. The actual track wiring is seldom complicated by the addition of a turnout because the r-t-r firms have a system of routing electrical power through the turnout regardless of which direction it is thrown. The only time you must add additional track wiring is when the addition of a turnout creates a wye or a reversing loop as part of the track plan. Wyes and loops are shown in Chapter 7; a loop in the figure-eight plan is found in Chapter 3; and wyes in the 9 × 9- and 10 × 10-foot plans are in Chapter 16. Each of the remote-controlled turnouts, however, has three wires of its own, and these must be connected to the turnout controller on your control panel and to the "AC" terminals on your power pack. On a complicated layout, which might have dozens of turnouts, it's a good idea to purchase a separate power pack for the turnouts and use another one to operate the accessories. The use of a turnout or an accessory can affect the speed of a train at a critical moment. For most 4 × 8-foot first-time layouts, a single power pack for all three—trains, turnouts, and accessories—is sufficient.

It is not necessary to solder any of the connections on your model railroad. Each of the r-t-r turnouts and most accessories have screws to attach the wires. However, there are

Fig. 6–2. Push the wires down through the hole and paint the exposed portions of the wires to match the surrounding "earth."

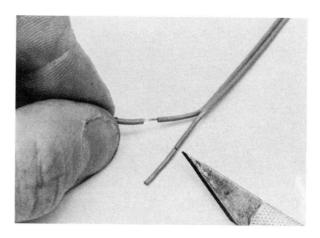

Fig. 6–3. Careful use of a sharp hobby knife will allow you to strip the insulation from wires without cutting the wire itself.

Fig. 6–4. Twist the ends of the wires and bend them into backward question-mark shapes before attaching them to the screws.

Each of the wire strands must be captured under the head of the terminal screws. If you leave a few of the hairlike strands free, they'll eventually find their way to the next terminal screw for that hard-to-locate short circuit. The twisted ends of the wires must be bent in a backward question-mark shape, as shown in Figure 6–4, with the loop just $\frac{1}{32}$-inch or so larger than the diameter of the screw threads and about that much smaller than the diameter of the screw head. The reverse question-mark shape loops the wire, so the action of

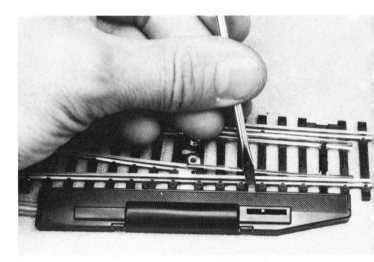

Fig. 6–5. Pry outward and upward to snap the tabs clear.

right and wrong ways to perform that seemingly simple task. I suggest that you use a sharp hobby knife to cut through the insulation on the wires, rather than using a conventional wire stripper. You can "feel" the point when you reach the wire with the hobby knife, so you can avoid even knicking the delicate hairlike strands of wire. It takes some practice to get the feel of cutting just the insulation and not the wire, but it's a technique that will always work once you learn it.

You'll need to remove only about $\frac{1}{4}$-inch of insulation. If you remove much more, you'll have an excess of wire, and it might touch a nearby terminal screw and cause a short circuit. If you remove too little insulation, it will be difficult to get the terminal screw to grip the wire. When the insulation is off, twist the wire strands together immediately by rolling the exposed end of the wire between your fingers. Watch those ends carefully until you get each terminal screw tightened; retwist the wire if the individual strands start to wander about.

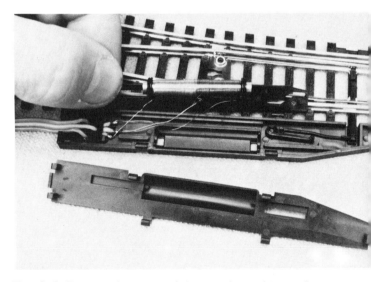

Fig. 6–6. Remove the cover of the switch machine and clean any dirt from inside.

the tightening screw head will tend to pull the wire around the screw for an even tighter joint. *Any* other bend or even straight-in installation of the wire on the screw terminal will result in several of those individual wire strands popping out from beneath the screw head. This may all sound like a lot of bother, but, really, it's just as easy to do it the right way once you learn how.

There will undoubtedly be times when you need a wire longer than that supplied with the turnouts. Save any leftover wires for just that purpose, or buy some additional hook-up wire from an electronics hobby store. (The technique for splicing wires is illustrated in Chapter 7.) Do try to match the color of the two wires you slice so you can trace any short circuits or loose connections by wire color. Be sure you have at least three inches of "slack" in the wire between the turnout and the controller and/or the power pack. You might have to lift the turnout slightly to adjust or relocate it or move the turnout controller. The extra length of wire will give you enough "room" to make such changes. The extra length may also be needed, someday, if you build a master control panel and need to splice in extra wire length to reach the new control panel.

The Train that Never Derails

There will never be such a thing as a train, real or model, that never derails. However, you can come very close if you pay careful attention to the alignment of your track and to the operation of your turnouts.

The ends of the turnout's moving switch points are just sharp enough to sometimes cause derailments. The flanges of the cars and locomotives tend to pick at the sharp corners of the switch points and derail. If you have a turnout that causes persistent derailments, you may want to trim just $\frac{1}{32}$-inch of the corner of the switch points, as shown in Figure 6–7. Do not trim any more than that

Fig. 6–7. Trim the ends of troublesome switch points to a slight 45-degree angle to help eliminate derailments.

or you'll make the point-picking problem even worse. Don't tempt the fates either; if your other turnouts are working without causing derailments, then leave them and their points alone!

Many model railroaders place a hat pin or a map pin into the layout at every place a derailment has occurred. The pin reminds them where to look for trouble (see the Derailment Troubleshooting Chart in Figure 6–8) when it comes time for an evening of maintenance. Cars or locomotives that are persistent derailers are placed on a shelf for attention at the same time. If you follow this kind of maintenance, you will soon locate and eliminate all of the troublesome spots on your layout.

Vanishing Switch Machines

Nothing on a real railroad even resembles the switch machine beside a model railroad's turnouts. You'll increase the realism of your

Fig. 6—8 Derailment and Track Troubleshooting

Trouble	Probable Cause of Trouble	Solution
Train derails frequently at one particular place.	1. Offset rails at joiners.	1. Align rails and rail joiners with steel ruler and needlenose pliers.
	2. Excess plastic "flash" or wisps from ties on inside edges of the rails.	2. Trim "flash" with a hobby knife.
	3. Plaster, glue, or some foreign object stuck to track.	3. Remove it.
	4. Ends of rails burred or rough.	4. Smooth the tops and inside edges of the rails with number 400 sandpaper.
Train derails at turnout.	1. Switch points not throwing far enough to make firm contact with "through" rails.	1. Remove any foreign matter from area around points and check the action of switch lever inside the switch machine.
	2. Turnout twisted or bent, so all rails do not align in both "main" and "siding" turnout positions.	2. Bend the turnout into perfect alignment.
	3. Coupler pins hitting switch rails or frog.	3. Cut pins to proper length, as outlined in Chapter 14.
	4. Any of four problem areas for "regular" track.	4. Correct, as outlined above.
Train derails everywhere.	1. Running the train too fast.	1. Run it slower.
Turnouts do not throw.	1. Turnout buttons on remote-control unit wired incorrectly.	1. Be sure wires are connected exactly as shown on the turnout's package and to "AC" terminals on the power pack.
	2. Button on turnout control not depressed when it is moved into position.	2. Simple operator error. Remember to *both* slide and push the button to actuate remote-control turnouts.
	3. "AC" portion of power pack not functioning.	3. Touch the wires from an r-t-r street light (test light) to just the "AC" terminals of the power pack. If light does not glow, have your dealer check the power pack.
	4. Turnout control is faulty, or contacts inside are dirty.	4. Touch the street-light wires to screws number 1 and 2 (the center screw) while you move the switch lever to the left and to the right and press it down. The light should glow. Touch the street-light wires to screws number 2 and 3 while you slide the switch lever to the right and push it down. The light should glow. If the light does not glow with the button to the right *or* left and depressed, replace the switch controller.
	5. Mechanical portion of the turnout and switch points may be bent or clogged.	5. Remove any debris from points and from switch machine and align switch parts.
	6. Hair-size wire inside remote-control switch machine broken.	6. Have wire soldered together at an electronics store.

layout considerably, then, by hiding those switch machines. Do not try to cover up the switch machines with the plaster scenery. The switch machines are so close to the track that the steps of some locomotives and the sides of others actually rub the switch machine for a moment, so there is no room for the added thickness of scenery on the rail side of the switch machine. The best trick is to paint the switch machine with the basic brown earth color I suggested for the Homosote beneath the track. When you mask the switch points during the ballasting, keep the switch machine clear so that it will receive some of the wash of flat black and earth colors used to weather the rest of the track. You'll be amazed at how well the switch machines blend into the layout when their colors match the scenery. It's not so obvious in the photographs because the switch machines' shape is still visible but the camouflage-with-paint technique does work.

You can go a step further, with some of your switch machines, and hide the portion that is away from the track with bits of ground foam-rubber leaves to simulate weeds and

Fig. 6–9. Disguise terminal track connections and switch machines with paint, ground cover, and ground foam-rubber "weeds."

bushes. A few scraps of balsa wood or some old brass rail can be cut and piled on the back side of switch machines where there are no adjacent tracks. The switch machine will then become just part of the pile of wood or rail. Be careful, when working with glue around the switch machine, that no glue finds its way inside the switch machine or anywhere near the switch points.

CHAPTER 7

Control Panels and Wiring

YOU CAN BUILD a complete model railroad with dozens of turnouts, and you can wire it with just two wires clipped to a single terminal track, *if* you want to operate only one train and *if* you do not include any reversing loops or wyes in the track plan. The design of most snap-together HO scale turnouts (Atlas, Bachmann, IHC, Life-Like, Model Power, Peco, and Roco) and crossings routes the

track power directly through the switch or crossing, so many of the "gaps" you may have heard about are unnecessary. The common rail wiring system for two-train operation is another wiring shortcut that allows you to use just one additional wire (and one rail gap) for each electrically isolated block. The wiring for your railroad in miniature should be only as complicated as you want it to be.

Walk-Around Control

The method of walk-around control can make your entire railroad seem more realistic without any real expense or labor. Walk-around control is the process of placing the throttle (speed control and reversing switch) on a tether or extension cord so you can walk around your layout to follow your train. It was developed about twenty years ago for large shelf-style around-the-room layouts, such as the 10×10-foot track plan in Chapter 16. With it the operator has the ability to run the railroad from a single control panel in the manner of a real railroad dispatcher or towerman, and it also offers him the chance to be an "engineer."

Walk-around control will have a far greater effect on your attitude toward your models than you could imagine. Even a simple model will seem to be many times more true to life when you are moving along beside it

Fig. 7–1. A walk-around control allows you to stay right beside your train for an "engineer's" eye-view of the operations.

with the throttle and reversing control in your hands. The controls for the turnouts and the blocks (for two-train operation) are still located on control panels, but those panels are located near the yards or towns or other concentrations of complex trackwork. On basement-filling layouts, the turnout and block controls are strung out all along the edge of the benchwork just in front of the tracks they control.

The mechanics of walk-around control are simple enough: an additional throttle and reversing switch are built into a box small enough to be held in one hand. That box is generally referred to simply as the "throttle."

Each brand of throttle has its own specific wiring instructions but most can be connected with four long (10 to 20 foot) wires to the four terminals on the back of most power packs. Those four wires are the "tether" cable for the walk-around throttle. You will be able to walk along beside your train for the length of that cable. Position the power pack near the center of the edge of the layout (for example, on the end of the layout at "Emmett" in Figure 16–3 or near the circled letter "I" in Figure 16–5). If you use a 12-foot long set of four 16-gauge insulated wires, you will be able to have just a single connection for the walk-around throttle's tether cable. The 12-foot tether cable will allow you to walk beside the train anywhere on those two layouts.

For larger layouts, with the capability of operating two or more trains, the layout must be divided into electrically isolated blocks and wired as shown in Figure 7–3. You will need to provide sockets, located around the edges of the layout about every ten linear feet, as shown in that figure and in Figures 7–14 and 7–15.

Your dealer can order walk-around throttles for you. The least expensive ones will have only the throttle and reversing switch, but some may also have a "pulse" control on-off switch for better slow-speed control of the trains; some even have built-in coasting or "momentum" so the train feels like it really weighs thousands of tons.

All of the walk-around throttles are designed to be held in one hand with the throttle knob or switch operated by a thumb or forefinger of that same hand. That leaves your second hand free to operate the block switches or to uncouple the cars from the train as shown in Chapter 14.

Two-Rail Wiring Basics

It's to the credit of the engineering efforts of the model railroad manufacturers that they have managed to make the "electrical system" of their trains look so much like the tracks of the real railroads. The rails of the tracks on your model railroad lead a double life. They guide and support the flanged wheels of the locomotives and rolling stock just like real railroad rails. The rails of a model railroad, however, also function as exposed "wires," which are part of the electrical circuit that carries the power to the electric motor in the locomotive. One of the rails is "positive" and the other "negative," and these carry the current to and from the locomotive. If the positive rail ever touches the negative rail, it will cause a short circuit. The plus and minus rails would appear to cross at every turnout or 90-degree crossing track. The r-t-r turnouts and crossings, however, are designed so that the "plus" rail passes beneath the "minus" rail at the frog (the plastic center of the turnout where the rails cross). A thin piece of plastic molded into that plastic frog insulates the two rails. An insulating gap has been placed between the turnout's moving switch points and the rest of the rail, so no short circuit can occur there.

"Frog" Systems

The r-t-r design is called the "insulated frog" system, and its greatest advantage is that it allows you to connect the track wiring on either side of the turnout and to mix in any quantity of turnouts and still have power (but no short circuits) anywhere on the track system. If you try to use another brand of turnout that has a "live frog" design with an r-t-r turnout, you may create a short circuit in your layout. The "live frog" turnouts must receive electrical power from the "point" (or single-track) side of the turnout. If you do have other brands of turnouts, it's best to use them for stub-ended industrial sidings or yards. In these places, the turnout can be at the end of the track. A discussion of the more complex wiring needed for the "live frog" system appears in Volume I of *The Model Railroading Handbook*. If you must mix the two designs, you'll have to use that more complex type of wiring.

Wyes and Reversing Loops

The r-t-r turnout and crossing design contains one problem that can't be eliminated. A short circuit is created whenever the track is arranged to form a reversing loop or a wye, such as those in this chapter. The reversing loop or wye is designed to allow you to turn a train around without removing it from the tracks. If you think about the logic of reversing a complete train, you'll realize (the diagrams will help) that the "positive" rail *must* touch the "negative" rail and vice versa. You may accidentally include a reversing loop or wye in a free-lance track plan; a diagonal track across an oval layout, with turnouts on both ends of the diagonal, will create a reversing loop like that in Figure 7–12. A similar, but less obvious, reversing loop is part of the

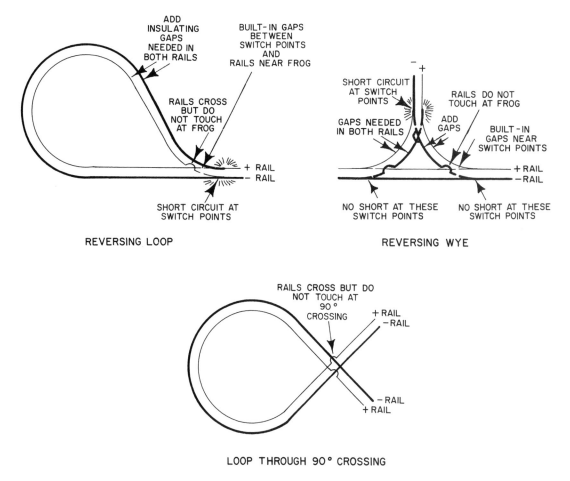

Fig. 7–2. Short circuits will occur at wyes or loops unless gaps are cut through both rails.

figure-eight 4 × 8-foot track plan in Chapter 3. Wyes are included in both the 9 × 9-foot and 10 × 10-foot track plans in Chapter 16. Generally, you will want to include a wye or reversing loop on the layout just to add the variety of clockwise and counterclockwise operation without hand-carrying the trains.

A wye or reversing loop must have a section of track that is used for the actual "reversing" action. The diagonal track on the typical reversing loop and, sometimes, the stub end of a wye are the obvious portions of the track that will be used mostly just during the time when the train is being reversed. A connection between a main line and a branch line, such as that in Figure 7–11, is a third example of where a "reversing section" might be located. In every case, the "reversing section" must be isolated electrically from the rest of the layout by cutting right through *both* rails on *both* ends of the reversing section.

You can substitute the insulated plastic rail joiners for metal rail joiners rather than cutting the rails if you wish. The rail joint created with plastic rail joiners is not quite as rigid as that done with metal rail joiners, so I recommend that you actually cut the rails whenever

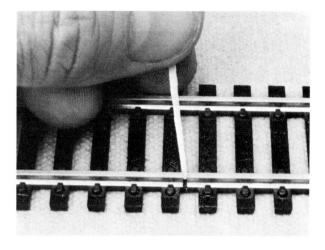

Fig. 7–4. After a gap is cut through the rail with a razor saw, the gap should be filled with epoxy or household cement.

there is room. Sometimes it may be necessary to place a gap between turnouts if there is space for only an insulated rail joiner. In that case, cut the gap with a razor saw and apply a dab of five-minute epoxy or household cement (but not plastic cement) into the gap. This will prevent the rails from moving back in contact with one another.

The "reversing section" must be fed with electrical power, but an electrical reversing switch must be placed in the circuit between the wires from the power pack and the connections at the track, as shown in Figures 7–10, 7–11, and 7–12.

Use a toggle or slide-type DPDT switch as a reversing switch by crossing the wires on the back as shown in Figures 7–10, 7–11, 7–12, and 7–20. Atlas makes a pair of pre-wired DPDT slide-type switches, the "Twin" (Fig. 7–21). Any of the three can be used to control the operation of trains through the "reversing sections" of the track. When the train enters the reversing section, it will either stop or proceed, depending on how the reversing switch on the power pack is set in relation to the DPDT switch that controls the reversing section. If the train stops, then you must flip the DPDT switch that controls the reversing section until the train is just about to exit the reversing section. While the train is

Fig. 7–3. Insulated plastic rail joiners provide electrical gaps at reversing sections or blocks.

in that reversing section, the direction switch on the power pack must be flipped to the opposite direction. When the train leaves the reversing section, it will proceed onto the mainline. You must, of course, change the turnouts to route the train so it won't derail as it moves through the reversing loop or wye to reverse direction.

If the train proceeds through the reversing section, then you do not have to flip the switch. The DPDT (direction or reversing) switch on the power pack must, however, be flipped each time the train leaves the reversing section.

The short length of the "reversing section" may not allow you to use one of the terminal track sections to connect the wires to the track. In that case, an electronics hobby or television repair shop may solder a few feet of wire onto two metal rail joiners so the rail joiners can serve as a "terminal track" anywhere you need them (some hobby shops also sell pre-wired rail joiner connector). You could have a half-dozen sets made in case you need them later for two-train wiring. It is not necessary, incidentally, to solder simple wire-to-wire connections if you carefully twist both the individual wire strands and the ends of the two wires together, as shown in Figure 7–8. Be sure to twist both of the wires so you

will not have just one straight wire with the other curled around it. Bend the twisted ends back over the insulated part of the wire and wrap the joint with about an inch of plastic electrical tape. Bend the last $\frac{1}{8}$-inch of the tape back onto itself (sticky side to sticky side) to form a tab. The tab looks sloppy but you'll be glad to have it when it comes time to unwrap the tape to make a wiring change or repair.

Troubleshooting

For your first layout, I suggest a relatively simple trackplan with no more than six or eight turnouts and a single train. Try as many aspects of the hobby that you feel might interest you, from track-laying to "waybill" operations. Once you've completed the wide range of projects possible, you'll know if you want to attempt the more complicated wiring required for two-train operations and other more advanced model railroading possibilities.

Even with a simple layout, however, there is the chance for operating problems. "Locomotive and Electrical Troubleshooting" (Figure 7–6) includes several solutions to problems that can be related to track wiring. You can use one of the 12-volt bulbs (with built-in wires) sold by hobby stores to illuminate buildings or passenger cars as a "test light." Touch the bare wire ends from the bulb to the rails, as shown in Figure 7–7, and the bulb should glow if the power pack, throttle and on-off switches are all turned on. The same bulb can be used to see if the power is reaching the terminals of the walk-around throttle and the terminals on the power pack.

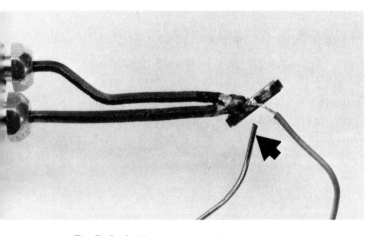

Fig. 7–5. Solder (arrow) can be used to attach track wires to metal rail joiners where space does not permit a terminal track.

Two-Train Control

Two trains can be operated on the same layout by simply dividing the track into two or more "blocks" in a manner similar to that

Fig. 7–6 Locomotive and Electrical Troubleshooting

Trouble	Probable Cause of Trouble	Solution
Locomotive does not run (and headlight does not glow).	1. Power pack not plugged in, or the outlet is faulty.	1. Plug in the power pack or check an appliance in the outlet.
	2. Track wires may be attached to the "AC" terminals of the power pack.	2. Connect the track wires to the two "DC" terminals.
	3. Wires may be improperly connected to the track terminals.	3. Check the "rules" and diagrams in Chapter 7.
	4. Insulated rail joiners may not be in correct positions.	4. Check the "rules" and diagrams in Chapter 7.
	5. Locomotive may be off the track.	5. Rerail the locomotive.
	6. Wheels or track rails may be dirty.	6. Clean the tracks.
	7. Nails, wires, tinsel, or other metals may be causing a short circuit by laying on the track.	7. Remove the material.
	8. Locomotive may be sitting on the plastic frog of a switch or crossing; on an insulated rail joiner; on a track with an operating-signal man or operating crossing gates.	8. Move the locomotive.
Locomotive does not run (but headlight does glow).	1. Check all of the above probable causes. Number 2 is the most likely.	1. Be sure to turn the power pack off immediately while you search for and correct the problem.
Locomotive does not run, and none of the above 8 checks solves the problem.	1. Use an operating light or 12-volt lamp bulb as a "test light." Touch the two wires to the "DC" terminals of the power pack with the "throttle" on. If the light glows, the pack is fine.	1. If the light does not glow with the power pack plugged into a working outlet and with the throttle full on, have the pack checked by your dealer's service department.
	2. Touch the test-light wires to the terminals on each of the terminal tracks with the throttle full on and the "Blocking Switch" (if any) for each block turned on. If the light glows, the problem is likely in the locomotive. If the light does not glow, there is a break in one or both of the wires from the power pack to the terminal.	2. Replace the wires.
	3. Place the locomotive on the terminal track that you just checked and found to be working. If the locomotive runs, then the problem is a loose or missing rail joiner or incorrect wiring.	3. Check every track joint and see that any complex wiring is correct according to the "rules" and diagrams in Chapter 7.
	4. If the locomotive does not run on a terminal track you know is getting power, and you have performed every other troubleshooting check, the problem is likely to be the locomotive. Try another locomotive as a double-check; if it does run, the fault lies in the first locomotive.	4. Have locomotive checked by your dealer's service department.
Locomotive runs but in a series of jerks and stops.	1. Dirty track or locomotive wheels, or, on some steam locomotives, dirty truck-pivot area.	1. Clean everything as outlined in this chapter.
	2. Loose wire connections or loose rail joiners.	2. Check EVERY one in the areas behind and in front of places where the locomotive stalls, and check the terminal track and the power pack wires.
	3. Lack of lubrication on the locomotive (but this is highly unlikely).	3. Lubricate as outlined in this chapter.
	4. Worn motor brushes.	4. Replace as shown in Figures 10–26, 10–27, and 10–28.

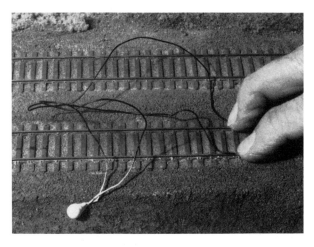

Fig. 7–7. Use a 12-volt light bulb with built-in wires to check for electrical current flow to the rails.

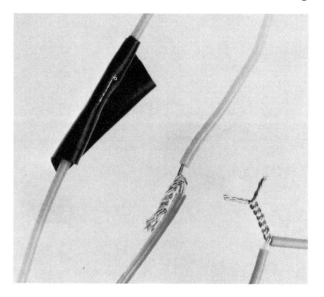

Fig. 7–8. Twist the wires to be joined together (right), bend the ends back (center), and wrap them with electrical tape to leave a tab (left).

used for reversing loops or wyes. The two-train wiring and rail-gapping is much simpler, though, than that required for reversing sections *if* you use the "common rail" wiring system. Most model railroad books and magazines suggest the use of a single power pack with two throttles for two-train operation. That system dates back to the days when a power pack cost as much as $50 or more. Today, it's just about as inexpensive to buy two complete power packs as it is to buy or add on that second throttle. You'll save countless hours of wiring and even more time troubleshooting any short circuits with the double power pack "common rail" wiring system shown here.

"Common Rail" Wiring Systems

With the "common rail" wiring system you designate one rail as the "common" and connect a single wire to that rail through the usual terminal track. The only trick to the application of the system is to be absolutely and positively certain always to remember which rail is "common" regardless of how the track twists or turns. If you have a complex layout, I suggest that you tear off some short strips of masking tape and place them temporarily on top of the "common" rail every

few feet until all of the wiring is complete and the layout is operating with no short circuits.

Notice that a power pack with two throttles will NOT work as the only power pack for "common rail" wiring. You must purchase an additional power pack for operating that second train with this system. (The wiring system for two-throttle power packs is shown in Volume I of *The Model Railroading Handbook*.)

"Blocking" the Track

You will need to cut additional insulating gaps in the rail opposite the one you have designated as "common" to divide the track into "blocks" for independent control of two trains. Cutting gaps in just one rail means that just one wire need be connected to supply power to each of the "blocks" of track between the gaps. Even on a medium-size layout, that can mean almost a fifty percent savings in wire and in complexity. Each of those blocks needs to receive power; the SPDT or "Blocking Switch," wired as shown in Figure 7–14 will do the job. The Atlas "Connector" switch (Fig. 7–21) has three

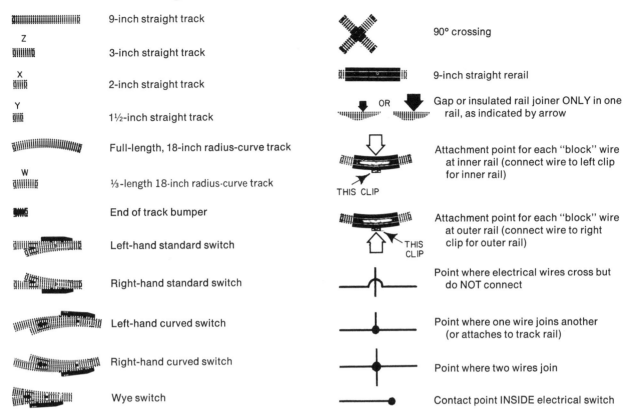

	9-inch straight track		90° crossing
Z	3-inch straight track		9-inch straight rerail
X	2-inch straight track	OR	Gap or insulated rail joiner ONLY in one rail, as indicated by arrow
Y	1½-inch straight track		Attachment point for each "block" wire at inner rail (connect wire to left clip for inner rail)
	Full-length, 18-inch radius-curve track	THIS CLIP	
W	⅓-length 18-inch radius-curve track		Attachment point for each "block" wire at outer rail (connect wire to right clip for outer rail)
	End of track bumper	THIS CLIP	
	Left-hand standard switch		Point where electrical wires cross but do NOT connect
	Right-hand standard switch		Point where one wire joins another (or attaches to track rail)
	Left-hand curved switch		
	Right-hand curved switch		Point where two wires join
	Wye switch		Contact point INSIDE electrical switch

Fig. 7–9. Key to symbols on track plans and wiring diagrams.

SPDT slide switches in one box. The Atlas "Selector" (Fig. 7–21) has four SPDT slide switches, each with a center-off position. Similar SPDT slide switches are available from Model Power, Peco and Roco. Electronics stores, such as Radio Shack, sell SPDT and DPDT switches like those in Figure 7–20.

Blocking Switches

There's somewhat more logic in having the "Blocking Switch" decide which train, rather than which track block, will operate. If you reverse the wiring direction of the switch, so the one wire connects to the block, one each of the two wires can connect to the two power packs. This is the system used in Figure 7–13. You will need almost twice as many SPDT or blocking switches, but the layout wiring will actually be simpler this way

once you add a third, fourth, or fifth block. This system also avoids any possible chance of your trying to "switch" both power packs into the same track, because the blocking switch can only be turned to one power pack at a time. All of the wiring connections you'll see in this book are based on the possible use of both this type of block-selection system and on "common rail" wiring.

The wiring diagram in Figure 7–13 is somewhat more complex than it needs to be for just two power packs and two blocks because it includes the wires you'll want for any number of additional blocks; for example, "A" and "B" connect to future blocks "S," "T," "U," and so forth exactly the same way the two wires from either "Q" or "R" blocking switches connect. The diagram also includes the locations for wiring the optional connector plugs and sockets for "plug-in" power

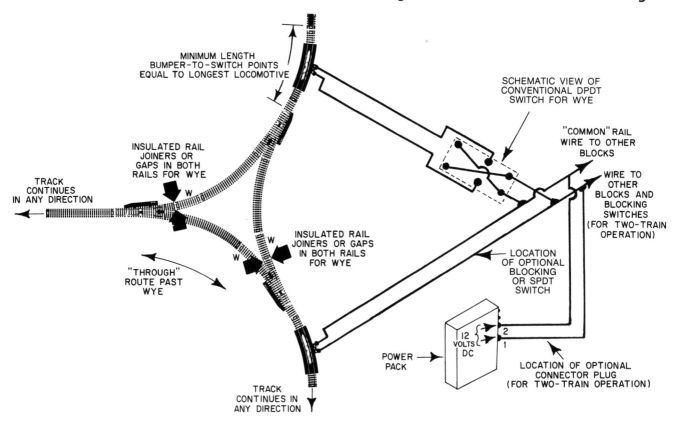

Fig. 7–10. Wiring diagram for stub-end reversing-wye trackage.

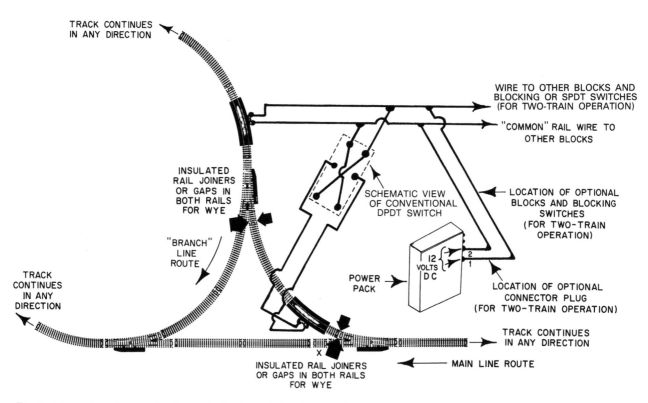

Fig. 7–11. Wiring diagram for the main line/branch line "through" reversing-wye trackage.

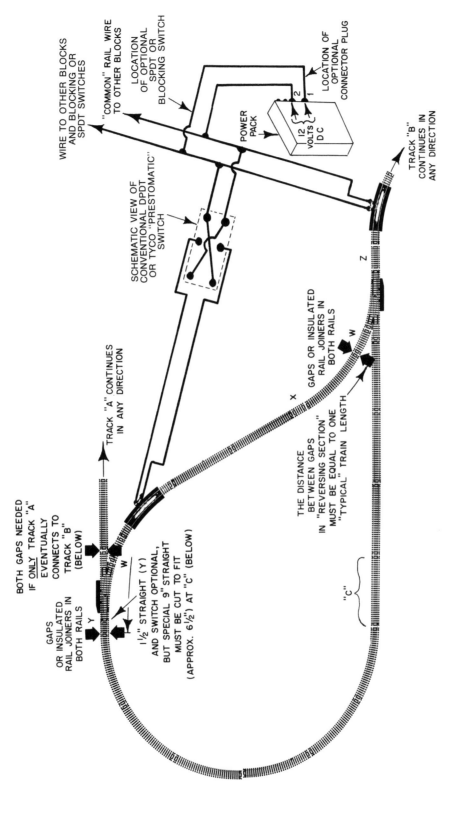

WIRE TO OTHER BLOCKS AND BLOCKING OR SPDT SWITCHES

"COMMON" RAIL WIRE TO OTHER BLOCKS

LOCATION OF OPTIONAL SPDT OR BLOCKING SWITCH

LOCATION OF OPTIONAL CONNECTOR PLUG

POWER PACK

12 VOLTS D C

2

1

SCHEMATIC VIEW OF CONVENTIONAL DPDT OR TYCO "PRESTOMATIC" SWITCH

TRACK "A" CONTINUES IN ANY DIRECTION

TRACK "B" CONTINUES IN ANY DIRECTION

BOTH GAPS NEEDED IF ONLY TRACK "A" EVENTUALLY CONNECTS TO TRACK "B" (BELOW)

GAPS OR INSULATED RAIL JOINERS IN BOTH RAILS

1½" STRAIGHT (Y) AND SWITCH OPTIONAL, BUT SPECIAL 9" STRAIGHT MUST BE CUT TO FIT (APPROX. 6½") AT "C" (BELOW)

Y

W

GAPS OR INSULATED RAIL JOINERS IN BOTH RAILS

THE DISTANCE BETWEEN GAPS IN "REVERSING SECTION" MUST BE EQUAL TO ONE "TYPICAL" TRAIN LENGTH

X

W

Z

"C"

Fig. 7–12. Wiring diagram for reversing-loop trackage.

73

pack connections to make walk-around control easier. The actual wire connections for the connector sockets (and plugs) are shown in Figure 7–15. Figure 7–14 shows the origins of the wires. Notice that block "A" must have a different connection to socket "A" than the connection to block and socket "B." The plugs, which connect to those sockets, are attached to the walk-around throttles through 8- to 20-foot-long tether wires. Those plugs are wired in the same way so that either walk-around throttle can be plugged into either socket "A" or socket "B." The wiring to the sockets makes "A" different from "B." You can add additional pairs of "A"

and "B" sockets along the layout (so you don't have to have such long tether wires on the throttles) by extending all three wires—"A," "B," and "C"—on and around the edges of the layout to sockets wired like "A" and "B," as shown in Figure 7–14. You can install any number of additional pairs of sockets or any number of additional blocks with the use of these wiring diagrams.

Reversing Sections

The "reversing sections" of the reversing loop or wye track arrangements should have both an SPDT blocking switch—to allow use

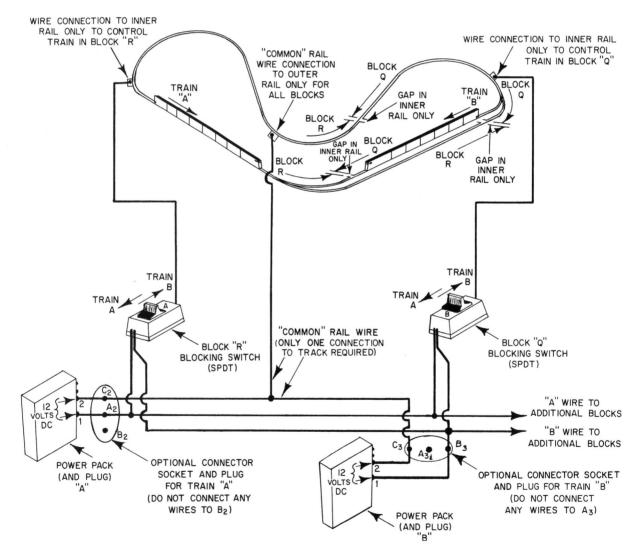

Fig. 7–13. Wiring diagram for true two-train control.

by either train (or throttle) A or B—and the DPDT (reversing) switch. The arrows in the wiring diagrams in Figures 7–10, 7–11, and 7–12 show where the SPDT (blocking) switches should be installed. Briefly, another C (common-rail) wire connection is needed for each "reversing section." The two end wires on a slide-type DPDT switch (Fig. 7–20, right) will connect to the C wire and to the "block" wire from the blocking (SPDT) switch; the two upper wires will connect to the two terminals (track rails) on the track.

If you find the whole concept of wiring the reversing wyes or reversing loops too complicated to understand at this point, just cut the gaps in the rails (there's *no* way around that!) and buy another power pack to operate only the "electrically isolated" reversing section of your layout. You would simply turn control of

any train ("A" or "B") over to the "reversing section" power pack during that portion of the train-reversing moves.

Control Panels

The more complicated your layout becomes with additional switches, blocks for two-train control, and animated accessories, the more you'll need a control panel. It's best to include a control panel in the layout design from the very beginning. If you make the control panel large enough, you'll have a ready place to mount the switch controls when you add additional switches.

I suggest you make a frame for the panel from 1 × 2 lumber and the face from $\frac{1}{4}$-inch plywood. You'll need so little material that it might actually be cheaper to have a cabinet

Fig. 7–14. You can include a "plug-in" walk-around control by providing a pair of telephone sockets at several locations on the layout.

CONNECTING PLUG AND SOCKET WIRING

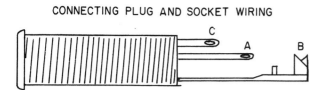

CONNECT WIRES: C_2, C_3, ETC., TO C TERMINAL
A_2, A_3, ETC., TO A TERMINAL <u>ONLY</u>
FOR POWER PACK "A" SOCKETS
B_2, B_3, ETC., TO B TERMINAL <u>ONLY</u>
FOR POWER PACK "B" SOCKETS

Fig. 7–15. Wiring diagram for sockets and plugs for walk-around control. Note: Socket only is shown. For plug wiring connect either of the walk-around throttle's wires to both A and B. Connect the second walk-around throttle's wires to C on plug.

shop make your control panel (or control panels) than to do it yourself. Of course, you will have to drill the holes for the wires and screws that will connect the controls to the face of the panel. Paint the face of the panel flat black. Leave the top half of the panel clear so you can use draftsman's $\frac{1}{8}$-inch-wide striping tape (or colored plastic "hardware" tape cut into $\frac{1}{8}$-inch strips) to put a schematic diagram of your layout on the panel. Use decal or dry-transfer numbers and letters (available at most artists' supply stores) to designate the blocks and the track switches. Put matching letters and numbers right on the electrical

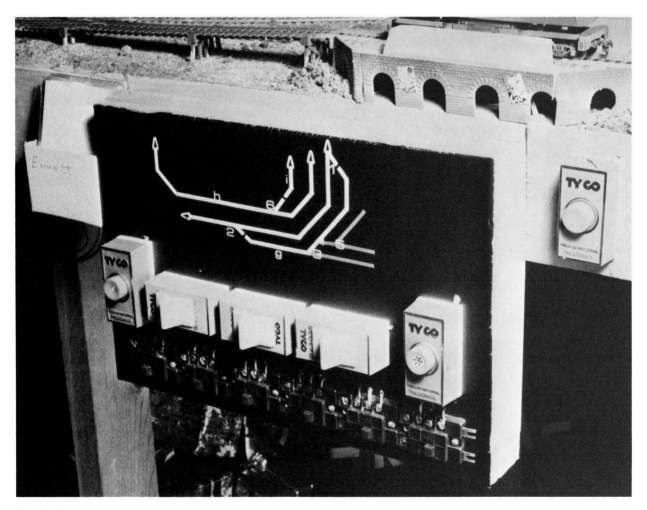

Fig. 7–16. One of the three control panels ("Emmett") for the Burlington Northern layout, illustrated in Chapter 16.

switches themselves. You might also want to get some decal or dry-transfer arrows or other symbols to mark the panel and the electrical switches.

The control panel shown in Figures 7–16 and 7–17 is one of three panels used to operate the 9 × 9-foot layout in Chapter 16. This particular panel has the block switches for blocks "g," "h," and "i," the switch controllers for the six switches in the towns of "Bedford" and "Emmett," which are nearest to the panel, a push-button SPDT switch (far left) to "kill" the power in hidden track "i," and a push-button SPDT switch (marked with an asterisk) wired according to the instructions furnished with it to work as a remote-control "uncoupler." The card-file box to the left of all three control panels holds the envelopes for the "Waybills," described in Chapter 7. The push-button SPDT button to the far right of the panel is the one furnished with the Tyco Dump Car set, which is immediately above the button. The control panel is mounted on the layout so the portion with no wires (the track diagram) is against the 1 × 4 table side, and the lower backside of the panel is accessible for checking the wiring or to add additional controls.

Fig. 7–18. The control panel at "Duncan" on the Burlington Northern.

Holding Tracks

The wiring system described here has no provision for shutting the power off in any block. It only turns off the power pack itself. This is fine if you have only two locomotives and the two power packs to run them. When you add a third locomotive, however, you need some place to "park" it when the other two are in operation. The blocks "a" and "b" in the engine terminal of the 9 × 9-foot layout in Chapter 16 are there to hold loco-

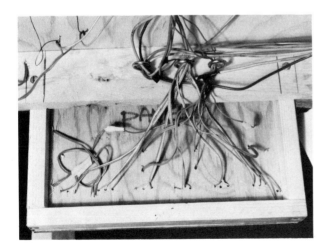

Fig. 7–17. The back side of the "Emmett" control panel. Note the three screw-in hooks that gather the wires.

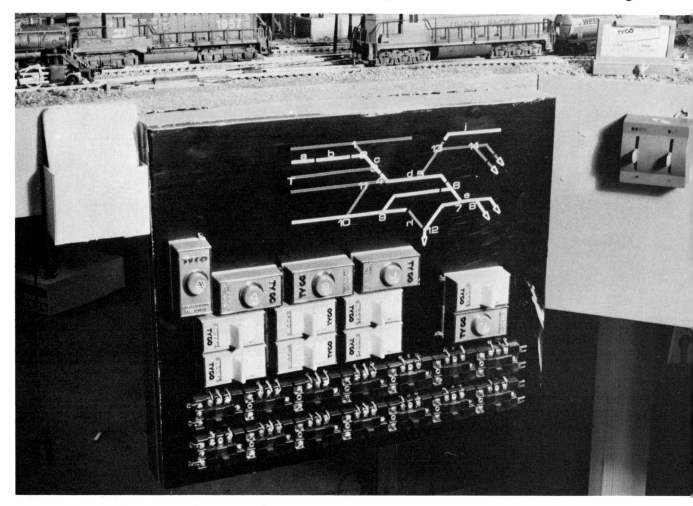

Fig. 7–19. The "Alliance" panel on the Burlington Northern is the most complex because it controls more blocks and more switches.

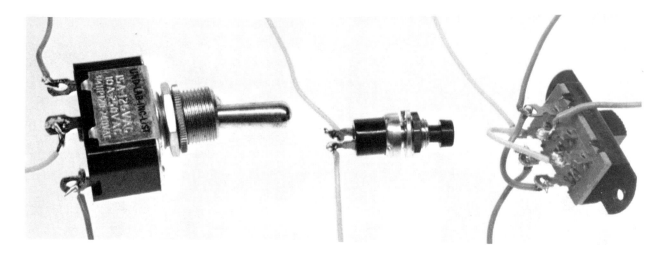

Fig. 7–20. Electronics hobby shops, such as Radio Shack or Allied Radio, carry these toggle-type switches: SPDT (left); push-button SPST (center, a simple on-off switch); and slide-type DPDT switch (right). You must solder the wires to them, as shown, before mounting them in holes bored into a control panel face.

Fig. 7–21. Hobby shops carry pre-wired Atlas electrical switches, including the bank of four center-off SPDT switches (left) called the "Selector," the trio of SPDT switches (center) called the "Connector" and the pair of center-off DPDT switches (right) called the "Twin." Each switch includes wiring instructions, wire-mounting and switch-mounting screws.

motives; blocks "j," "f," and "i" are long enough to hold a locomotive and a complete train. A SPST push-button style switch (Fig. 7–20, center) is inserted into the wire leading from the blocking switch for those blocks to the track. The button will then be used to control the flow of power to that isolated block so that the locomotive runs only while the button is being pressed. Install an insu-lated rail joiner in the rail opposite the "common rail" (Fig. 7–12) to isolate each of these locomotive-holding blocks to be controlled by the push-button SPST switch. With this system, you can park a locomotive in one of these electrically isolated blocks and forget about it until you want it; the locomotive will only leave that block when you hold down the button controlling that block.

Do's and Don'ts for Wiring and Control

Do use extreme care in cutting the insulation from wires so that the delicate individual wire strands are not broken. Twist the strands together as soon as the insulation is pulled free.

Don't attempt to squeeze the wire tight enough to break through the insulation or to simply slit the length of the wire to pull back the insulation.

Do purchase a separate power pack to control switch (turnout) machines and lighting as well as a separate power pack for each additional train (when you want to operate two or more trains at once).

Don't attempt to use one power pack for more than one function. Some of the power packs, however, do have provision for separate control of two trains. A third power pack will still be needed for switch machines and lighting.

Do at least consider the advantages of a separate throttle for walk-around control so you can walk along beside your train with its controls in your hand.

Don't attempt to make your own walk-around control. The available units are simple enough to attach with four wires to the back of most power packs, using the wiring diagram supplied with the walk-around control.

Do drill holes in the tabletop or roadbed so all wiring can be routed beneath the table so it will be accessible even after all the scenery is in place.

Don't run wires on top of the table or beside the tracks.

PART III

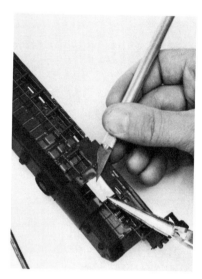

Tools and Techniques

CHAPTER 8

The Workbench

YOU CAN BUILD a model railroad with nothing more than a hammer, a screwdriver, and a knife. A lumberyard will precut the legs for sawhorse table supports and supply sheets of $\frac{1}{2}$-inch-thick, 4 × 8-foot plywood and Homosote. Ready-to-run structures are available as well as ready-to-run locomotives and cars, so all you really need to do is nail down the track, attach the wires, position the buildings and drape some plaster-soaked paper towels here and there for hills with sifted-on ground cover, such as that described in Chapter 12. The 4 × 8-foot plans in Chapter 3, particularly the figure-eight-shape plan, will provide plenty of operating action, and you will hardly have to build anything. Most model railroaders, however, find the hobby fascinating because it does offer endless opportunities to "build things." It's just nice to know that the hobby is versatile enough so you do have the choice.

Roughly three categories of tools are used for model railroading: the basic assortment for laying track and painting ready-to-run equipment; tools for advanced structure or locomotive conversions involving the actual cutting, fitting, and assembly of plastic parts;

and the array of woodworking tools needed to assemble "open-grid"-style benchwork. (The tools for building benchwork aren't really model-building tools at all, however, so these are discussed separately in Chapter 4 in the explanations of how to build benchwork.) There are some very basic modeling techniques and some specific tools you'll need to use on your real railroad in miniature.

The Basic Tools

The tools that are the most important are the ones that are necessary to lay the track, assemble plastic building kits, and perform any necessary maintenance or adjustments on the rolling stock, locomotives, and track. You may already have many of the tools around the house, but it would be better to get a specific set for the exclusive use of building and maintaining your model railroad. You can make some minor substitutions for the tools I suggest in terms of sizes; a five-inch pair of needlenose pliers will do just as well as a seven-inch pair. However, do not try to second guess the list. Don't, for instance, substitute common pliers for needlenose pliers or a pocket knife for an X-Acto hobby knife.

One final bit of experience garnered from more than thirty years of similar mistakes; spend the extra few dollars to get the very

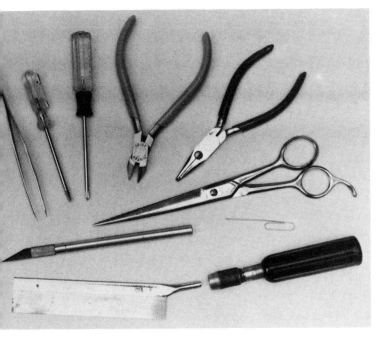

Fig. 8–1. The basic model railroading tools.

best tools at a hobby or hardware store rather than picking up "dollar" bargains. The better tools will probably last a lifetime, so their cost on a per-year basis is only pennies:

Basic Model Railroading Tools

pointed tweezers
small standard screwdriver
small Phillips-head screwdriver
flush-cut diagonal cutters (small)
flush-cut diagonal cutters (to cut rail—
    optional)
small needlenose pliers
scissors
paper clips (or Kadee's coupler-height
    gauge)
X-Acto Number 1 hobby-knife handle
    with extra Number 11 blades
X-Acto Number 5 hobby-knife handle
X-Acto Number 235 razor-saw blade

The use and purpose for most of these tools will be obvious to anyone who has assembled a train set. Some of them, though, are intended for rather obscure purposes.

The flush-cut diagonal cutters are sold by many hobby, hardware and electronics sup-

ply stores. Like most diagonal cutters, they are designed to cut wire by virtually squeezing through it to produce a "cut" that has a 45-degree bevel on both sides. The "flush-cut" diagonal cutters have angled cutting surfaces on their jaws, so that the angle is on just one side of the cut; one side produces a perfectly "flush" or vertical cut. Do not attempt to use them for cutting the track rails. This will dull the cutting surfaces. Some hobby shops also sell larger flush-cut diagonal cutters that *are* designed to cut brass or nickle silver rail (Fig. 5–6). The small flush-cut diagonal cutters are intended to cut wires with a minimum of pulling and damage to the individual wire "threads." Their most important use, for a model railroader, will be to cut the windows and other plastic parts for structure kits from the molding sprues, or "trees," of scrap plastic. If you cannot find flush-cut diagonal cutters, buy regular diagonal cutters and use them for cutting wire.

The X-Acto Number 1 hobby-knife handle and Number 11 blades can be used to cut these structure parts from their sprues. Do not attempt to pull or break the plastic parts away from their sprues; there's a good chance you'll break the part rather than the sprue! The paper clip's purpose is to serve as a gauge for adjusting the height of toy train couplers on rolling stock or locomotives as shown in Chapter 14. You can also use paper clips to apply tube-type cement for plastics to some hard-to-reach corner, as well as to scrape away excess cement.

The X-Acto Number 5 hobby-knife handle and the Number 235 razor-saw blade are the tools you need to cut the rails for custom-fitting snap-together track on some layouts, if you do not wish to purchase the second pair of large flush-cut diagonal cutters. Custom-fit track sections are necessary with some track plans, and a cut-to-fit end-of-track piece for a siding can often mean the difference between the siding holding one car or two. You can save money and have a smoother flow of track on your "second" model railroad layout by substituting three-foot lengths of flexible track for long stretches of sectional track. The flexible track will seldom fit in any layout without at least one of the rails being cut to fit. It's somewhat tricky to get the flexible track shaped into smooth curves, so I suggest that you build at least one layout with conventional track. You will probably use the razor saw most for cutting plastic walls and other structure parts for building "conversions" such as some of those discussed in Chapter 11.

Special Plastic-Working Tools

You may want to spend some time creating the special "conversion" structures that will set your railroad in miniature apart from all others. Similar techniques can be used, along with the techniques in Chapter 10, for unique locomotive and rolling-stock "conversions." The X-Acto razor saw is the basic cutting tool for these custom-built models, and the Number 1 knife and Number 11 blade can be used for final trimming and finishing. The pointed tweezers and tube-type as well as liquid cement for plastics that are needed to assemble box-stock kits will work just as well for any "conversions" involving the use of two or more models. The secret to success in making conversion models, however, lies in seeing that your modified parts fit at least as well as the stock-kit components, and that means you'll need a few more tools.

Plastic-Working Tools

X-Acto Number 1 knife with Number 11 blades

Fig. 8–2. Special plastic-working tools.

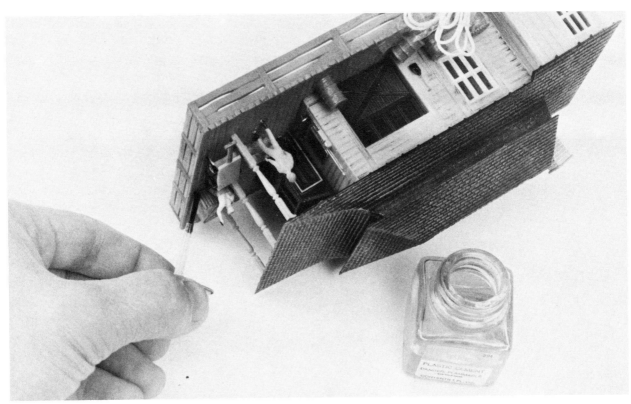

Fig. 8–3. Liquid cement for plastics can be used to dissolve glue joints on ready-built buildings, as well as for assembly work.

12-inch-long steel ruler or straightedge
   draftsman's plastic triangle
medium-cut large flat-mill file
file card or brass-bristled suede shoe
   brush
bench vise (with adjustable head), such
   as a PanaVise
liquid and tube-type cement for plastics
tube of patching or "spot" automobile
   body putty

The steel straightedge or ruler and plastic triangle are necessary in order to guarantee that all of your cuts are straight and true. The mill file will help to keep the surfaces true as well, but it's most useful for filing 45-degree bevels on the mating corners of walls cut to length so they can be assembled in the same manner as those in a stock kit.

If you are going to work with locomotive, rolling-stock, or structure-conversion pro-

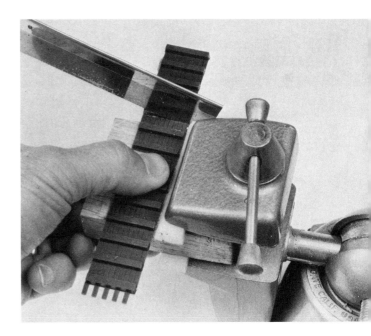

Fig. 8–4. The PanaVise type of swivel-head vise allows you to position the sawing block for more comfortable working conditions.

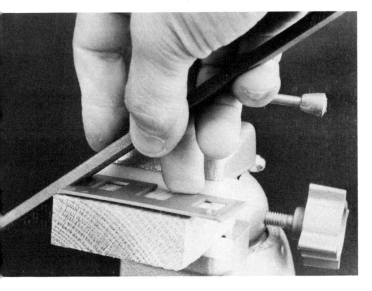

Fig. 8–5. File the edges of modified building walls to a 45-degree bevel so they can be joined tightly to other walls.

jects, where you need to cut plastic parts, I recommend that you consider purchasing one of the bench vises with an adjustable head, such as the PanaVise. You can also use the vise for making more precise and safer cuts to shorten and fit track sections. The vise should not be used to actually clamp the plastic pieces but, rather, to clamp a short scrap of 1 × 3 or 1 × 4 wood. The wood serves as a firm and stable backing for the part you are cutting, while your fingers serve as clamps to hold the plastic against the wood by squeezing the plastic part and the wood backing together. The vise keeps the wood stable and secure, and the adjustable (or swivel-style) head allows you to position the block comfortably both for clamping by hand and for cutting or filing. You can use the same technique with a conventional bench vise, but you'll have to contort your body into some rather uncomfortable positions to

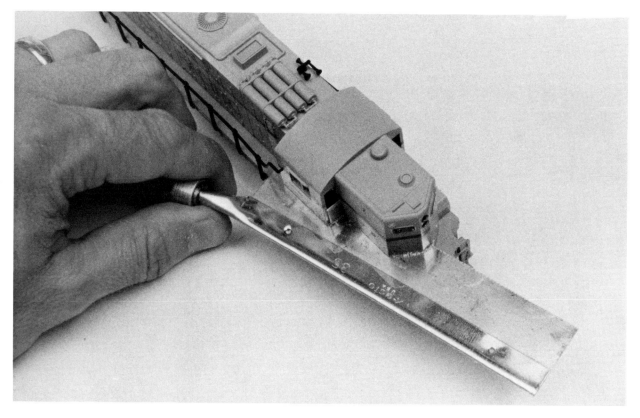

Fig. 8–6. The razor saw makes a knife-thin cut with a minimum amount of effort.

clamp with one hand while cutting or filing with the other.

The nice thing about model railroading, particularly in HO scale, is that you don't need much more than a 2 × 3-foot workbench area. An old desk or table would be an ideal workbench for your modeling, or you could purchase a breadboard from a lumberyard and use it as your work surface with a shoe-box to store your tools. You should have a sturdy table to back up the breadboard, so stay away from card tables, TV trays, and the like. If you don't have a strong, stable structure, your finished models will probably look as wobbly as your workbench.

Lighting for the Workbench

The most critical model building "tool" is proper lighting. Try to arrange your work-bench area so you have at least two sources of light in order to avoid having to work in your own hands' shadows. It's best to have the same type of lighting for your workbench as you have for your layout area. This will guarantee that the colors and subtle weather-ing shades you apply at the workbench will look the same way on the railroad itself. I prefer incandescent light bulbs (the screw-in kind) for layout lighting because they give a softer light and they can be dimmed for eve-ning or night effects by adding a conventional wall-dimmer switch in the circuit. It's best to have an electrician add that dimmer switch so you don't run the risks of injury or fire hazard possible with 115-volt house wiring. The disadvantages of incandescent lighting, however, are that it can make the work area uncomfortably warm, and it requires more electricity to equal the light output of fluorescent tubes.

CHAPTER 9

Rolling Stock Super-Detailing

THE ORDINARY FREIGHT CAR is what real railroading in miniature is all about. Freight cars provide a living for the real railroads, and the simulation of the car and its movements is what makes model railroading come alive. I'll show you how you can operate freight cars in the same way the real railroads do it (but without any of the paperwork) in Chapters 14 and 15; there you will find all the information you need to get your fleet of freight cars into a shape that at least resembles a real railroad. It isn't possible to duplicate the thousands of freight cars that move in and through each town on a real railroad. Only a club layout is large enough to duplicate the hundred-car trains of the prototype. But part of the "art" of model railroading is making just a relatively few freight cars look like many, and to make them at least appear to be carrying something to somewhere.

You won't find one freight car in a thousand on a real railroad that's as bright and clean as those in a model train set. It only takes one night in the dew and one day of dust or rain to "weather" a real freight car, so their freshly painted look never lasts very long. If you become accustomed to visu-

alizing what a real railroad looks like, you'll discover that many of your cars look identical, except for the amount of weathering and the car numbers. Brightly painted "toy" train cars will never look realistic unless you weather them.

It's far too obvious that you don't have "enough" cars on your layout when each one is so obviously different from the rest. If you match weathering effects on a few cars with different factory paint colors, they will blend together in the same way the real ones do. Don't be afraid to buy two or three identical cars rather than two or three different ones the next time you add to your rolling-stock fleet. You can apply slightly different weathering hues to them if you like and change at least one of their numbers by using decals. You'll increase the realism of your railroad far more than you can imagine simply by matching the "mix" of identical versus unusual cars on the real railroad.

Repainting Techniques

Most of the ready-to-run cars are painted to match the bright colors of real-life railroad cars. However, in a typical real-life railroad train or train yard, only a few of the cars are that bright. Most freight cars are painted in the reddish-brown color which is so typical of the majority of real railroad cars. That reddish brown can vary from an almost chocolate brown to a cedar or redwood color, depending on the railroad and the year the car was painted. The color is so common because the paints used at the turn of the century could be colored for almost no cost by using powdered clay; and that's how the "earthy" colors came to be.

Matching Colors

You can match a couple of the shades, "Boxcar Red" or "Roof Brown," using spray cans of Testors or Pactra paints. Testors' "Dark Brown" will appear to be "Roof Brown" if the finished model is then sprayed with Testors' clear "Dullcote." The slightly redder "Boxcar Red" can be approximated by spraying the "Dark Brown"-painted finished model with Pactra's "Clear Flat." The "Dullcote" seems to darken most colors about one shade, while the Pactra "Clear Flat" does not change the color but adds a semimatte finish. You can buy a bottle of any real railroad color from Floquil or Scalecoat and apply it with a paint brush, but it's a lot easier and quicker to use spray paint. Floquil makes some aerosol railroad colors. Hobby shops and some art supply stores sell an airbrush that is a miniature version of the spray guns used to paint automobiles. The airbrush, with its own air compressor, can be used to spray Floquil, Scalecoat, or SMP bottled paints. You may find some other brands of clear flat finish that will give the same type of finish as Testors', but you *must* experiment by spraying them on a test surface with both the paint and the decals you use. Most brands of clear flat spray paint will cause decals to wrinkle or curl, and they might even do the same to the paint itself!

Repainting a model freight car or locomotive means that you must also apply new letters, heralds, and numbers to the model after the paint dries. You should also remove the original letters, heralds, and numbers, however, because they *will* show through the paint in the form of a raised outline all around the markings. Common rubbing alcohol and a cotton swab or tissue will remove most markings. Dip the swab or tissue in the alcohol and rub the lettering or numbers on the side of the car with it for a moment until the marking is "erased." The inks used on most models are alcohol-based and can be removed quite easily with this technique. However, some inks may have to be sanded, using Number 600 sandpaper.

Removing the Original Paint

The original paint on model railroad cars is very difficult to remove. You can try an oven cleaner, such as Easy-Off, or automobile brake fluid, but you could ruin the model rather than removing the paint. Several types of plastic are used on model railroad cars and on the locomotive bodies too. A paint remover that doesn't dissolve one body, though, might melt another.

You *must* apply a coat of primer to give the surface some "tooth" so you can keep the

Fig. 9–1. Remove the trucks, couplers, and the underframe before painting any car or locomotive.

Fig. 9–2. Rub the lettering with a cotton swab dipped in alcohol to remove the lettering before painting.

applications of that final color coat as thin as possible. I have found that the Magic brand of primer sold by Standard Brands and the Tempo primers sold by some hardware and automobile-parts stores work quite well. Some primers will attack paint or plastic, and most are so thick that they obscure most of the rivets and other fine details. You'll have to experiment with the primer you want to use (even if it's one of the two I've had good luck with) to be certain it won't attack the paint on your particular model. Test spraying on the inside of the body or near the bottom of one of the car ends will reveal whether or not the primer will cause the paint beneath it to curl or crinkle.

Spray Painting

There's a bit of an art to spray painting with an aerosol can. First, wash the models in

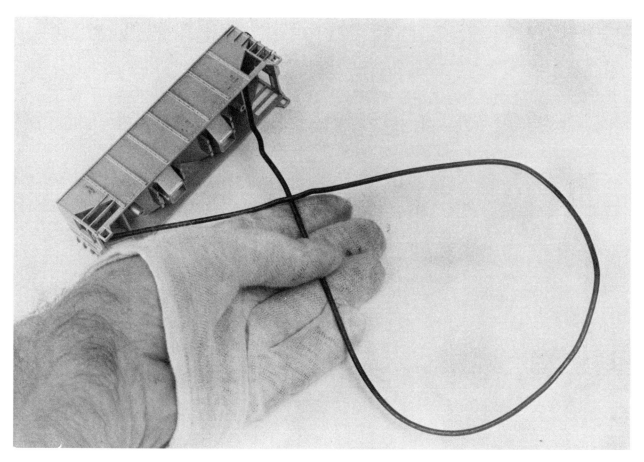

Fig. 9–3. Bend a coat hanger to this shape so it will have spring-grip on the car. Protect your holding hand with a glove.

detergent before any painting, rinse them, and allow them to air dry to remove all traces of grease and fingerprints. Then, you will need some sort of a handle to hold the model so that you don't touch the paint. I use a wire coat hanger straightened and rebent to a small "e" shape so the inside of the car body is held under a spring tension by the wire. For smaller parts I attach masking tape, sticky side up, with smaller pieces of tape. The smaller parts can be placed on the tape, spray painted, and left there until the paint dries. I wear a disposable plastic work glove on one hand for holding the coat hanger and the scrap of wood, and I spray the car or parts with the aerosol can in my other hand.

To begin, hold the can under warm (never hot!) running water, and be sure to shake it vigorously for a count of at least 100. Practice your spray painting technique on some old cars until you can apply a thin and even coat of paint with no runs and no "orange-peel" textures. You'll find you can get a smoother coat if the model and the spray can are at room temperature (70°F). Begin the spray just off the model and pass it evenly over the model before releasing the button. Starting or stopping the spray directly on the model can produce splatters and runs. It's best to apply as many as a dozen very light coats rather than trying to do the job with just one; you'll almost always produce runs in the paint if you try to cover with just one or two coats. If you're finished with the spray can for an hour or more, invert the can so the nozzle is down and press down on the nozzle until just gas but no paint flows from the nozzle. The paint-pickup tube will be above the paint, with the can inverted, so this technique allows the can's own pressure to clean both the nozzle

Fig. 9–4. Apply several light coats of primer from a distance of about nine inches to get a smooth and even finish.

and the spray tube inside the can. Gloss paint makes a much better surface for the application of decals but you can achieve a glossy finish by spraying a coat of clear gloss.

Decals

A decal is nothing more than a number, name, herald, or other marking that is painted on a piece of glue-covered paper. The colored portion of the decal is then sprayed with several coats of clear gloss paint. When you soak the glue-covered paper in water, the glue dissolves and allows the decal to be pushed from the paper and onto the model. Because the decal is too thick to snuggle in tightly around rivets, seams, and other details, decal manufacturers, such as Champion and MicroScale, make decal-softening fluids that can be applied like so many drops of water. These fluids almost dissolve the decal back to its original "paint" state, so it really does look as though it's painted on.

The major decal manufacturers can handle direct-mail orders, and each of them offers a catalog for $5.00. I suggest you obtain all three makers' catalogs so you'll know what choices you have for relettering rolling stock and locomotives. A few decals are made for station and industrial signs as well as names, and these can be used if you want to make up your own railroad names. Contact the decal firms directly:

Champion Decal Company
    P.O. Box 1178
    Minot, ND 58701

Herald King
    % Miller Advertising, P.O. Box 1133
    Bettendorf, IA 57222-1133

MicroScale Industries
    P.O. Box 11950
    Costa Mesa, CA 92627

Wm. K. Walthers, Inc.
    P.O. Box 18676
    Milwaukee, WI 53218

How to Apply Decals

The decal must first be cut close to the printed portion with scissors or a hobby knife to remove as much of the clear border as possible from Herald King and Champion decals. MicroScale decals have a tapered edge to most of the clear decal films. This can be seen if you hold the decal so that light reflects off the shiny clear part. Cut the Micro-Scale decals apart near the outer edges of the clear portions. From this point on, the decal cannot be touched with a bare finger until the final protective coat of clear flat paint has dried. Use pointed tweezers to pick up the decal and dip it into warm water for just a moment. Set the decal on a blotter or on a paper towel for a few minutes while the glue dissolves.

When the decal can be moved on its paper backing, it is ready to be applied to the model. Hold both the decal and its paper backing exactly where you want the decal. Keep just the decal in place with the tip of the

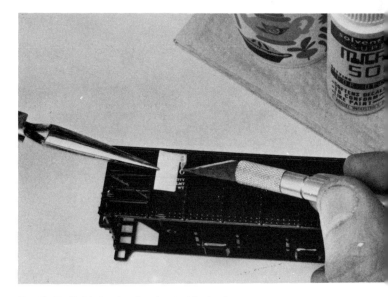

Fig. 9–5. Hold the decal with a hobby knife while removing its paper backing with tweezers.

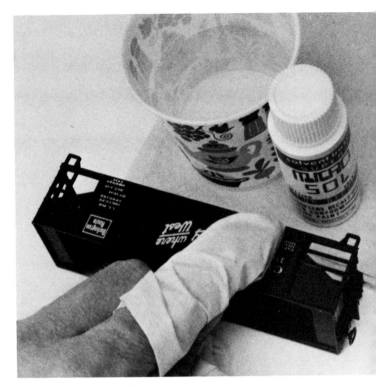

Fig. 9–6. Use tweezers to position both the decal and its paper, then hold the decal with a knife tip while you slide the paper from beneath it with tweezers.

Fig. 9–8. Gently dab the decal after it has been softened with "Micro Sol," or with any decal-softening liquid, to force it down around rivets and other details.

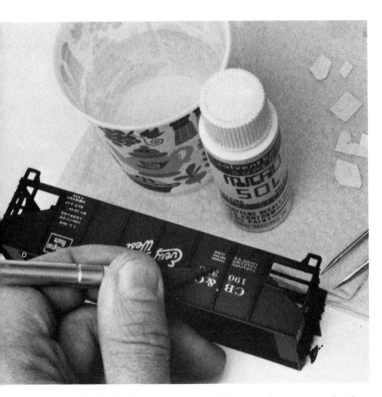

Fig. 9–7. Any trapped air bubbles can be punctured with a knife tip and the decal covered with a second application of decal-softening fluid.

hobby-knife blade while you pull the paper backing from beneath it.

Apply a thin coat of Champion's "Decal-Set" or MicroScale's "Micro Sol" to the decal with a Number O-size paint brush. If the area that is beneath the decal is textured with rivets or other details, it's wise to wet the area with the decal-softening fluid. Allow the fluid about 15 minutes to dry, and, if necessary, dab at the decal lightly with a finger wrapped with a tissue to force the decal down over the surface. Don't push too hard or the decal will "grab" the tissue; just dab at it. It might take as many as six applications of the decal-softening fluid, applied over a period of an hour or more, to get some decals to snuggle tightly around curved or highly detailed surfaces. When the decal-softening fluid has dried overnight, scrub the surface of the decal lightly with a cotton swab dipped in water to remove any traces of the decal-softening fluid or the decal glue. Let the model dry overnight again and apply a protective spray-on coat of Testors "Dullcote," Pactra "Clear Flat," or some other spray-on flat finish clear paint that you have pretested to be sure it will not attack either the paint or the decals. The final coat of paint will match the finish or gloss (or lack of gloss) of the decal to the rest of the model, and it will help to disguise those clear edges of the decal so only an expert could tell it was a decal rather than painted-on lettering.

Weathering and Aging Tips

I cannot tell you how to weather a model car, locomotive, or structure. The only way you'll learn is to study the techniques. You'll have to go out into the real world to study how weathering really looks, and you'll have to practice the techniques I offer to learn how to use them properly.

Weathering is a term used to describe a final coat of very thin paint that is applied to the model to simulate the effects of sun, wind, dirt, and rain. The paint can be just about anything from artists' water-base acrylics to artists' oil colors to artists' pastel chalks powdered on sandpaper and brushed onto the model. If you have access to an artist's airbrush (an $80 to $300 miniature spray gun like those used to paint cars), you can use spray-on Testors or any of the other bottled model paints. Excellent weathering effects can be achieved with oils, acrylics, or pastel chalks applied with a paint brush or a fine-pore sponge in a dabbing technique. The paint, however, must be thinned with about 95 parts water (for acrylics) or turpentine (for oil colors), so that the color will be barely visible.

Sand and Dust

There are really only two secrets to the art of weathering a railroad miniature. First, keep the paint thin enough so that you can apply two or three coats without obscuring the lettering and numbers on the car or locomotive. Second, use photographs or very recent memories of the real thing as your guide to where and how much of the weathering colors to apply. You'll find that light beige or gray will be useful in simulating the sun-bleached effects of nature on any color car, locomotive, or structure. Those lighter shades can also be used on darker cars to simulate dust from desert areas, such as the Southwest. Many Southern Pacific cars, for instance, have a beige tint to their surfaces from traveling through the desert dust and from the effects of the hot Southwestern sun. Black or dark brown are the colors to use to simulate steam locomotive soot, diesel locomotive exhaust stains, and coal dust on your models. You'll see examples of all three different types of weathering in the color illustrations.

You should try to simulate as many different types of weathering as you can on your models, about half of them having weathering patterns common to the area you are modeling. Most of the cars you'll see in the coal-mining regions are stained with coal dust, and most of the cars that serve in limestone areas are streaked with gray, and the Southwestern cars are beige-tinted. Vary the degree of the weathering, from the barest trace that might collect on a "new" car to the years of grime that collect on an older car. If you apply too much weathering to a car or two, do as the real railroads do and paint over the number in the original car color and add a fresh decal number.

Wood and Rust

The weathering techniques can be used to weather track and to simulate wood flat-car floors or industrial loading platforms. Paint the "wood" surface a very light shade of beige, and then apply a wash of dark brown with a sponge, streaking the wash in the di-

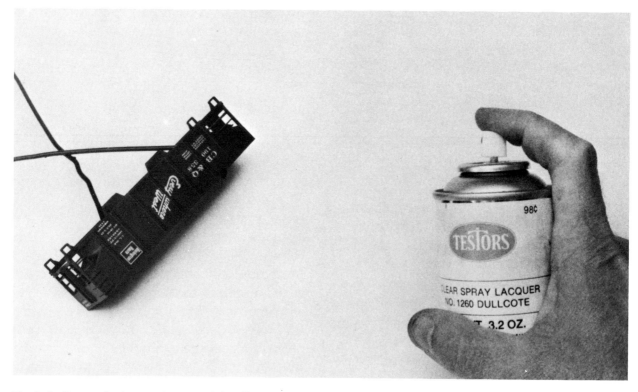

Fig. 9–9. Spray a final protective coat of clear flat paint over the decals; their finish will match that of the model.

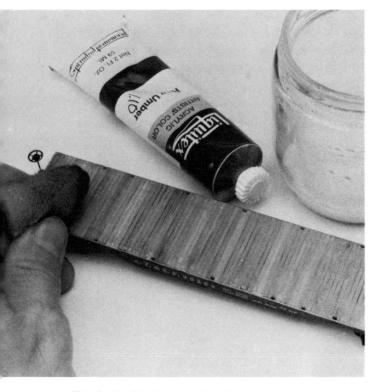

Fig. 9–10. Simulate wood grain by wiping over the beige-painted surface with water-thinned dark-brown streaks.

rection of the grain. Make every other board or tie or so a darker shade and just touch a few of them to leave mostly the faded-wood look of the light beige. Paint the track rails with dark red-brown to simulate rust, and add drops of "rust" to flat-car floors or loading docks to simulate rusted nails. Scrape just the tops of the rails gently with a knife blade to remove any paint from the electrical pickup surfaces, and do keep the rust-colored paint away from the moving parts of the switches. You can make your sectional track look like it was laid on real wood ties with individual spikes by using these weathering techniques.

Freight Car Loads

I suggest that you add some type of load to all of your flatcars, but you should load only half of the hoppers or gondolas. Ways to simulate loads for hoppers and gondolas ap-

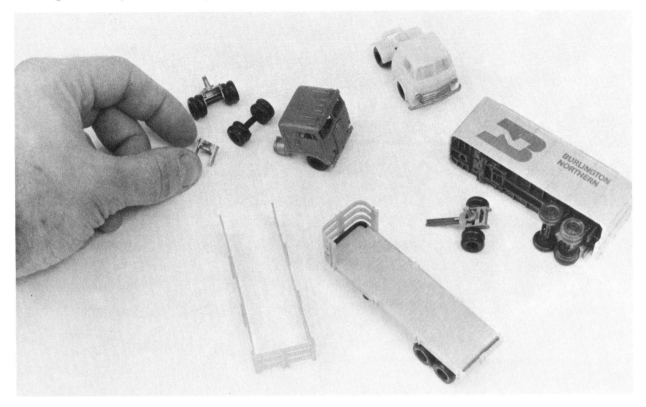

Fig. 9–11. A tractor truck has been cut apart to make a dolly for a double-trailer and a tandem-axle van. Cut the fence from a cattle trailer to convert it into a flatbed.

Fig. 9–12. The converted tractors and trailers in action at the "Duncan" grade crossing.

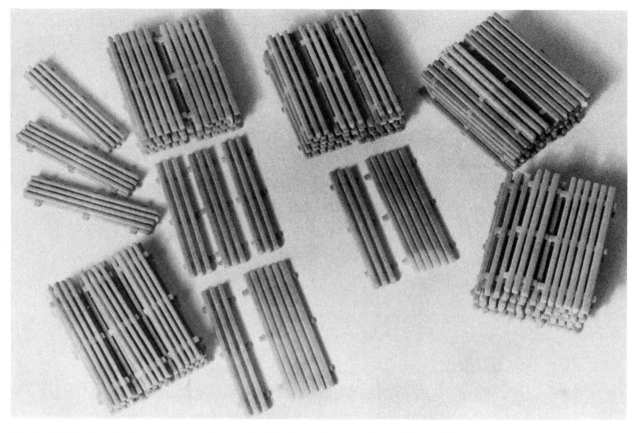

Fig. 9–13. The lumber from two sawmills was piled in alternating rows of two-wide and three-narrow, as shown at left.

pear in the "Loads-In Empties-Out" section of Chapter 15. The r-t-r "action" cars are the type that can be loaded and unloaded without your hands touching the cargo. The log-dumping cars are a typical example, but the dumping principle is also offered, by the r-t-r firms, in coal, ore and even box-dumping versions. The flat cars with removable highway trailers also fall into this "action" category when one of the "hands-off" loaders or unloaders is used.

Coal is available in several sizes or grains from hobby stores, or you can powder real coal by putting it in a cloth bag and hitting it with a hammer. Cut a piece of cardboard to fill the car interior so only about a $\frac{1}{4}$-inch of coal is needed to fill it. Pour in the coal so the

Fig. 9–14. These four flatcars are fully loaded; remove at least $\frac{1}{3}$ of each load so the cars can simulate "unloaded" cars or "loaded" ones for improved switching-action credibility.

Fig. 9–15. Partially loaded flatcars lend more authenticity to your models than empty or fully loaded ones.

peaks of the piles are level with the car sides but no higher. Spray the loads with water from a plant atomizer or one of the lever-style plastic hair-spray bottles. Mix equal parts of white glue and water and apply it to the water-wetted load with an eye dropper. You may need to add a few drops of liquid detergent to the white glue and water to keep it from sitting on top of the coal loads.

Flatcars are more realistic in operation if they are partially loaded. This way, if you leave a Trailer Train type of flatcar at an unloading dock for a scale "day," you can pick the "unloaded" car up again without anyone wondering much about it. A completely empty flatcar is far too obvious to serve as a "loaded" car unless, of course, you really do want to load and unload those cars with r-t-r action accessories.

Be sure to tie down any loads of lumber or other loose commodities. You can use 7-pound test nylon fishing line dyed black with common Rit dye. The nylon line can be woven through the various stake pockets along the sides of the flatcars and tied at just one place out of sight on the bottom of the car. Thread is too coarse and has too many hair-like strands to be realistic "rope" or "cable" in HO scale. Chapter 15 includes some ideas on using highway trailers and intermodal containers for flatcar loads.

Rolling Stock Maintenance

Rolling stock must be free-rolling, not wobbling as it rolls down the track, with trucks that are free to swivel so the cars don't derail on curves or turnouts. All couplers must be the same height, with no low-hanging uncoupling pins. In addition, all rolling stock must be able to travel anywhere on the layout without derailing.

The "Derailment and Track Troubleshoot-

99

Fig. 9–16. Easy-to-build kits are available for modern articulated "spine" cars that carry one trailer per car. This is Athearn's five-car kit.

ing Chart" (Figure 6–8 in Chapter 6) describes the problems that cause derailments. Most often, the problem will lie with the track rather than the rolling stock. Still, if a single car derails and no other cars have problems, inspect that car carefully for possible causes of derailments.

The most frequent cause of derailments on rolling stock is coupler pins that hang down so far that they snag at turnouts or crossings. Chapter 14 includes information on how to be sure the couplers are mounted properly.

The second most common cause of derailments by freight cars is dirt, which usually is attracted to freight car wheels and bearings

Fig. 9–17. This Athearn boxcar was weathered with powdered artists' pastel chalks by George Booth, then fitted with Kadee couplers.

by oil. Virtually all of the HO scale freight car models and kits include plastic trucks made of a slippery plastic that should never require lubrication. Oil in the ends of the axles on freight cars merely attracts dust and dirt and turns it into a sticky substance. Excessive oil or grease on locomotives can also dribble onto the rails to be picked up by the wheels of the rolling stock. You can, then, avoid most dirt by simply not lubricating anything but the metal bearings and gears of the locomotives—with the least amount of oil or grease possible.

If you find a sticky residue on the wheels, scrape it off very gently with a hobby knife or the blade of a small screwdriver. The wheels can be removed from most model railroad trucks by simply spreading the plastic sideframes apart between your fingers so the axle and wheel set falls out. With the wheels removed, the bearings for the pinpoint axle ends can be cleaned with a toothpick dipped in paint thinner. Work outdoors and avoid any fire or sparks when using any flammable fluids. Do not use a knife to scrape the bearings clean or you may scratch the bearings

Fig. 9–19. Use a hobby knife and a scrap of wood to slice about $\frac{1}{64}$-inch from the truck pivot to eliminate side-to-side rocking.

and reduce the free-rolling qualities of the trucks.

If you find that the cars rock from side to side as they roll down the tracks, one of the truck pivots must be tightened. The lower-cost rolling stock that have trucks with a split pin that snaps into the bolster in the floor are difficult to correct. Sometimes, you can spread the pin slightly but not enough so the truck cannot pivot freely. On models that have trucks mounted with a separate press-in pin or with a screw, the underframe often can be modified at the truck pivot (bolster). Use a hobby knife to slice about $\frac{1}{64}$-inch from the truck pivot. With this material removed, the screw for that truck can be tightened enough so the truck will only pivot. Leave the opposite truck alone so it can wobble from side to side as well as pivot. The single pivoting (but not rocking) truck will keep the car level and the rocking truck will allow the trucks to follow uneven or rough trackwork without derailing the car.

Some of the least expensive cars may have thin wisps of plastic around the extreme outer edges (the flanges) of the wheels. This plastic

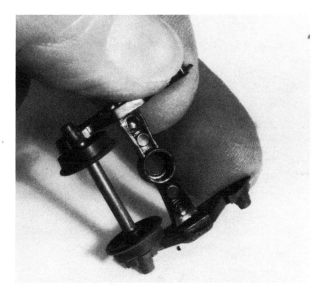

Fig. 9–18. Spread the sides of the truck apart between your second and third fingers to remove the wheels.

is called "flash" and occurs during the manufacturing process. You can remove it with a sharp hobby knife. For really free-rolling freight or passenger cars, cars that have the sound of real railroad wheels, replace the wheel and axle sets on all your freight cars with metal wheels and axles. Hobby dealers can supply these wheelsets for any HO scale model.

CHAPTER 10

The Locomotive Factory

MOST MODEL LOCOMOTIVES are ready-to-run replicas of real steam and real diesel engines. Virtually all the three-dimensional details that appear on the real thing appear on the model. There are several ways, how-

Fig. 10–1. A wash of flat black acrylic and water will make vents and louvers appear to be open.

ever, that you can make these locomotives seem even more like the real thing. A "wash" of 95 parts water and 5 parts black acrylic can be used to fill in the hollows of louvers and grills. This will make it appear as though there really could be engines inside the diesel bodies.

Every steam and diesel locomotive, even those at the head ends of passenger trains, have some degree of weathering such as that described in Chapter 9. Locomotives are even more likely to become dirty than rolling stock, but the patterns of the dirt will be different indeed. Again, photographs from railroad books and visits to real railroad yards will show you just where and how the real locomotives collect their dirt.

That black acrylic wash can also be applied to the trucks, ends and lower areas of the locomotives to simulate dirt and grime. You'll see an example of the light gray "wash" applied to one steam locomotive and three or four varieties of diesel weathering on the models in this book, but there are hundreds of other variations on the full-size locomotives.

You may also want to repaint and apply decals to your locomotives to match another railroad, or you may want to create your own railroad colors and markings. The most complicated alterations you might want to make on your railroads' locomotives will be to use "conversion" techniques, which combine

Fig. 10–2. Beige and light gray water-thinned acrylics will give steam locomotives a weathered appearance.

two locomotives' parts to make two other locomotives that are not available as ready-to-runs.

Maintenance

If you keep your track clean and do not operate your layout on the floor, the amount of maintenance needed on your locomotives should be minimal. The major problems that affect model locomotives are oxidation of the metal wheels and track; grease and oil mixed with dirt on the wheels and track; dirt, lint, dust, and other debris around the motor and gears of the locomotives. The only part of your locomotives that is likely to show even visible signs of wear might be the brushes on the motor, but they should last for hundreds of hours of operation. Most of the damage that occurs to model locomotives is the result

of an inexperienced modeler trying to repair something that wasn't broken in the first place. The second most frequent causes of damage are, of course, accidental trips from table to floor, and accidental footwork around those floor-level layouts.

The only maintenance or repairs you should make are to see that the wheels (and the track rails) are kept spotlessly clean, that the motor and gears are cleaned frequently, and that only a small amount of grease or oil is added to replace what you wipe off in the process of cleaning the mechanism. If you have a perfectly clean engine, and if you have gone through all the troubleshooting steps in this chapter, and your locomotive still does not run, then you should take it to your hobby dealer to determine if he, one of his customers, or even the factory itself, offers repair service. At worst, you can disassemble the

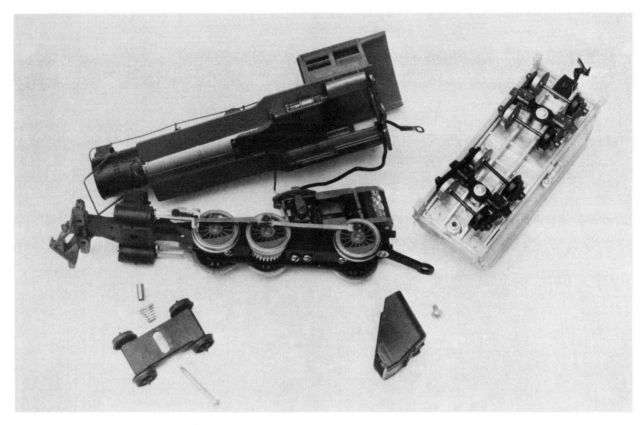

Fig. 10–3. The superstructure can be removed from this Mantum 4–6–0 steam locomotive by removing one screw from the center of the pilot truck and then sliding the superstructure to the rear.

Fig. 10–4. Use both hands to spread the diesel body apart far enough so the power truck will snap out.

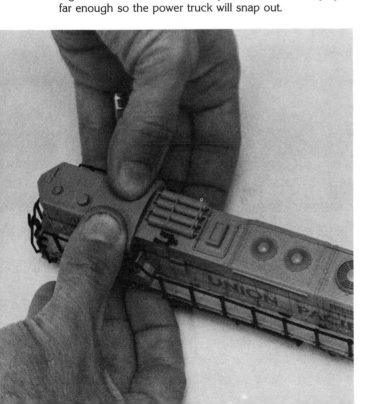

motor so the locomotive will roll, then use it as a "dummy."

Disassembling

The locomotive body must be removed from the diesels and from a steam locomotive for access to the gears and other working parts. The sides of most brands of diesel bodies must be removed by spreading the body apart with quite a lot of pressure to snap the trucks or chassis from beneath them. It's a good idea to have someone help, so one of you can spread the body while the other tries to wiggle the trucks free. The motor is contained in the tender on some Tyco and Bachmann steam locomotives, and it can be removed in the same manner as the motors in the diesels.

Screws hold the body to the superstructure

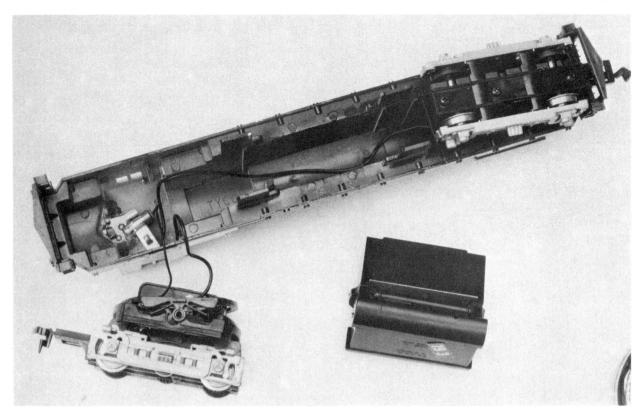

Fig. 10–5. The center "fuel tank" and weight snaps out of the Tyco or Bachmann body just like the trucks. Be careful not to stretch or break the wires or the light-mounting pins.

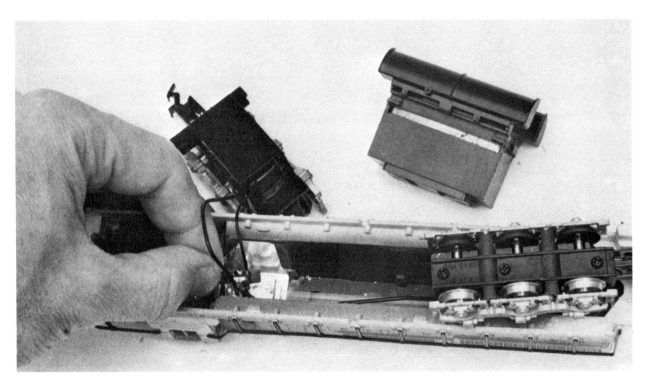

Fig. 10–6. At least one truck must be removed to gain access to the inside of the body to replace a burned-out light bulb.

on most steam locomotives and on some diesels. These screws must be removed to gain access to the motor and gears. You can determine the correct screws by examining the underside of the model. A screw always leads up toward the smokestack, and it must be removed, in addition to one or two more usually toward the rear of the locomotive. Some diesels have four screws in the bottom of the chassis that must be removed to free the body. Remove the front screw, but just loosen the other likely screws a half-turn while you wiggle the body to decide which ones are the right ones. The rear of the cab, on some models, has a tab and a slot that attaches the rear of the superstructure to the chassis. Be extremely careful when you remove the body so you don't break any of the wires leading to the motor or light bulbs. If you do, the wire will have to be resoldered. You can find someone in an electronics hobby store or in a television repair shop to do the soldering for you if you do accidentally break a wire.

The Chassis

Most of the model locomotives operate very nicely as shipped by the factory. Often, the models will run more smoothly and more quietly after 20 or 30 hours of operation in one- or two-hour sessions. If the locomotive is running erratically, or if you simply like to fiddle with mechanical objects, the chassis can be disassembled for cleaning and inspection. Each brand of locomotive, however, has a different method of attaching the body to the chassis and of attaching the trucks and motor to the frame.

Tyco Diesels

Most Tyco diesels have a single powered truck with a self-contained motor. The second truck is simply free-rolling, although it is carried in the same style of plastic frame as the powered truck and can look similar. To remove the trucks, simply spread the sides of

Fig. 10–7. Most Tyco (and some Bachmann) diesels have their trucks mounted on a plastic gimbal or carrier like this one.

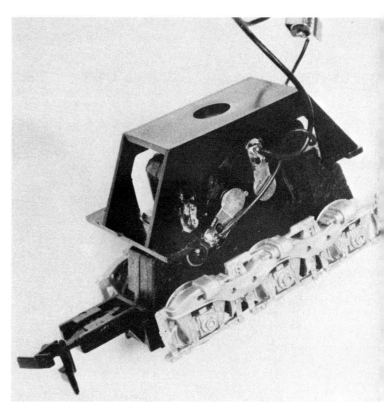

Fig. 10–8. The motor configuration in most of the Tyco diesels with six-wheel trucks is similar to this one from the SD–24 diesel.

the body apart by pulling them with the tips of your fingers below the running boards. The fuel tank should be removed first by simply pulling it down while the sides of the body are spread apart. The trucks can be pulled downward next. The trucks snap into a plastic bracket or gimbal that, in turn, snaps into the body. There is no frame other than those brackets for each truck.

Bachmann Diesels

Most of the Bachmann diesels have a powered truck and a free-rolling truck similar to those in the Tyco models. The Bachmann models, however, have a plastic frame. To remove the frame, complete with trucks and fuel tank, simply spread the sides of the body outward by prying with the tip of a screwdriver against the underside of the running boards. The complete chassis can then be pulled down and out of the body. Plastic caps cover the bottom of the trucks. The caps can be removed by simply prying the end tabs down gently by pushing downward on the coupler

pockets. In fact, the trucks and gears can be cleaned and lubricated without removing the body; the body need only be removed if you want to clean and inspect the motor.

Model Power and ConCor Diesels

The bodies on most Model Power diesels can be removed by prying outward on the bottom edges of the body with either your fingertips or, if you can reach inside, with the tip of a screwdriver. Spread the body, and the complete chassis should fall from the bottom of the body. It is, however, possible to clean and lubricate the gears without removing the body. Pry gently upward on the plastic tab on the inside ends of the truck and the cap covering the bottom of the truck should snap away to reveal the wheels and gears. The wheels then can be removed. When reassembling the wheels, be careful that the two copper strips contact the backs of each wheel. The ConCor diesels have a similar chassis and truck so you can use these methods to disassemble them.

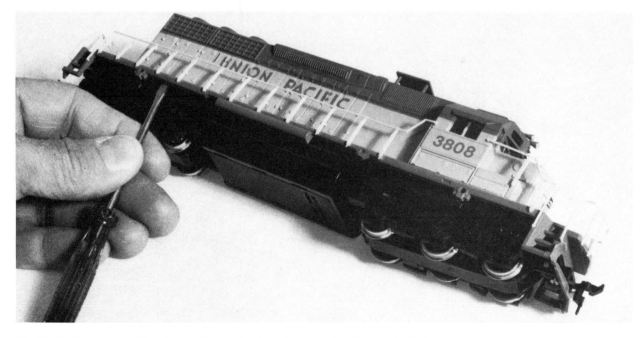

Fig. 10–9. Use a screwdriver to pry the running boards outward to free the body from most Bachmann diesels like this SD40-2.

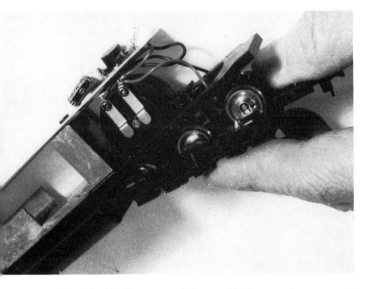

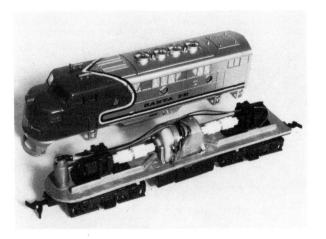

Fig. 10–12. Spread the sides of the body apart to remove the chassis from most Model Power diesels like this F3A.

Fig. 10–10. Pry out and down with the coupler, on most Bachmann diesels, to remove the bottom cover from the trucks.

Fig. 10–13. Pry gently on the inside tab of the truck bottom cover to remove the cover from most Model Power diesels.

Fig. 10–11. With the bottom cover removed, the wheels and gears can be removed from the Bachmann truck for cleaning and regreasing.

Athearn Diesels

Athearn has two distinctive methods of mounting the body to the chassis. The later production SW1500, GP38-2, GP40-2, GP50 and SD40-2 have bodies that mount with four tabs extending through the chassis into the fuel tanks. To remove these bodies, insert

Fig. 10–14. With the bottom cover removed, the wheels and gears can be removed from the Model Power trucks.

Fig. 10–15. This Austrian-made SD40 is typical of the chassis used in a number of IHC, Life-Like, and Model Power locomotives.

Fig. 10–16. Insert two screwdrivers into the rectangular holes in the newer Athearn fuel tanks to free the body-mounting tabs.

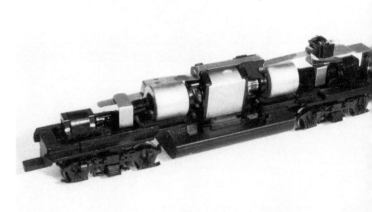

Fig. 10–17. This GP40-2 chassis is similar to most of the current production Athearn diesels.

Fig. 10–18. Insert a screwdriver from below the chassis to pry and push the truck retaining cover free.

Fig. 10–19. Lift the worm gear, with its two bearings and two thrust washers, from the top of the Athearn truck.

two medium-size screwdriver blades into the slots in the bottom of the fuel tank to engage the tabs. Pry both tabs out while you gently pull upward on the body until you can feel the body slide free on that side. Hold the body firmly while you insert the two screwdrivers in the slots on the opposite side of the fuel tank to free that side of the body. The body then can be lifted free.

The earlier Athearn diesels have bodies that are held in place with two pins that fit into tabs on the sides of the running boards on each side. Use a screwdriver or your fingertips, as described for the Bachmann and Model Power diesels, to pry the sides of the body or running boards out to free the body.

The trucks on all Athearn diesels are held in place with a half-circle clip. Before removing the clip, gently pry outward on the long metal band on the top of the chassis to snap it away from the motor and from beneath the metal clips on the top of each truck. To remove the clip from the top of each truck, insert a screwdriver between the chassis and the truck and pry out on the bottom of the clip. If you try to remove the clip from the top of the chassis, you can break the retaining tabs. When the clips are removed, look

carefully at the position of the worm gear, the washers on the ends of the gear, and the square bronze bearings so you can reassemble those parts in the proper order. The spur gears on the trucks are accessible after the worm gears are removed. To disassemble the trucks, remove the clip from the bottom of each truck using a screwdriver to pry outward on the clip's side flanges from the top of the truck.

Cleaning and Inspection

Most HO scale diesel and steam locomotives have some type of metal wiper that contacts either the wheels or the trucks to carry the electrical current from the rails to the motor through the wheels or drivers. Most Tyco, Bachmann, ConCor and Model Power diesels have a small copper strip that contacts the back of each wheel. Remove the wheels and notice how far the copper strip moves. That strip should move about $\frac{1}{16}$-inch so that the wheel forces that copper strip inward $\frac{1}{16}$-inch. Thus, the strip provides pressure on the back of the wheel when the wheel

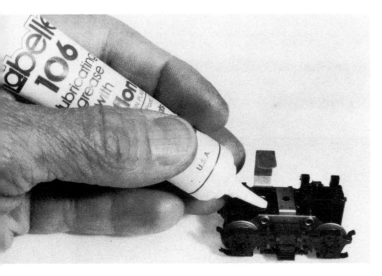

Fig. 10–20. Use LaBelle Number 106 grease to lubricate the gears in any model locomotive. This is Athearn's GP38-2.

Fig. 10–21. Use LaBelle Number 108 oil to lubricate the bronze bearings on the Athearn worm gear shafts and for any motor shaft.

moves from side to side in the truck. If necessary, bend the clips in or out to achieve that contact. The backs of the wheels and the contacting portion of the copper strip also must be clean.

Use a hard rubber eraser like those sold by Life-Like, Model Power or Bright Boy to clean the wheels and the strips. If there is black grease inside the trucks, remove the wheels and gears and clean them in paint thinner.

Use grease and oil that will not dissolve plastic. Hobby shops carry LaBelle brand Number 106 grease and Number 108 oil that is plastic-compatible, but you may find other brands as well. Just be sure the label indicates that the grease or oil will not harm plastics. Apply one pin-head-size dot of LaBelle Number 106 grease to each gear tooth. Also apply one drop of LaBelle Number 108 oil to the bearings on each end of the motor. All of the other bearings are plastic and should not be lubricated.

Cleaning and Inspecting Athearn Diesels

Athearn diesels have a more complex electrical pickup system. A metal strip runs across the top of the motor to contact similar metal strips on the top of each truck. Those strips must be bent so there is pressure between them. Remove the strip from the motor, then push it back in place with the ends resting above the strips on the tops of the trucks. The ends of that long metal strip should be at least $\frac{1}{16}$-inch above the strips on the ends of the truck. When the long metal strip is pushed back under the strips on the ends of the trucks it will have enough pressure to maintain contact. Be sure the contacting portion of the long metal strip and the metal strips on the tops of the trucks are clean by polishing them with one of those hard rubber erasers.

The Athearn trucks have a second electrical contact where they mount to the frame. Remove the trucks, as described earlier, and inspect the rubbing faces on the bottom of the frame and the metal strips that serve as the pivots for the trucks. Again, polish both areas with a hard rubber eraser. If they are extremely dirty or rusty, scrape the surfaces clean with a sharp screwdriver blade.

The Athearn motor also maintains an electrical contact with the chassis. To inspect that contact, remove the motor using a screw-

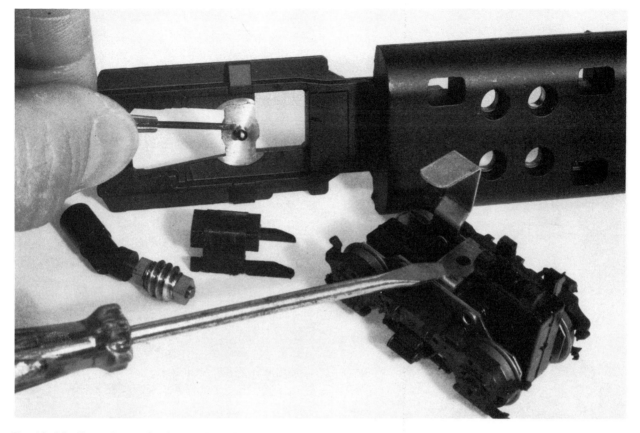

Fig. 10–22. Use a sharp-edged screwdriver blade to scrape dirt from the pivot surfaces of the Athearn chassis (left) and trucks (right).

Fig. 10–23. Use a screwdriver to press against the bottom of the plastic mounting tabs to remove the motor from any Athearn chassis.

driver to push upward through the four round holes in the bottom of the chassis to free the flexible plastic motor mounts. With the motor out, you can see a bare metal strip down the center of the chassis. That area must be perfectly clean. Clean the copper tabs on the bottom of the motor, too, and bend them, if necessary, so their ends extend at least $\frac{1}{8}$-inch below the bottom of the motor. Those copper strips contact that bare metal strip in the bottom of the chassis.

Those areas of metal strip-to-frame contact can cause erratic operation of Athearn diesels. If you know how to solder, the performance of any Athearn diesel can be made more reliable and free from hesitation by soldering short lengths of 18-gauge insulated electrical wire from the copper strip on the top of the motor to the top tabs on the trucks. Two more wires also can be soldered from

Fig. 10–24. Use a sharp-edged screwdriver blade to scrape dirt from the motor contact slot in the Athearn chassis.

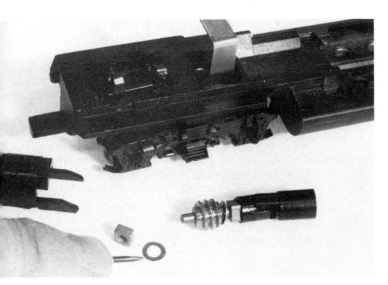

Fig. 10–25. The thrust washer on the outer end of the Athearn worm gear shaft. Add another washer if the model surges on downhills.

the copper strip on the bottom of the motor to the vertical edges of the metal strips that serve as the pivot points for the Athearn trucks. With this series of four wires, you are running wire connections directly from the motor to the trucks to bypass the frame itself.

Athearn diesels can surge or stumble on steep downhills with a heavy train. Sometimes this can be caused by too much end play in the worm gears. To reduce the end

play, add a second Athearn Number 99201 thrust washer (available to dealers from Walthers and other wholesalers) to the stub end of the worm gear shaft (Figure 10–25). When you reassemble the worm gear, however, be sure that you can detect a perceptible end-to-end movement. If there is no end-to-end movement (end play), remove the washer.

Cleaning the Motor

The only parts of the motor that should require attention are the commutator and the motor brushes that rub on the revolving commutator. I do not recommend that you attempt to replace the brushes or clean the commutator in the motors used by Life-Like or Model Power because the motors are enclosed (and dirt is unlikely to enter). It is difficult to disassemble these motors without breaking the holding tabs. If the motor does not run, even with the wires from the power pack touched directly to the frame contact strips on the motor, replace the motor.

The brushes on the Athearn motors are accessible by simply removing the copper clips that snap onto the top and bottom of the motor. Pry up one end while holding the center of the copper strip down so the spring

Fig. 10–26. Use a pipe cleaner dipped in paint thinner to scrub the commutator clean. This is a typical Athearn motor.

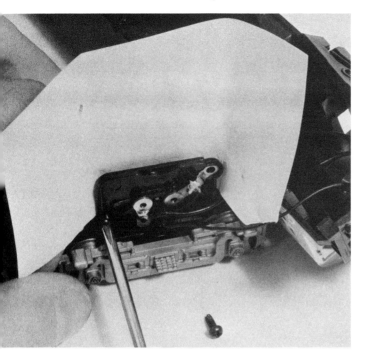

doesn't eject the round sintered copper motor brush. Gently lift the strip, then the coil spring, and remove the brush from the bottom of the round hole beneath the spring. If the brush is shorter than $\frac{1}{16}$-inch, replace it with Athearn's Number 90037 motor brush. The commutator can be cleaned without removing the brushes. Simply dip the end of a pipe cleaner in some paint thinner and gently scrub the round copper commutator as shown in Figure 10–26.

The brushes in Tyco and some Bachmann motors can be reached by removing the sides of the trucks as shown in Figure 10–27. Insert a business card, as shown, to keep the brushes in the outer half of the frame. Gently tilt the frame out and carefully lift the card so the brush springs will not force the brushes to fly out of the chassis. Use a piece of lint-free cloth or a pipe cleaner, dipped in paint thinner, to clean the face of the commutator. If the brushes are thinner than about $\frac{1}{16}$-inch, they should be replaced with brushes ordered directly from Tyco or Bachmann. It usually takes many hundreds of hours of

Fig. 10–27. Insert an index card to hold the spring-loaded motor brushes while installing the cover plate and the screws when new motor brushes are needed on Tyco or some Bachmann diesel locomotives.

Fig. 10–28. The motor brushes on some steam locomotives are held in place only by the hair-pin-style wire brush springs.

Fig. 10–29. The newer Mantua steam locomotives, like this 2-6-6-2 articulated, have a round "can"-style motor.

operation for motor brushes to wear, however, so it is highly unlikely that they should be worn enough to need replacing.

The motor brushes in some of the older Tyco and Mantua steam locomotives are visible on motors similar to those in Figure 10–28. Again, the brushes should be replaced if the round copper brush soldered to the end of the brass strip is thinner than $\frac{1}{16}$-inch. The wires are soldered to the brushes on most of these motors, however, so you may want to ask your local hobby dealer if he can replace the brushes for you or if he has another customer that might be able to do the work. Some of the Tyco steam locomotives have the motor in the tender and their drive system is virtually the same as that used in the Tyco diesels. Still other Tyco, Bachmann and Model Power steam locomotives have a fully enclosed motor like that shown in the Mantua 2-6-6-2 articulated locomotive in Figure 10–29.

Assembling the Locomotive

The assembly of the locomotive is the reverse of the disassembly. You must be particularly careful about the wheels, however. One wheel of each diesel wheel pair, one driver of each steam locomotive drive pair, and one wheel of each steam locomotive tender wheel pair is insulated so the wheels will not create a short circuit. The insulated wheel will have a plastic washer in its hub or, with some steam locomotive drivers, a thin band of white or red fiber or plastic near the rim. All the insulated wheels must be on the same side on the front truck and on the opposite side of the other truck on diesels. On steam locomotives, the insulated drivers must be on the opposite side (or contact the opposite rail) from the insulated wheels on both tender trucks.

If you discover that a locomotive travels in the opposite direction from all the others, that problem can be corrected by removing the wheels or drivers and turning them end-for-end and then replacing them.

Cleaning the Parts

Use a tissue soaked in lighter fluid, lacquer thinner, or solvent to remove the grease and grit from the wheels and the gears. Be sure to work in a well-ventilated area, away from fire or flame and away from any electricity that could cause a spark interacting with those

Fig. 10–30. Use a screwdriver blade to scrape clean the surfaces of diesel wheels or steam locomotive drivers or tender wheels.

volatile and poisonous fluids. Wear rubber gloves to protect your hands and goggles or safety glasses to protect your eyes. Wood toothpicks can be dipped in one of the fluids to reach the tight areas. Small wood sticks can be used, in the same way, to dislodge the worst dirt from wheels. Never scrape wheels with metal objects. You might scratch them, and the scratches will collect even more dirt more quickly. Never use steel wool on any of your model railroad equipment; the tiny strands will be attracted to the motor magnets and switch rails and could cause short circuits. You should need to do a thorough cleaning job only once a year or so unless you're running your trains on the floor. For most tabletop layouts, a twice-a-year wheel and rail cleaning with a typewriter or ink eraser is all that will be needed.

Troubleshooting

The Locomotive and Electrical Troubleshooting chart in Chapter 7 (Fig. 7–6) includes the probable causes of trouble that can occur in the track and the power pack as well as in the locomotive. All three components are part of the same electrical circuit. I suggest that you use a 12 volt model railroad light bulb as a trouble-shooting "test lamp."

Do's and Don'ts for Model Locomotives

Do clean the locomotive wheels and polish them with an ink eraser or the track cleaning erasers sold by Life-Like, Model Power and Bright Boy.

Don't allow dirt to accumulate on locomotive wheels since it can cause erratic electrical pickup and unreliable speed control.

Do clean the bearings, axles and gears of the locomotives to remove any dirt, lint or excess oil or grease.

Don't apply oil or grease to *any* plastic bearings. Use oil (like LaBelle Number 108) on metal bearings and grease (like LaBelle Number 106) on plastic or metal gears.

Do remove or mark any locomotives or cars that derail regularly for later inspection so the fault can be found before the next operating session.

Don't just hope that a derailment-prone locomotive or car will eventually fix itself.

Do inspect the couplers on all locomotives to be sure they are at the proper height for coupling and that the uncoupling pin does not hang down too far.

Don't continue to operate locomotives or cars with faulty couplers since they may derail or catch on the turnouts to cause damage and derailments.

Do use the Trouble-Shooting Chart in Chapter 7 (Fig. 7–6) and check each step, in the order presented, to pinpoint the cause of derailments or poor locomotive performance.

Don't assume you know the cause of a problem without checking the alternatives on the Trouble-Shooting Chart.

The Locomotive Paintshop

The same techniques described in Chapter 9 for painting rolling stock will work equally well on locomotives. On most diesel locomotives, however, the painting might become slightly more complicated because you may want to use a two-color paint scheme to match a particular prototype or for your own railroad. Use Scotch "Magic Transparent Tape" for masking. It's thinner than regular masking tape, and you can tell whether or not it's "stuck" by just looking to see if the part shows through the tape. Paint the lighter color first on most two-color paint schemes.

The black shade on the Burlington Northern diesels is actually dark gray acrylic primer. This is a shortcut that saves the detail-hiding thickness of another coat of paint. You might be able to find a primer in a light gray or a light brown or even in white for the "second" color on other railroad paint schemes. Apply a strip of Scotch "Magic" tape all around the model, with one edge of the tape forming the color separation line between the existing color and the one you are about to spray on. If the color separation line

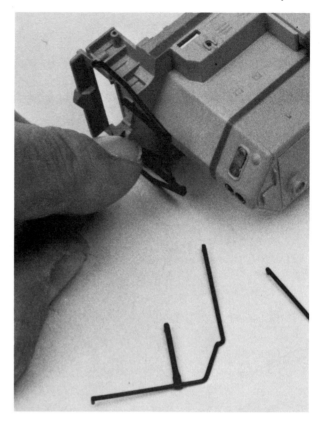

Fig. 10–32. The end or side handrails can be removed by carefully prying them from the body with your fingernail.

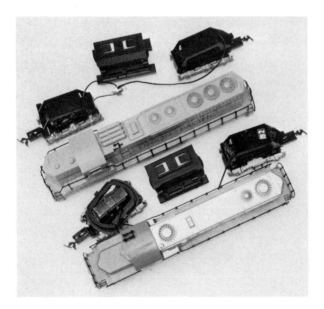

Fig. 10–31. The trucks, wires, light bulbs, and fuel tanks should be removed from the Tyco bodies before painting.

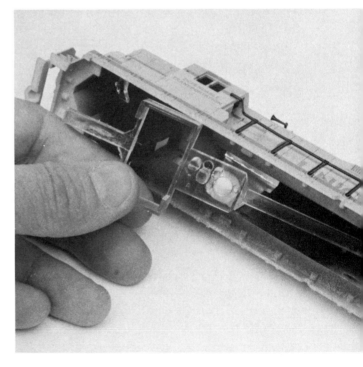

Fig. 10–33. Remove the clear plastic light lenses and windows from inside the body shell before painting.

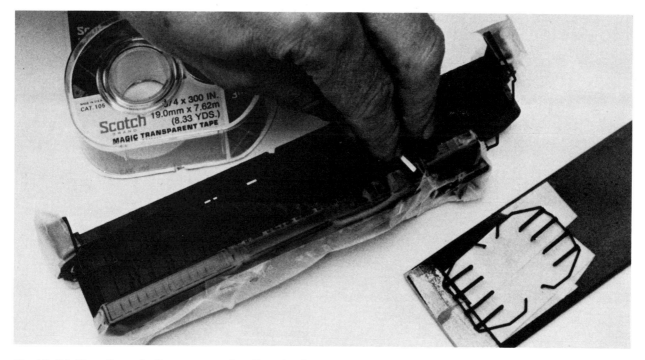

Fig. 10–34. Tape the end rails to a scrap of cardboard with masking tape doubled over so the sticky side is up. Use a matchstick to get the Scotch "Magic Transparent Tape" to stick tightly into the corners of the body.

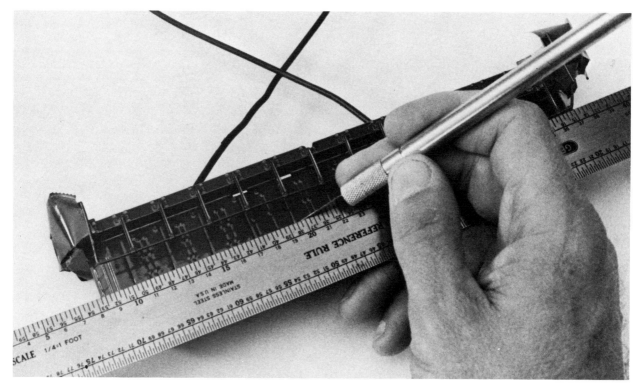

Fig. 10–35. Slice along the edge of the painted masking tape before peeling the tape back.

has V or Z shapes, you may want to cover the whole area with the tape and cut through it to make the design; then you can remove the excess tape along the cut lines. You might also want to remove the end and side railings to make masking easier. I removed just the last posts from the side railings and the complete end railings to mask the end platforms so they would be black rather than green.

Spray on the second color and let it dry for at least a day. Use a new Number 11 blade in your X-Acto knife to slice carefully along the edge of the "Magic" tape so the second color won't stick to the tape. Do not rely on just the tape to make a clean color separation edge because it will leave a ragged and rough line when it is removed. When you do pull the tape away, double it back over itself as shown in Figure 10–36 to minimize the chances of lifting the original color. If there are some zigs and zags in the paint separation line, touch them up with either (or both) colors applied with a Number 0 paint brush. When the paint

is dry, the model can be decorated with decals purchased from the firms listed in Chapter 9 and with those same techniques. It will be necessary to use plenty of decal-softening fluid to get those decals to snuggle tightly around the louvers and rivets on any diesel body.

Locomotive Conversions

When you have mastered the art of repainting and decaling your own diesel locomotives, you may want to go a step further to

Fig. 10–37. Remove all the handrails and make the first cut with the saw blade snug against the steps in front of the cab.

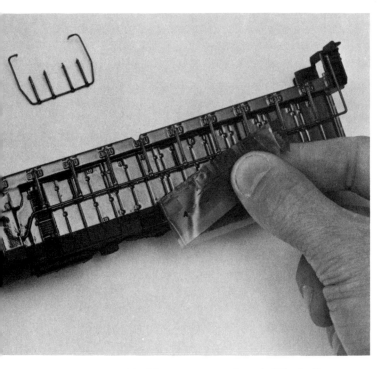

Fig. 10–36. When removing Scotch "Magic Transparent Tape" from a two-color paint job, pull the tape back over itself so that it won't lift the second color with it.

Fig. 10–38. Position the second cut so the peeled-away flap stays on the body. Cut through each side, then across the top. Tape the loose ends of both long handrails aside.

create duplicates of real locomotives that are not available as ready-to-run models. The Number 1957 is one in a series of twenty "high nose" GP–9 diesels that the Chicago, Burlington & Quincy Railroad purchased in 1954. The original numbers were 270 through 289, and they were originally painted black with gray roofs and red and yellow trim. MicroScale's Number 87-15 decals can be used for this early scheme (an illustration of the paint scheme appears in Volume I of *The Model Railroading Handbook*) as well as for the later red, gray, and white scheme, such as that on the ConCor or Tyco SD-24. Tyco is the one shown in the color section.

The green, black, and white Burlington Northern scheme first appeared in 1970, when the CB&Q merged with the Great Northern, the Northern Pacific, and the Spokane, Portland, and Seattle railroads. The number 6253 Burlington Northern diesel model is a replica of a rare beast on the Burlington Northern; they modified a single

Fig. 10–39. File both faces of the cut areas smooth with a medium-cut flat-mill file.

SD–24 with what is called a "chop nose." The chop nose or low nose SD–24 is fairly common, however, on other real railroads. Number 6253 was part of a series of fifteen locomotives built for the CB&Q in 1959 and later renumbered 500 through 507, 509 through 515, and, finally, renumbered 6240 through 6247 and 6249. The box-stock Mantua on Tyco Burlington SD–24 is an accurate model of this series right down to the number 502.

The models of number 1957 and 6253 were built by cutting off the cab and nose of a Tyco or Mantua GP–20 and ConCor or Tyco SD–24 so the two cabs and noses could be interchanged. This conversion provided the high nose needed for a scale-model GP–9 (actually a much more common prototype than the GP–20) and the low nose for the unusual chop nose SD–24. Figures 10–37, 10–38 and 10–39 show how the cuts were made with a razor saw and smoothed with a mill file. Tube-type cement was used to reas-semble the noses after a careful check was made to see that the power trucks (motors) would clear.

The top of the mounting bracket for the Tyco (SD–24) power truck was filed down about $\frac{1}{32}$-inch to clear the new low hood. Masking tape was used to hold the noses to the new bodies, and the glue was allowed to dry for a full week before the tape was re-moved. The glue seams were trimmed with a hobby knife and primer and paint were ap-plied. The ends of the handrails next to the cabs were cut flush with the sides of the cab, because the "new" holes in the cab didn't line up with the handrails of the "old" bodies at those four points. The air horns from the hood of the SD–24 were mounted on the roof of the GP–9.

The decals are MicroScale's Number 87–25, and, since only some Burlington Northern diesels have the safety stripes on the nose, only the SD–24 received them. The decal and paper with the stripes were cut to fit

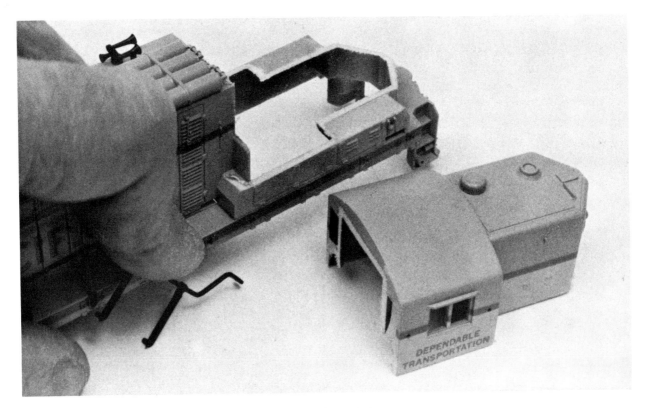

Fig. 10–40. Cut both the GP–20 and the SD–24 bodies at identical places.

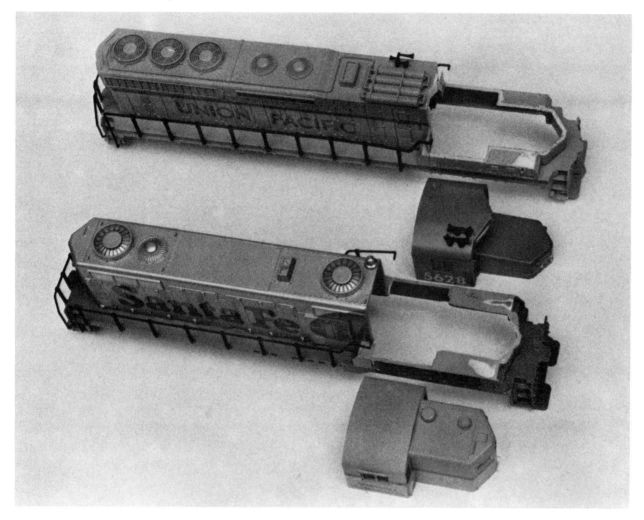

Fig. 10–41. Carefully fit the GP–20 cab to the SD–24, and vice versa, before applying any glue.

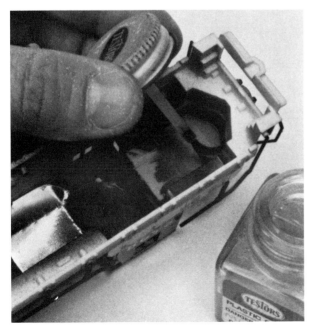

Fig. 10–42. Apply liquid cement for plastics to the inside of the glue joints.

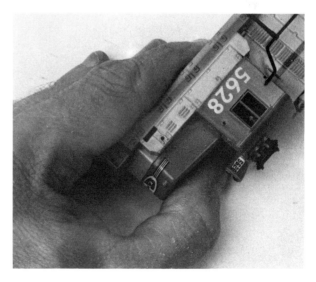

Fig. 10–43. Hold the body and cab together tightly for 10 minutes or so to give the glue a chance to form a bond.

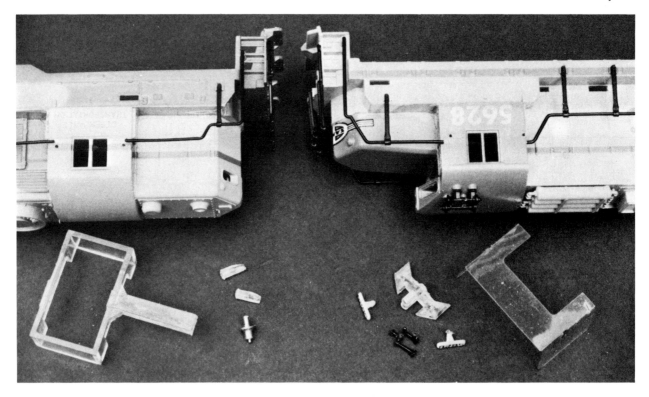

Fig. 10—44. Cut clear window pieces to fit the proper cabs.

Fig. 10—45. The Tyco truck-mounting bracket that goes beneath the low hood end of the SD—24 must be shaved and filed to fit. The metal frame on the ConCor SD—24 chassis must be cut with a hack-saw to clear the low hood.

Fig. 10–46. The handrails that fit into holes in the sides of the cab on the GP–20 (in this illustration) and SD–24 must be cut off so the handrail ends just rest on the surface of the cab sides.

Fig. 10–47. The Burlington Northern only applies the "zebra" safety stripes to the ends of a few diesels. This is a "high hood" SD–24 at Denver on the Colorado & Southern portion of the Burlington Northern in 1972.

Fig. 10–48. The two diesel bodies duplicate prototype diesels right down to the proper numbers and the white rectangular "lift-here" tabs.

the nose area before the decal was dipped into the water.

The subtle differences between the modified chop nose SD–24, the ConCor or Tyco SD–24, the modified GP–9 and the stock Tyco or Mantua GP–20 provide the kind of realism that makes a model railroad just that much more like its prototype. Some modelers add extra details, like snowplows, roof lights, and end hoses to super-detail their diesels. Hobby shops sell these parts under the Cal Scale, Custom Finishing, Detail Associates, Details West, Overland and Precision Scale labels.

Some modelers, like Leonard Frere, want diesels for their model railroads that are different from anything built by the real locomotive manufacturers. Leonard likes the angled roof edges of the F40PH, F45, and FP45

types of diesels. He wanted a short, eight-wheeled version of the F45 or FP45 (twelve-wheeled diesels) for his HO scale railroad. He simply cut down the length of an Athearn F45 to fit the Athearn GP35 chassis by cutting off the rear of the body, removing enough of the remaining rear of the body so it would fit the shorter GP35 chassis, and gluing the rear of the F45 back in place. His completed model, painted in Burlington Northern colors and decals, looks very much like an eight-wheeled freight version of the F40PH sitting to the left. There was no real "F40" (as Leonard calls his conversion), but this is what it would have looked like. Other modelers have lengthened the GP30 to make the never-built twelve-wheeled "SD30." It is, after all, your model railroad; you can build and operate just about any type of locomotive you wish.

PART IV

Scenery and Buildings

CHAPTER 11

Structures

THE CONSTRUCTION of buildings is almost a hobby within a hobby. The buildings on a model railroad add an immeasurable look of "life" to the scene, and imply industry and action. The buildings also provide the reasons for the railroad's operations because they suggest that the freight and passenger cars really are carrying commodities. All those structures, though, are really scenery in that they "decorate" the miniature railroad layout. Each of the structures on your model railroad serves two functions: to make the railroad seem more like a living thing and to provide a background or scene for the movements of the trains. The contrast of the angular stationary structures and the movement of the similarly shaped locomotives and cars makes both the moving and the static model more true to life.

You'll be a big step ahead of the game of improving the realism of your model railroad if you really do consider the buildings to be scenery. Structures, of course, are like any other aspect of real-life scenery; each one is a bit different from the next, just as one tree or one hill is different from another. You expect to see dozens, maybe even hundreds, of almost identical boxcars or hoppers or even locomotives on a real railroad. You can expect to see identical pieces of rolling stock or locomotives on a model railroad too. Usually, a model railroad "suffers" from quite the opposite problem; far too many of its cars and locomotives are different from one another, and this often creates a circuslike atmosphere. The rule of realism suggests the use of as many of the same style, same color freight cars as you can afford, but this must be reversed when it comes to structures.

Try to do everything imaginable to make every structure different from every other structure on your railroad, and, of course, try to make each one different from every structure on everybody else's railroad!

Custom-Modified Buildings

Very little effort is involved in making each and every building you buy or build a "custom" creation. It's well worth the trouble, however, to make even a minor modification that will alter the appearance of the structure enough so at least it doesn't look like all of those in the ads and catalogs. Modifying a building can begin with your first kit-assembly job. The plastic structure kits, such as those in the r-t-r series, can be assembled in just an evening or two with tube-type and liquid cement for plastics.

129

Fig. 11–1. Buildings are "conversions" of two or more separate structure kits. Note the two reflected in the "magic" mirror.

Painting

The prelude to any assembly should be painting, even though the parts are almost always supplied in two or three or more colors. Unpainted plastic has a certain transparency that is visible and immediately identifiable to even a casual visitor. However, if you paint the plastic before assembling the pieces, an expert model builder won't be able to tell if its plastic or wood, or even real brick or stone or concrete.

Testors is just one firm that makes a subdued rainbow of "flat" colors, and these are perfect for painting the structures on a model railroad. The bottled Testors paints are intended for military figures, but the flat-

finish dark greens, beiges, browns, grays, and blues are precisely the colors you want for your model railroad structures. Most of these paints are offered only in bottles, but they're easy enough to apply with a brush because one coat is usually enough to cover the plastic. Testors also has flat black, flat white, and flat red in spray cans, and some of the primers (which don't "eat" plastics) come in light and dark gray and brown, so you can find most of the colors you'll need in spray cans.

Spray or brush-paint the windows and doors for the structures while they're still attached to the molding sprues or trees. The easiest way to paint most buildings is to as-

Fig. 11–2. The eastern end of the town of "Alliance" on the Burlington Northern layout in Chapter 16. The mirror is out of the picture to the far left.

Fig. 11–3. George Booth repainted this ConCor passenger station and added a new name with dry transfer letters. The passenger cars are Model Die Casting's "Harriman" series.

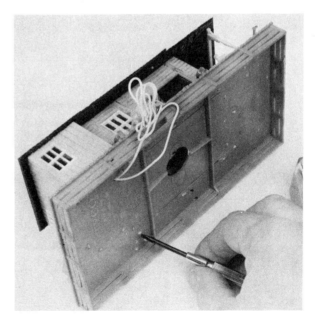

Fig. 11–4. The scale-model people and other details can be removed from the various r-t-r buildings for use elsewhere on the layout. Coat the mounting pegs in liquid cement for plastics and push them out through the bottom.

Fig. 11–5. Some of the figures can be pried loose with a knife blade after the glue joint is softened for an hour with several applications of liquid cement for plastics.

Fig. 11–6. The chimney holes in the roof of the Tyco Arlee Station kit were filled with leftover parts of the roof. The roof was cut to fit the Tyco or ConCor Freight Station with the Arlee Station roof supports to become the Alliance Freight Station.

Fig. 11–7. Two Tyco Freight Station kits (without their roofs) and the platform from the Tyco Piggyback Flatcar set.

semble all the outer walls without the windows. Let the glue dry overnight on all the seams, and prefit the roof, but don't glue it on. The building can then be spray or brush-painted in a hurry because there's no "tiny" painting to be done. Paint the windows a contrasting color, the details like downspouts or smokestacks a third color, and the roof a fourth color. Let the paint dry overnight too.

You cannot use plastic cement to glue a painted surface to another painted surface or to plastic, so the windows, details, and roof will have to be installed with one of the cyanoacrylate cements, such as Aron-Alpha, Hot Stuff, Zap or Super Glue, or with five-minute epoxy. If you feel you must use plastic cement, then scrape the paint away from the

areas that will be joined and glue the parts in place by installing them and holding them there with a knife blade while you brush on some of the liquid cement for plastics. Use the cyanoacrylate cement or epoxy to glue the clear-plastic window "glass" in place. The plastic cements (either tube-type or liquid) will etch or craze the clear plastic.

The "Live-There" Look

Each of the structures on your layout should be surrounded with "earth," so they look like they belong. Brush or trowel the brown-colored plaster you use for scenery (see Chapter 12) around the Homosote tabletop before the building is installed, and push the structure into the still-wet plaster. About $\frac{1}{16}$-inch of the plaster is deep enough. Be sure the building is level when you sink it into the plaster. You can then use the same dirt and grass effects that you select for the rest of the scenery to blend the area around the building into the rest of the "world" (or to blend the rest of the world into the building area if you installed the building before the rest of the scenery).

Weathering

The last step is the most important; the building *must* be weathered by spraying it lightly and from a distance of about two feet with a flat paint that comes close to matching the surrounding scenery. Spray a bit more of the paint near the edges of the roof to simulate rain-washed dirt that accumulates near the rain gutters, and spray a bit more near the base of the building to simulate where rain would have splattered mud around the base of the building. Practice this "weathering" technique on an old shoe box until you can determine just how far away you can hold the spray can to get the effect of dust.

The entire town or industrial area should receive this roof and foundation treatment. You might want to select a different "weathering" shade for different towns. The town of "Alliance" on the Burlington Northern layout in Chapter 16 has an overall touch of beige to match the nearby dirt. The area around the "Corning Mine" has a very light touch of black to simulate rain-washed coal dust, and the town of "Emmett" was given a weathering tint of dark brown. This overall weathering is the single most important step in making your layout look real.

Structure Conversions

Only so many variations can be made on a structure by painting it. If you really want the majority of your buildings to look different

Fig. 11–8. An alternate way to disguise the odd roof on the Tyco and ConCor freight stations is to add a second story, similar to this one on the Phoenix (Arizona) Model Railroad Club layout.

Fig. 11–9. This small freight house is cut from the plain end of Bachmann's illuminated Freight Station to make the building about one-third its original size.

from any others, you're going to have to learn the technique known as "conversion," or "kit-bashing." The two Burlington Northern diesels in Chapter 10 were created through the conversion process, and this process is even easier to apply to structures.

The fundamental principle of structure conversions is that the finished product should look unlike anything you can buy. The actual conversion could be as simple as adding a new roof to the Tyco "lighted" ready-built or ConCor kit-built Freight Station or as complex as constructing a structure like the "Alliance Company" from two Tyco, Model Power, or Pola Old-Time Factory kits. I have deliberately attempted to make most of the buildings on the Burlington Northern layout as different as possible so that you can see the effects of the conversion process—and the simplicity of the actual work. You can refer to the photos in the various chapters for scenes of the buildings and to the "satellite" view in Figure 16–4 in Chapter 16 to locate the specific structures. The key to that view (Fig. 16–4) shows both the r-t-r "action" accessories, like the log or ore car-dumping devices, and the highway trailer loading or unloading accessories. The other structures

might be kits, part of a kit or a combination of two or more kits. The modified kits are shown in this chapter.

I recommend that you purchase a Walthers catalog from a hobby shop. With the catalog, you can get a better idea of what the box-stock buildings look like. Refer to the current catalog to find out what is available; the listings that appear on the bottoms of some of the boxes show kits that are now sold under a number of different brand names. See page 145, under Buying Structures, for an explanation of the brand labels.

The Tyco or ConCor Freight Station has a pagoda-style roof that is rare in real life but as common as Santa Fe diesels on model railroads. You can alter the appearance of that structure completely by replacing its roof with

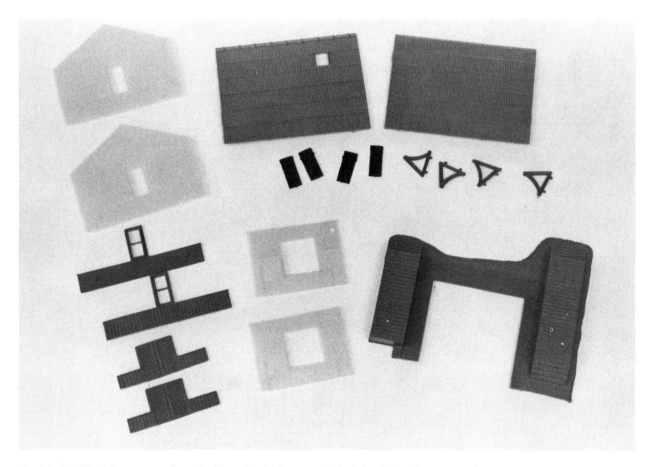

Fig. 11–10. The leftover parts from the Tyco, Model Power, or Pola Arlee Station kit were used, with the corrugated roof from the Tyco, Model Power, or Pola Pickle Factory kit, to assemble the Engine, Tool & Supply Co. structure near "Emmett."

Fig. 11–11. The parts from a Tyco, Model Power, or Pola Aunt Millie's House and a Tyco, Model Power, or Pola Hardware Store were modified to build the Duncan Feed & Fuel grain elevator. The leftovers became the Railroad Boarding House at "Alliance." Most of these plastic kits, made by Pola, are available from several manufacturers, often with a different identifying name.

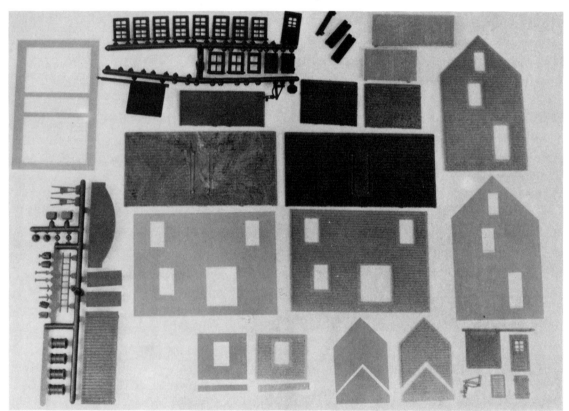

Fig. 11–12. The Tyco, Model Power, or Pola Firehouse kit has parts useful for a number of different kit-conversion structures.

one cut from two Tyco, Model Power, or Pola Arlee Station kits. The r-t-r "lighted" buildings are an excellent and inexpensive source of scale-model people for all parts of your railroad. Remove the people, in the same way you would remove the roof, by applying about six coats of liquid cement for plastics to dissolve the factory-glue joints. Let the glue soak in for about an hour (but no more) and then gently pull and pry away the parts you want. I disassembled two of the freight stations just for the people and the roofs. The small roofs were joined together and cemented to plastic sign posts to make the Emmett Trailer Train dock.

The walls and windows from a Tyco, Model Power, or Pola Hardware Store and Aunt Millie's House were mixed together to make the Duncan Feed & Fuel grain elevator and the Railroad Boarding House at "Alliance." The end walls from one of the "lean-tos" were

Fig. 11–13. The Tyco, Model Power, or Pola Railroad Hotel kit can be used as an industry if the porch is converted to a freight-car unloading platform. The floor of the porch must be raised to the top of the railings during assembly.

notched with a razor saw to clear the roof for the grain elevator's cupola. The parts in the illustration (see Figure 11–11) are the ones used for the grain elevator; the leftovers became the railroad boarding house.

Albert Hetzel created the Ford & Sons Ice Co. building by using only the long walls from two Tyco, Model Power, or Pola Firehouse kits with chimneys and some other parts from two Pickle Plant kits. The leftover doors from the two firehouses and one of the leftover cupolas from the pickle plants were used with two Sawmills and one Piggyback Flatcar platform to make the single-stall Engine House. Only the darker-colored buildings from the sawmills were used. The various modified parts (all cut with a razor saw) for the Engine House are shown in Figure 11–15. The brick lean-to came from a Firehouse kit.

The lesson here is that each and every kit must be viewed as nothing more than a "lumberyard" full of walls and roofs and doors and windows that can be cut and combined in almost endless ways. You can train yourself to do this by assembling a few struc-

Fig. 11—14 (left and right). The Ford & Sons Ice Co. was assembled from two Tyco, Model Power, or Pola Firehouse kits.

Fig. 11—15. Some parts from the Tyco, Model Power, or Pola Pickle Plant and the Sawmill were cut to be "converted" into a single-stall Engine House at "Alliance."

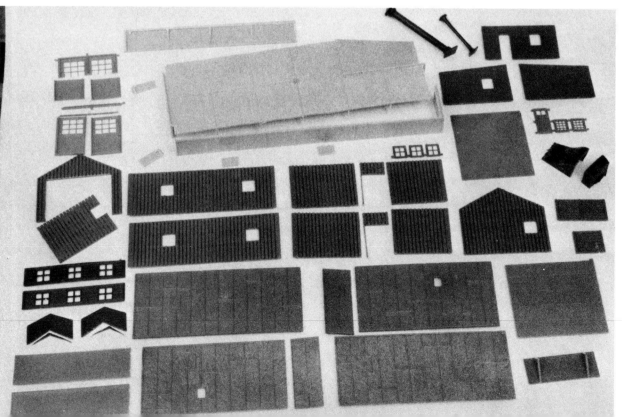

Fig. 11–16. A typical eastern coal mine. Note the different sizes or grades of coal. (Photo courtesy Association of American Railroads.)

Fig. 11–17. The Tyco, Model Power, or Pola Coal Mine kit was modified so the central section was on top of the mine shaft portion to help disguise the fact that the tracks disappear into a tunnel.

Fig. 11–18. Empty hoppers are fed into the Corning Mine on the right track, and loaded hoppers are picked up on the left track. The outside staircase is from the Tyco, Model Power, or Pola Crossover/Signal Bridge kit.

Fig. 11–19. One Tyco, Model Power, or Pola Stockyard and one Ma's Place were used to provide the parts cut, as shown, for the three dwellings owned by Corning Mining.

ture conversions like these. Then you can spot potential conversions just by looking at the catalog photos of the stock structures. All of the leftover parts can be placed in a scrap box if you can't figure out what to do with them right away. The Lumber Supply Co. was made from the two remaining buildings from the two sawmills, Company Furniture was made from the leftover Pickle Factory main building, Sons Winery was assembled from the tank end of one of the Pickle Factory kits, and Alliance Coal & Fuel uses the sawtooth-roofed structure from one of the sawmills and the other Firehouse brick lean-to.

Fig. 11–20. The three dwellings owned by Corning Mining.

Fig. 11–21. Klass Gunnick and Duncan Harvey built this two-level mine. The upper portion is the Tyco/Pola Freight Station, the angled center is from two Tyco/Pola Coaling Stations, and the lower loading bay is a ConCor Container Transfer Crane.

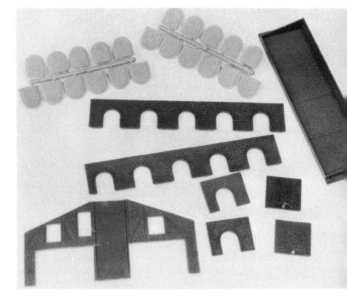

Fig. 11–22. The Alliance Company is a project for experienced kit-conversion builders. Two Tyco Old-Time Factory kits were cut and fitted to make the two-story structure, with the leftover arches cut, as shown, for the Emmett Coke Co. ovens.

The Mining Supply Co. is a classic; Albert Hetzel used two Tyco, Model Power, or Pola Interlocking Tower kits with a new flat roof for that one. He used the "passenger" halves of the back walls (opposite the bay window) of the Arlee Station to make the simple Alliance Station. The leftover roof pieces (the chimney sides) were filled with scrap pieces of plastic shingles for the roof on the Lighted Freight Station at "Alliance." The leftover "baggage" ends of the Arlee Station kits were used to make the Engine Tool & Supply Co. with a roof from the Pickle Factory kit.

The three dwellings owned by the Corning Mine were made from one Tyco, Model Power, or Pola Ma's Place and the building (identical to Ma's Place) from the Stockyard. A lot of minor cutting and fitting was needed to make three buildings from two; Figure 11–19 shows the parts ready to be assembled. The leftover stock pens from the Stockyard kit became the cattle pens at "Emmett." The Corning Mine is the popular Tyco, Model Power, or Pola Mine, with the "lower" level cut to create an upper level and the various supports from the kit cut to fit. The Tyco, Model Power, or Pola Coaling Station

Fig. 11–23. A bottom side view of the Alliance Company before installation of the roofs reveals how the parts are assembled.

Fig. 11–24. Station and industry names for signs.

ALLIANCE	BUILDERS	ALLIANCE	BUILDERS
ARLEE	CHEMICAL	ARLEE	CHEMICAL
BEDFORD	COAL	BEDFORD	COAL
CORNING	COKE	CORNING	COKE
DUNCAN	CONCRETE	DUNCAN	CONCRETE
EMMETT	DAIRY	EMMETT	DAIRY
FALLS	FARMING	FALLS	FARMING
GURNSEY	FEED	GURNSEY	FEED
HASTINGS	FUEL	HASTINGS	FUEL
ISLAND	FURNITURE	ISLAND	FURNITURE
JUNCTION	GROCERY	JUNCTION	GROCERY
KIMBALTON	HARDWARE	KIMBALTON	HARDWARE
LAKE	ICE	LAKE	ICE
MASON	IRON	MASON	IRON
NEW	LUMBER	NEW	LUMBER
ONEIDA	MINE	ONEIDA	MINE
PADUCAH	MINING	PADUCAH	MINING
SPRING	OIL	SPRING	OIL
TIMBER	PACKING	TIMBER	PACKING
TREES	STEEL	TREES	STEEL
UDELL	STORAGE	UDELL	STORAGE
VALLEY	STOVES	VALLEY	STOVES
WOODWARD	SUPPLY	WOODWARD	SUPPLY
YOUNGSTOWN	WHOLESALE	YOUNGSTOWN	WHOLESALE
	WINERY		WINERY
BAKING		BAKING	
BOX	SUPPLY	BOX	SUPPLY
BREWERY	SONS	BREWERY	SONS
BREWING		BREWING	

AND AND AND AND & & & & & &   AND AND AND AND & & & & & &
CO.   CO.   CO.   CO.   CO.   CO.   CO.   CO.   CO.   CO.   CO.   CO.
COMPANY   COMPANY   COMPANY   COMPANY   COMPANY   COMPANY
INC. INC. INC. INC. LTD. LTD.   INC. INC. INC. INC. LTD. LTD.

ALLIANCE	BUILDERS	ALLIANCE	BUILDERS
ARLEE	CHEMICAL	ARLEE	CHEMICAL
BEDFORD	COAL	BEDFORD	COAL
CORNING	COKE	CORNING	COKE
DUNCAN	CONCRETE	DUNCAN	CONCRETE
EMMETT	DAIRY	EMMETT	DAIRY
FALLS	FARMING	FALLS	FARMING
GURNSEY	FEED	GURNSEY	FEED
HASTINGS	FUEL	HASTINGS	FUEL
ISLAND	FURNITURE	ISLAND	FURNITURE
JUNCTION	GROCERY	JUNCTION	GROCERY
KIMBALTON	HARDWARE	KIMBALTON	HARDWARE
LAKE	ICE	LAKE	ICE
MASON	IRON	MASON	IRON
NEW	LUMBER	NEW	LUMBER
ONEIDA	MINE	ONEIDA	MINE
PADUCAH	MINING	PADUCAH	MINING
SPRING	OIL	SPRING	OIL
TIMBER	PACKING	TIMBER	PACKING
TREES	STEEL	TREES	STEEL
UDELL	STORAGE	UDELL	STORAGE
VALLEY	STOVES	VALLEY	STOVES
WOODWARD	SUPPLY	WOODWARD	SUPPLY
YOUNGSTOWN	WHOLESALE	YOUNGSTOWN	WHOLESALE
	WINERY		WINERY
BAKING		BAKING	
BOX	SUPPLY	BOX	SUPPLY
BREWERY	SONS	BREWERY	SONS
BREWING		BREWING	

AND AND AND AND & & & & & & &   AND AND AND AND & & & & & & &
CO. CO. CO. CO. CO. CO.   CO. CO. CO. CO. CO. CO.
COMPANY   COMPANY   COMPANY   COMPANY   COMPANY   COMPANY
INC. INC. INC. INC. LTD. LTD.   INC. INC. INC. INC. LTD. LTD.

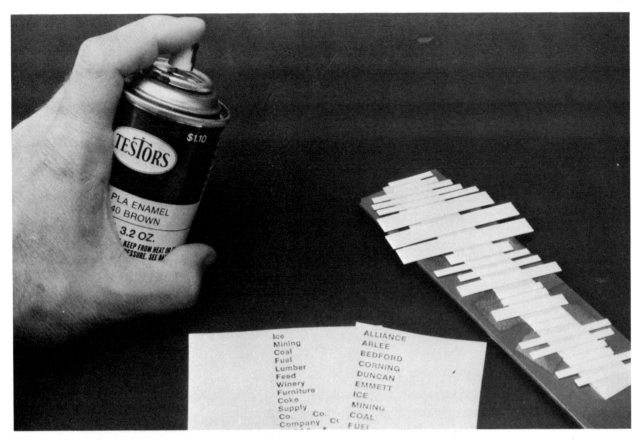

Fig. 11–25. Cut backings for the signs from file cards and hold them to a scrap of wood with masking tape, sticky-side-up, while you spray-paint them brown or gray.

Fig. 11–26. Cut the signs from Figure 11–24 and from the Tyco kits with a hobby knife and cement them to file cards with rubber cement.

supplied the raw materials for the wood tunnel portal in Figures 12–25 and 12–26 in Chapter 12.

Structures that Speak

The weathering steps suggested earlier will help bring those painted plastic buildings into the realm of reality. You will want to carry it a step further, however, to make those buildings come to life. Populating the buildings with people will help add that "breath" of life. And the final touch will be added when the various signs of the buildings and industries are in place. These include the railroad station signs, a few advertising posters, and perhaps a billboard or two. Make a photocopy of the signs in Figure 11–24. Then you can cut out the various signs to supplement those supplied with the majority of the buildings.

You can piece together the names of all the industries on the Burlington Northern and hundreds of others from the words on that page. Cut the words out and paste them to pieces of a file card or postcard with rubber cement. If you want a color, add it with a felt-tip pen. Spray the signs with a light coat of Testors "Dullcote," and, when they dry, attach them to your buildings with five-minute epoxy. When the waybill tells your Pedlar Freight's switching crew to spot a car at Ford & Sons Ice Co., all the crew needs to do is find the right car and look for the industry's sign. Your "empire" is now a part of the real world.

Buying Structures

Virtually all the structures and bridges used on the Burlington Northern HO Scale Layout (Fig. 16–4) are Tyco, Model Power, ConCor, or Pola kits, selected because they are both well-detailed and available in areas of the country that may lack complete hobby shops. Most of these kits are made for Tyco by Pola. Pola, however, also sells HO scale structures under their own name, as well as under the AHM, IHM, ConCor, Walthers, and Model Power labels. If you compare these brands of kits, you'll often find the same kit with, perhaps, a different front or color or with a change in the arrangement of multiple-building kits. In some cases, the simulated material of the walls of the kit are different. The names and brands of the kits change quite often, so it's nearly impossible to provide a number-by-number interchange, but you can spot the shapes of the models if you

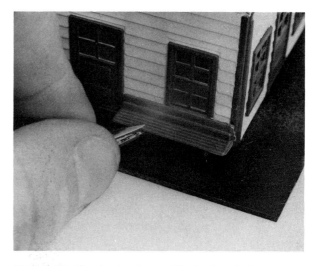

Fig. 11–27. Use the detail parts, like this bench, from any kit or ready-built structure in order to add additional character to other structures.

Fig. 11–28. Most conversions are meant to make a smaller structure out of a larger one. This freight warehouse, however, was made by combining three Life-Like Al's General Store kits. (Photo courtesy Life-Like Products.)

look carefully. There are other brands of kits, particularly those produced by ConCor and Walthers, that are just as detailed as the Pola kits but are models of completely different structures. The Atlas, Bachmann and Life-Like plastic kits are also similar to the Pola kits in construction and ease of modification.

Do's and Don'ts for Model Buildings

Do use cement for plastics to assemble even the snap-together building kits.

Don't rely on just a few plastic tabs or pegs to hold a plastic building together.

Do paint every building on your layout so each looks like solid material rather than translucent plastic.

Don't use buildings just as they come from the box. Paint the building and or the trim a different color.

Do modify all the buildings, before you assemble them, so they are at least a bit different from the stock kit and, thus, unique to your model railroad.

Don't use buildings exactly as found in the kits; they will look like the buildings on every other model railroad. With freight cars, that's realistic because freight cars travel from town to town. Buildings, however, are unique to specific areas.

Do apply enough dirt around the base of any building so the building appears to be resting in the earth.

Don't drop buildings on top of the layout so they look like oversize children's building blocks sitting on carpet.

Do arrange buildings in small groups to match the style of industrial, downtown or residential areas with open areas of scenery between clusters of buildings.

Don't spread houses, stores and industries at random around the layout.

CHAPTER 12

The Earth in HO Scale

IT'S NO WONDER that model railroaders have to devise so many construction, design, and operating tricks to make their miniatures look like the real thing. The whole construction process is backward when you compare the building of a real railroad to the building of a model. We arrange the world to suit our tracks, while the real railroads must arrange their tracks to fit the world. Nobody is a "natural" scenery expert. The only way to learn about scenery is to look at it—*really* look at it. Don't try to place your railroad in the Rocky Mountains if you can't get there to see what they look like, or, at the very least, if you're not willing to study books on geology and geography at a college library. Nature is one of the more difficult things to duplicate unless you have a model or sample readily available.

The Field Trip

Try to select geography that is either near your home or that you can visit at least once a year. Take some photographs and make some plan-type sketches to show the scene in the photographs. Let those photographs

encompass the terrain for a quarter-mile or so on either side of the tracks, and take some close-ups of just the cuts and fills and bridges next to the tracks. It's a good idea to even take some samples of the soil both for color and to actually use on your layout.

Pay particular attention to the way cuts (through mountains or hills) and fills (over valleys or streams or hollows) begin and how they blend in with the edge of the track and with the surrounding terrain. These are the most difficult-to-capture aspects of real scenery. It's relatively simple to use latex rubber molds to cast rocks or to spread plaster around a hillside. However, the abrupt change from almost vertical sections of scenery to the gentler slopes and the edges of the railroad right-of-way are not so easy to capture on a model railroad. If you have a color photograph, some samples of the rocks and soil in the area, a bird's-eye-view sketch of the area, and a few notes to tie it all together, then you're prepared to make a model of the area.

I must recommend that you try to include at least three or four of these real-world vignettes in your scenery. Finish them before you complete the rest of the scenery so you'll learn the feeling of creating scenery. The rest of the layout's scenery can then be "freelanced," drawing on the experience you have with those proven-to-be-genuine scenes from the real world. Please do not try to

147

duplicate any of the scenery you see on other model railroads; you'll be translating only what someone else has interpreted to be "real," and you'll lose much of the realism in the process.

Go directly from your research in the real world to the methods and techniques that other modelers have developed. You don't have to invent new ways to make scenery. What you do have to do is to try to capture the shape and color and texture of the part of the real world that you have selected as your prototype. You will need to make several trips back to that "source" for information you forgot to get the first time and, perhaps, to collect more dirt and rocks for the layout. While you're on those field trips, you can also collect rocks to be used as molds (this will be discussed later in this chapter) and a variety of weeds and twigs to be used for tree trunks and bushes on your layout.

The Full-Scale Mock-Up

Model railroaders have developed a very simple scenery system that, like the Homosote roadbed, requires an industrial compound that you may have to search for. There is a special building plaster called Hydrocal that becomes virtually as hard as rock after it sets; in fact, it becomes a type of alabaster. Some building-supply firms will order it in 100-pound bags if you ask them. Hydrocal is almost self-supporting; no chicken wire or screening is necessary as with other systems. Woodland Scenics sells smaller packages of Hydrocal through model railroad dealers. If you cannot find Hydrocal, then settle for the best grade of regular gypsum plaster you can find. You'll need gypsum plaster for some of the details described later in this chapter; the finished Hydrocal is too hard to carve into rocks and erosion gullies.

Fig. 12–1. Use a tall boxcar and a long locomotive or passenger car to check clearances on the mock-up scenery.

Topography

The scenery system that was developed for use with Hydrocal only requires piles of wadded-up newspapers to create the shapes of the hills and mountains and valleys. You will need some sort of $\frac{1}{8}$-inch or thicker Masonite or plywood "profile" boards to match the shape of mountains and valleys where they meet the edge of the table. You will also need a few vertical braces to support the tops of the hills or mountains in the center of the layout. The system allows you to actually mold the shapes of the hills and valleys with old newspapers before you apply any plaster.

The basic humps and lumps are wadded-up newspapers. The almost final surfaces of the hills and valleys are then shaped by draping wet newspapers over the wads of newspapers. If you see that a hill is too high or a cut is too close to the tracks, all you have to do is shove the newspapers aside. Strips of masking tape will help to hold the wads of newspapers down, and strips of tape can be used to make a netlike support to carry the newspaper wads over any large gaps or access holes in the benchwork.

Be sure to operate the highest boxcar and the longest locomotive or passenger car you have over the railroad while the scenery is still in the "mock-up" stage. This will allow you to determine whether there is enough clearance through all the cuts and tunnels. Often an overhanging pilot on a diesel locomotive or the skirt on a passenger car will hit scenery placed too close to the track.

Tunnels

Every model railroad can benefit from the use of tunnels because they help disguise the fact that the trains really don't travel as far as they should and that they really don't connect with the outside world. Here, again, you'll find yourself working in the opposite direction of the real railroads, which try to avoid the expense of a tunnel whenever possible. Very few model railroads are large enough to have a mountain that's gigantic enough to warrant a tunnel; the real railroads would have used cuts in almost every example you see on a model railroad. If you expect those "molehills" to look like mountains large enough for a tunnel or two, you'll have to be careful to apply the practices the real railroads use, although in somewhat smaller than true HO-scale proportions.

You'll see that there are several smaller buildings in the "Alliance" area of the Burlington Northern layout because the "clutter" of a dozen buildings is far more realistic than the three or four structures that would fill that size area if everything were in exact scale. The windows and doors are precise HO scale, and the proportions are correct for 1/87-scale people, but most of those buildings are closer to the size of a single-car garage than to that of the gigantic factories they represent. That same principle must be used for the hills and valleys on your model railroad. Use several smaller hills rather than one large mountain, for example. Copy the dirt or rock cuts through the earth that lead to every real railroad tunnel (including the rather deep cut leading to the top of each tunnel portal), but don't make the mountain above the tunnel as large. You can disguise the size of the mountain, to some extent, by "planting" smaller trees on its upper slopes to give the illusion of distance.

Portals

Each tunnel must have some type of tunnel portal. A few tunnels are blasted through solid rock, so the rock itself forms the shape of the portal. Most tunnels, however, have wood, concrete, brick, or stone portals and linings through the length of the tunnel. When you build the portal, don't forget to extend the material far enough into the tunnel to give the illusion that the tunnel is lined through its entire length. Real mountains aren't hollow like those on a model railroad, and that mass is what you are trying to duplicate.

Model railroad shops sell a large selection of simulated wood, cut stone and rock tunnels portals, or you can make your own. The expanded plastic foam that florists use for flower arrangements makes a fine material to use for tunnel portals. Carve the foam with a common kitchen steak knife to create the graceful arch over the top of the tunnel portal, and make the arch at least $3\frac{1}{2}$-inches high and the vertical walls at least two-inches wide ($2\frac{3}{4}$ inches if the tunnel is on a curve). The polyfoam portal can be covered with the same plaster you use for your scenery. Smooth on the plaster to simulate a concrete tunnel portal and lining, or rough it up to simulate a tunnel carved through solid stone.

A wood tunnel portal can be made by cutting the parts from a Tyco, Model Power, or Pola Coaling Station, as shown in Figure 12–25, with a razor saw. Use some three-inch-high strips of cardboard to simulate the vertical walls or linings of each tunnel for at least six inches into each tunnel. You can decide whether to include the tunnel portals in the mock-up stage and plaster around them, or to make the mountain look as though it really was there before the track and install the tunnel portal after the plaster is in place.

Plaster Mountains

When you're satisfied with your newspaper mock-up scenery, cover every inch of the tracks with wide masking tape. You can tape plastic trash bags over large flat areas, such as the "Alliance" yard and around any bridges. You will want to apply some plaster near the tracks on most flat areas to simulate hills and cuts, however, so use just the masking tape over the track in most places. You will also want to cut through the Homosote to

Fig. 12–2. Cover every inch of the track with wide masking tape to protect it from the plaster.

make any small lakes or streams at this stage, and, of course, all the bridges should be in place with plenty of space below them for the bottom of the river or stream.

The Hydrocal plaster will remain self-supporting if it is soaked in industrial-grade paper towels (usually brown or beige and much tougher than the household kind). Industrial paper towels are available from restaurant- and hospital-supply distributors. Perhaps you could persuade your local service station to sell you a few bundles. If you cannot find Hydrocal plaster, use common gypsum plaster, but build some $\frac{1}{8}$-inch plywood supports for the interior of the mountains before you finish the newspaper mock-ups. The mock-ups will help you to decide if more supports are needed. Use the mock-ups, regardless of what type of plaster you use, to help you to decide on the shape for the upper edges of the $\frac{1}{8}$-inch plywood or Masonite "profile" panels that should be nailed and glued to the sides of the benchwork (like those near the river and bridges on the Burlington Northern layout in Chapter 16). Two or three layers of

Fig. 12–3. Crumple and wad newspapers to form the shapes of the hills. If the newspapers are too bouncy, wet them with a mist of water.

Fig. 12–6. Dry-coloring pigment is available where you buy the Hydrocal plaster. Use enough of the coloring to make the plaster darker than you'd like because it will become much lighter when the plaster dries.

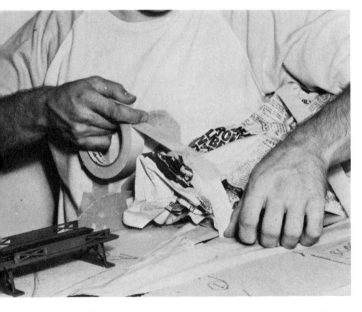

Fig. 12–4. Tape the wadded newspaper to the ⅛-inch Masonite profile boards on the edges of the layout.

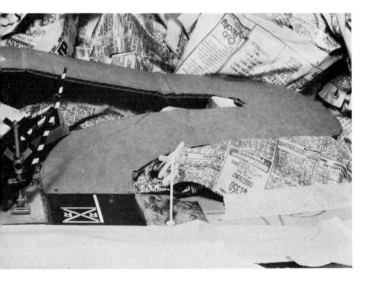

Hydrocal-soaked paper towels will be self-supporting but it may take four or more layers of paper towels soaked in conventional gypsum plaster to come close to the self-supporting strength of the Hydrocal method.

Mix the plaster in flexible plastic pans that you can throw away or purchase a large Pyrex glass mixing bowl. The Pyrex can be washed clean much more easily than regular glass, and it is somewhat stronger. Purchase some dark-brown powdered pigment for plaster from the same building-supply dealer who sells you the Hydrocal or gypsum plaster. Buy enough to give a light-brown color to all the plaster you purchase. The powdered pigment should have instructions to tell you how much is needed for that particular brand, or you can ask the dealer.

Pour about four cups of water into your mixing bowl and slowly sprinkle in about an equal amount of plaster while you stir. Always

Fig. 12–5. Roads through the hills can simply be cut from corrugated cardboard and taped in place before applying plaster.

Fig. 12–7. Add the plaster and the dry-coloring pigment to the water as you stir.

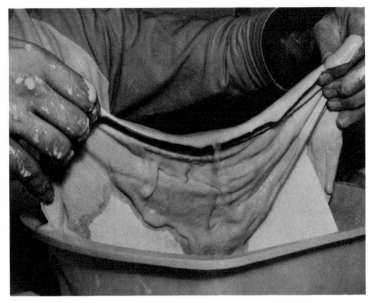

Fig. 12–8. Submerge each paper towel in the tub of wet plaster so that the plaster completely covers every inch of the towel.

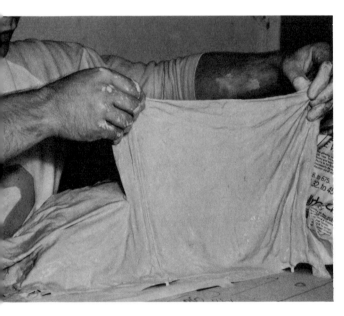

Fig. 12–9. Dip the paper towels in the wet plaster; then drape them over the mock-up scenery.

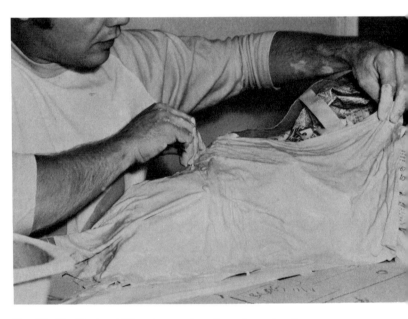

Fig. 12–10. Each additional paper towel must overlap the adjacent towel by at least two inches for strength. At least two layers of Hydrocal-soaked paper towels will be needed for self-supporting scenery.

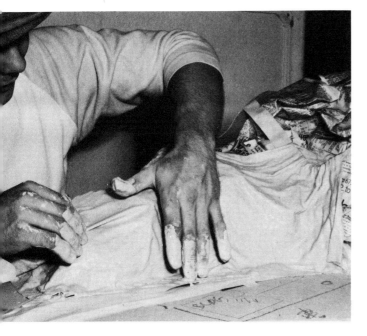

Fig. 12–11. Smooth each paper towel's plaster where it meets the masking tape over the tracks.

add the dry plaster to the water; not the water to the plaster. The exact ratio of plaster to water can vary considerably, so keep stirring while you add the plaster. You want a mix about the consistency of thick cream. When the consistency is right, stir in the proper amount of the dry pigment. With practice, you'll learn how much plaster is about right, and then you can stir in both the plaster and the pigment at the same time.

Submerge each paper towel in the plaster mix to thoroughly wet it and drape the plaster-soaked paper towel over your mock-up scenery. Overlap each additional paper towel about half-way across the area of the first one and place the third paper towel almost directly over the first. This interweaving technique will give you the three layers you need for strength. If you're using conventional gypsum plaster rather than Hydrocal, add two more paper towels to the area in the same overlapping pattern. Continue to add paper towels around the layout.

You will undoubtedly have to mix many batches of plaster to complete the scenery

work on any layout. The new plaster will stick nicely to the old if you continue the work on the same day. If the job takes more than a day, be sure to spray some water on the places where you will add new plaster to the old so that the two will bond together nicely. I suggest that you rub the surface of the last layer of paper towels with your hand during the last few minutes of the hardening or setting stage to roughen the surface. When you do this, the particles of just-hardened plaster will act like very rough sandpaper to roughen the rest of the surface. It's a bit hard on your hands, so apply some hand cream or salve to replace the natural body oils the plaster leaches out. The roughened surface can be used as is for just about everything, but for those almost vertical walls and cliffs, you'll want to carve or cast rock or erosion marks into the plaster.

Real Rocks

It's possible to carve simple rock structures like the layers of sandstone and the erosion marks that water makes on smooth earth cuts and fills. More complex rock structures are best duplicated with latex rubber molds taken from real rocks. Chunks of coal can often provide rocklike strata that is even more realistic than genuine rocks when applied to a model railroad. Spray the portion of the rock or the piece of coal you want to duplicate with silicone spray or with one of the nonstick cooking sprays, such as Pam.

Liquid latex can be purchased in cans from many craft-supply stores. If you cannot find the liquid latex, you can substitute plain white glue, but the resulting mold won't last for more than one or two "castings." Brush a thick layer of the latex or white glue over the rock, apply a layer of gauze or cheesecloth to act as reinforcement, and brush on another layer of latex or white glue over the gauze or cheesecloth. Repeat the process until you have a total of three layers of liquid latex or

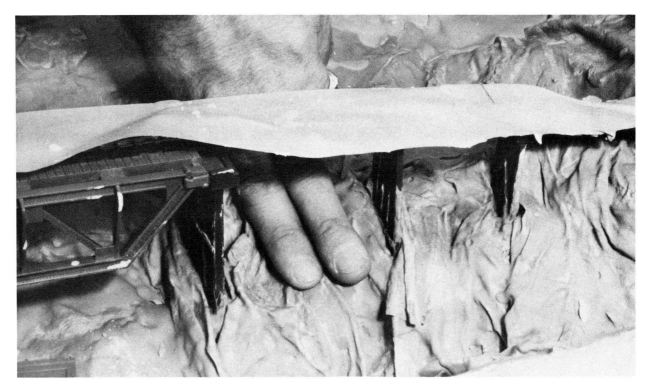

Fig. 12–12. Tuck the still-wet plaster-soaked paper towels in around the trestle bents to make the earth beneath the bridges. It would be wise to protect the bridges from the plaster with small pieces of clear plastic.

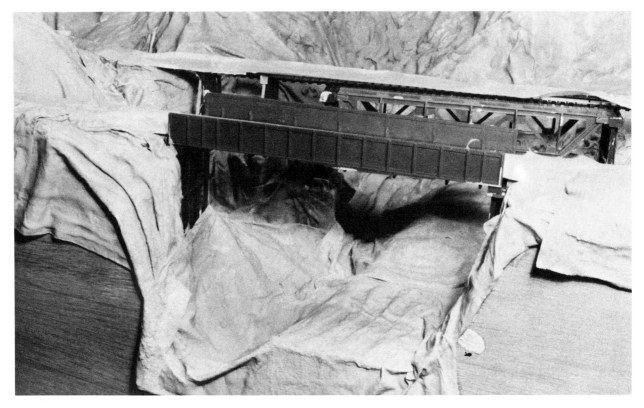

Fig. 12–13. The gaps between the paper towels and the abutment and trestle bents can be filled with a thick, puttylike mixture of plaster.

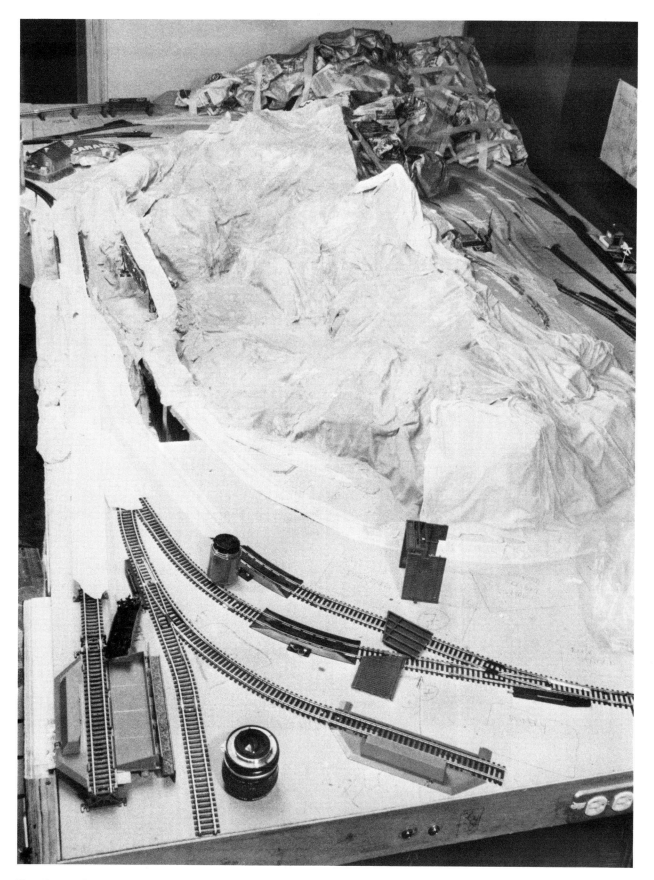

Fig. 12—14. Complete one area of the scenery at a time. If you're not satisfied with the shapes, simply add more wadded-up newspapers and plaster-soaked paper towels on top of the finished scenery.

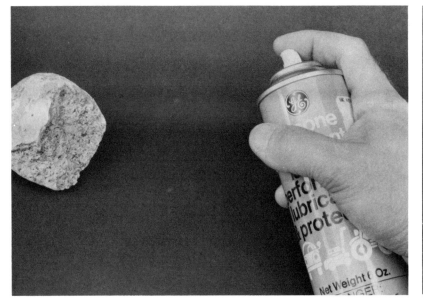

Fig. 12–15. Find a rock or a piece of coal with a suitable rock texture and spray it with several coats of silicone "dry" lubricant.

Fig. 12–16. Pour a thick layer of liquid latex or white glue on the silicone-treated rock surface.

white glue and two layers of gauze or cheese-cloth. Allow the mixture 24 hours to dry before gently peeling it away from the rock. You now have a mold of the rock, which can be duplicated in plaster.

Use gypsum plaster for the rock castings so that you can carve the edges to help them blend into the surrounding scenery. You might want to use a shade of gray or beige dry-color pigment for the rocks rather than brown. Use only about half as much of the pigment as you did to simulate dirt on the rest of the scenery so the rocks will be almost white. Mix the plaster until it is just a bit thicker than before (but it should still be pourable). Prewet the area where the rock casting will be placed with a spray bottle or plant atomizer. Pour the wet plaster into the mold and immediately slap the mold and the plaster against the place where you want the rock. Hold it there until you can feel the plaster harden (it will take only a minute or two) and immediately peel the mold away before the plaster is completely hard. You can add as many applications of rocks made from the same mold

as are needed to give the cliff the "face" you want. Overlap each casting slightly, and, perhaps, tilt each one a few degrees to give a slightly different appearance to each segment. You can, of course, use many different rock-casting molds on various parts of the layout or even on a single cliff "face." Remember that the rocks must match the texture of the rocks in the cuts and cliffs you see in the geographic area you have selected as the prototype for your layout. Crumpled aluminum foil can be used in place of the latex or white-glue molds to duplicate one specific type of rock texture with this same casting procedure.

Ground Color and Cover

Rocks can be colored by simply spraying on a wash of 95 parts water and 5 parts dark-brown or dark-gray acrylic paint. The wash will collect in the crevices and hollows of the rock castings and the almost white plaster will show through as highlights for some incredibly realistic rock effects. Brush equal parts of

Fig. 12–17. Cover the rock with alternating layers of liquid latex of white glue and gauze to make a mold for casting rock surfaces.

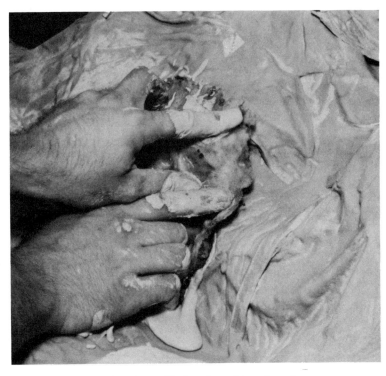

Fig. 12–19. Press the plaster-filled rock mold against the plaster scenery and hold it there until you can feel the plaster harden.

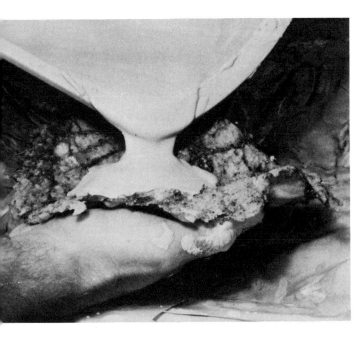

Fig. 12–18. Fill the rock mold with gypsum plaster.

Fig. 12–20. Overlap the next rock casting over the first to help disguise the seams between the two. Keep adjacent castings aligned so the major cracks or flaws in the rock are parallel to one another.

Fig. 12–21. Crumple aluminum foil and use it as a mold to create this type of rock texture.

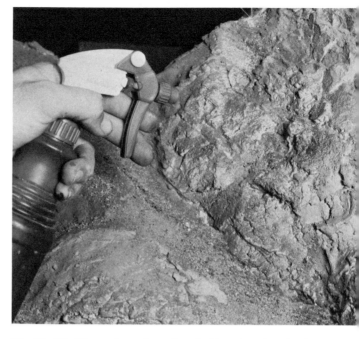

Fig. 12–22. The rock can be colored with an initial wash of black or dark brown Rit dye or acrylic color and water to highlight and accent the depressions and crevices.

water and white glue over the horizontal surfaces of the rocks, and use a strainer or flour sifter to sprinkle real dirt on those areas. Cover the areas of the scenery that are not occupied with buildings, track, or cliffs with real dirt in this same manner. When all the dirt is in place, you can remove the masking tape from the track and add whatever matching or contrasting shades of dirt you have selected for track ballast, as described in Chapter 5. Part of the earth and even some of the track sidings should be covered with grass and weeds, as described in Chapter 13.

Water

The material that produces the most realistic water with the least effort is the epoxy sold by craft shops for use in decoupage. This material differs from the resin sold to repair fiberglass boats in that the epoxy requires only a few drops of the catalyst per cup of resin, while the fiberglass material demands a nearly equal mix of resin and catalyst. The two look the same when cured, but the de-

Fig. 12–23. Slightly lighter tones can be dabbed onto the rock face to create the speckled appearance of some types of real rock.

Fig. 12–24. A typical wood tunnel portal on the Southern Pacific Railroad, 1978.

Fig. 12–25. The parts from a Pola, Model Power, or Tyco Coaling Station were cut like this to make a wood tunnel portal.

Fig. 12–26. The two "wings" on each side of the tunnel portal would normally be positioned as shown. The angle of the hill on the Burlington Northern layout suggests a reverse angle for the right-hand wing.

Fig. 12–28. The tunnel portal area after the sceney is completed.

Fig. 12–27. The plaster mountain covers the tracks just like a real mountain might, so a cut must be made (with a hardware knife) for the tunnel.

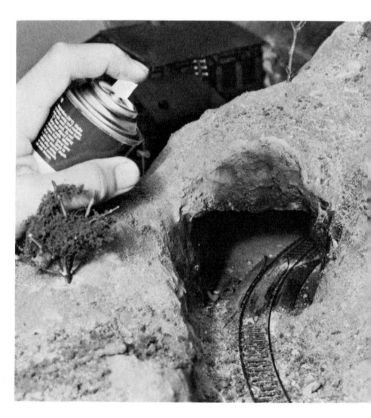

Fig. 12–29. Spray a light mist of black over the tops of each tunnel portal to simulate the stain from diesel exhaust or steam-locomotive smoke.

Fig. 12–30. Spray the area that will become the bottom of any stream or lake with several heavy coats of Testors Dullcote to seal the surface, so loose plaster or texturing materials won't form air bubbles in the bottom of the resin "water."

Fig. 12–32. The tiny hairlike interior of cattails can be used to make most realistic weeds in the edges of epoxy-resin lakes.

Fig. 12–31. Decoupage fluids, such as Envirotex, can be used for lakes or streams. Mix according to the instructions on the bottles or cans.

coupage epoxies do not produce the horrible odors of fiberglass resins while they cure. Both run like water until they cure or harden, so the bottom of any lake, river, or stream bed must be sealed and perfectly water-tight where you intend to pour the resin. If the river runs right to the edge of the table, you can build a "dam" by sealing the end with cloth silver-colored air-conditioner duct tape. If the stream is deep, back up the duct-tape "dam" with a temporary sheet of plywood or Masonite. Add any sunken boats, old tires, weeds, or logs that you want to see submerged. Spray the entire "submerged" portion of the river or stream with several coats of Testors Dullcote to seal any loose dirt or debris so that trapped air cannot form bubbles in the bottom of the epoxy-resin "water." Let the Dullcote dry for at least two days before pouring the epoxy resin.

Mix the resin and the catalyst exactly as

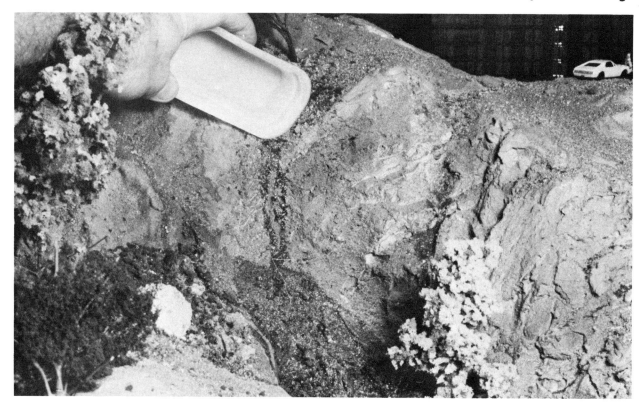

Fig. 12–33. Steep streams can be poured (or brushed) with as many as a dozen thin applications of epoxy resin.

Fig. 12–34. When the scenery is complete, the wadded-up newspapers can be pulled from beneath the mountains and hills.

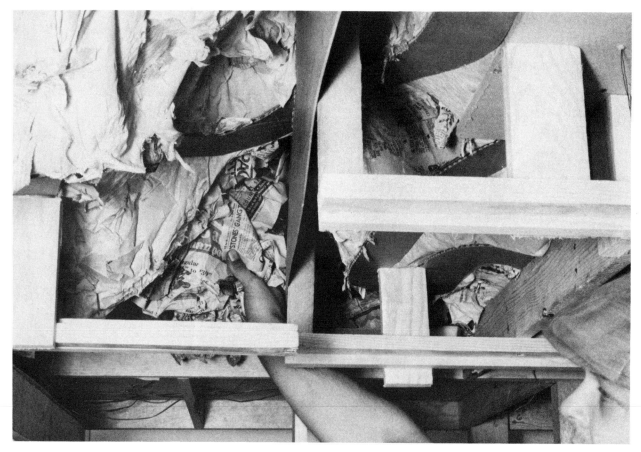

Fig. 12–35. This fast-flowing mountain stream was created using Artist's Gloss and Gel Mediums as shown in the color section.

shown on the side of the can. Mix several small batches so you can build up deeper water in layers that are no more than $\frac{1}{16}$-inch thick. If you try to pour too much of the resin, it will crack as it cures. You can add another "pour" to help disguise the crack, but it will never look quite right. You should be ready to insert a few weeds cut from hemp rope and a bit of ground foam rubber dyed green into the edges of the last layers of the resin while the resin is still wet. Wiggle a wooden stick around on the last layers, just as they are becoming hard, to simulate ripples on the water's surface. If you pick at the resin right through the hardening stage, you can even simulate rapids and white caps. Touch a few of the hardened tips with a wash of white oil paint and turpentine to give a white-water effect. Very steep streams can be cast by tilting the entire layout so that the stream itself is level. If you cannot do that, then build up the

Do's and Don'ts for Creating Scenery

Do have color photographs, postcards or magazine illustrations of the general area you wish to model beside the layout so you can match colors, shapes and plant/earth textures with model materials.

Don't attempt to create scenery by using only the packaged model scenery materials arrayed by whim.

Do use real dirt sifted through a fine wire screen to simulate dirt.

Don't use dyed sawdust or ground foam to simulate dirt.

Do check the clearances beside and above the tracks, at tunnels, and cuts through the hills by running the longest locomotives and the longest cars over the layout.

Don't build rock walls or cliffs so close to the tracks that long locomotives or cars will sideswipe the scenery and derail.

Do spray any of the too-bright greens with a fine mist of light beige wash (a mix of about nine-parts water to one-part beige acrylic paint plus a drop of dishwashing detergent) to blend the colors of the layout and avoid too much contrast between earth and leaves or grass under the relatively dim indoor lighting.

Don't settle for bright greens and deep browns as the only scenery colors.

Do apply ballast to any mainline tracks (and dirt to industrial sidings) but keep the ballast well away from the moving parts (the switch points) of all the turnouts. Glue the ballast in place with a mixture of nine-parts water to one-part Artist's Matte Medium with a drop of dishwashing detergent.

Don't use loose ballast and do not allow any glue or ballast around the points of any turnout.

stream by applying a dozen or more thin layers of the epoxy resin with throw-away paint brushes, which hardware stores sell for use with acids. Artist's Gloss Gel also can be used for steep streams.

Alternate materials to simulate water in small, shallow streams and ponds are Artist's Gloss Medium and Artist's Gloss Gel. The Gloss Medium is essentially an acrylic paint that dries clear and shiny. The Gloss Gel is thicker and shiny but it can be formed into peaks and lumps to simulate rapids, short waterfalls, and other fast-moving water. The color section of this book illustrates the use of Artist's Gloss Medium and Artist's Gloss Gel, but the techniques are similar to those you would use with decoupage epoxy resin and catalyst.

CHAPTER 13

Trees, Shrubs, and Other Greenery

MUCH OF MOTHER EARTH is covered with some type of living foliage and that's what prevents this planet's surface from becoming just a cloud of dust. The dirt and rocks, of course, underlie all that greenery, and that's why greenery is the last scenic effect to be added to a model railroad. If you're following the suggestions in this book, your entire model railroad is now covered (in your mind, at least) with either track, structures, ballast, rocks, dirt, or simulated water.

In practice, I suggest that you complete just a few square feet of the layout to this stage so you can apply your lessons to the rest of the railroad after you have learned them through practice. There's no real reason why you cannot create scenery in just one small corner of the layout, from the plaster stage right through "water" and foliage. When you feel like making more scenery, begin another section and gradually work your way around. I suggest that you place that precolored plaster just about everywhere in order to get the messy part over and done with. If you find later that you need to change a mountain or add a river, it's easy enough to break through the plaster to mock-up a change in the sce-

nery and cover it with plaster. Apply the final touches of foliage to only those areas where you're pleased with the rest of the scenery. Those "finished" areas will include the tracks and their immediate surroundings.

Ground Cover

Scenery begins at the ground. Far too many modelers skip right ahead to bushes and trees and wonder why their layouts look like deserts with trees on them. I suggest that you use at least two different kinds of ground cover in addition to real dirt: ground (chopped) foam rubber dyed green and $\frac{1}{8}$-inch-strands of polypropylene macramé twine. The real dirt and the ground foam can be held in place on the layout by spraying the area to be covered with a fifty-fifty mixture of Artist's Matte Medium and water. The ground foam rubber is available in a variety of "grinds" (sizes of the foam pieces) and colors to match summer foliage, as well as spring and fall colors, and the bright hues of flowers. The foam is even available in earth or dirt colors and it makes a surprisingly realistic substitute for sifted real dirt. Hobby shops carry the foam under the AMSI, Bachmann, Life-Like, Plastruct, Timberline Products, and Woodland Scenics labels. The foam can simply be sprinkled on trees, shrubs or ground that has been coated with white glue or Artist's Matte Medium.

165

Fig. 13-1. Use a plastic squeeze bottle to apply the strands of polypropylene "grass" to glue-soaked terrain.

Weeds and Grass

Polypropylene twine is available from macramé shops and craft departments. The twine must be cut into ⅛-inch lengths. Polypropylene is the only material that will retain the individual strands after it is cut this short. You can do this with other synthetic macramé or knitting twines, but they'll bunch together to form "clumps" very similar to tumbleweeds. Polypropylene, on the other hand, will simulate grass, hay, wheat, and similarly textured weeds. Buy dark green, light green, and avocado colors if you can. Faller, Kibri, Noch, Preiser, Vintage, and Woodland Scenics (available to dealers from Walthers), and Timberline Products (2029 E. Howe, Tempe, AZ 85281) sell similar materials, already cut.

A squeeze-bottle applicator is the best

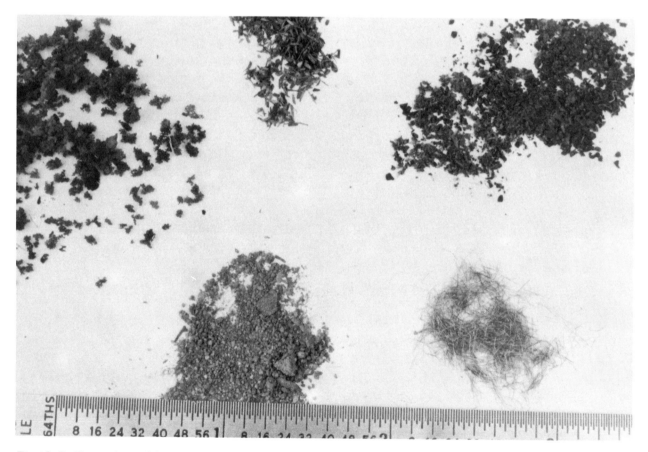

Fig. 13-2. Five scale-model ground covers (clockwise from upper left): Ground foam rubber, sifted sawdust, sifted coffee grounds, ⅛-inch cut strands of polypropylene twine, and real dirt.

Fig. 13–4. To simulate weeds, the larger ground foam-rubber particles can be sprinkled over scenery that has been prewetted with water and white glue.

Fig. 13–3. Apply most ground covers through a strainer, tapping the side of the strainer to sift the material.

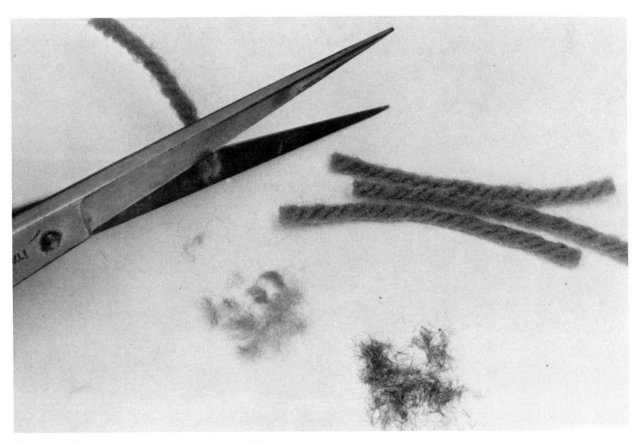

Fig. 13–5. The polypropylene twine cuts into individual strands (bottom), while most synthetics tend to collect in scale-model tumbleweeds (center).

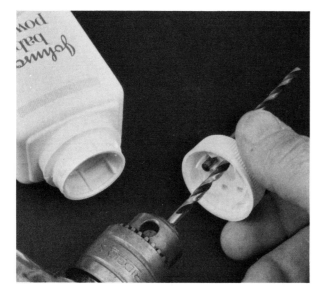

Fig. 13–6. Drill the holes in a baby powder lid to ⅛-inch diameter so the plastic bottle can be used as a squeeze-type applicator for the grass.

"tool" to use to apply the ⅛-inch strands because the squeezing action creates some static electricity on the strands, which makes them stand up like a crew cut when they come in contact with the glue. You may be able to find a flexible plastic container with a half-dozen ⅛-inch holes in the lid. A container from bathroom cleanser or table salt will do, or you can make your own from a plastic baby-powder bottle. Drill ⅛-inch holes in the lid, using a second drill bit to keep the two layers of the lid from rotating. When the lid is snapped back onto the bottle, each of the little sawtooth tabs must be positioned so they fit inside the neck of the bottle. Just squeeze the bottle to "spray" the simulated grass onto the glue-dampened "earth."

Fig. 13–7. Some natural growths for scale-model trees and bushes (clockwise from upper left): Peat moss, real grass roots, flowered baby's breath, bottle brush, dried Caspia, dried and dyed Caspia.

Trees and Bushes

Natural materials such as weeds and lichen mosses and even some root systems work well for simulating trees and bushes. In some cases, the tiny flowers or ends of the natural material are fine enough to be almost-to-scale leaves. However, most of these materials must be used only as the branch systems for the trees or bushes on a model railroad, with the actual leaves formed from finely ground foam rubber, dyed sawdust, or a combination of the two materials.

Branches and Twigs

The most critical part of most miniatures of trees and bushes are the tiny intermediate twigs that branch off from the main trunk to hold the leaves. These intricate structures must be glued onto most weeds before the ground foam or sawdust is applied, so those "leaf" materials can be glued to the "intermediate twig" material. The hairlike plastic "cloth" that is used for some types of packing insulation and for plastic scouring pads and Woodland Scenics' Poly Fiber are perfect materials for those twiggy portions of the trees and bushes. Macramé shops sell bulk skeins of a coarse-cottonlike material that some macramé rope is made from that can be substituted for the Woodland Scenics' Poly Fiber. The material is available in both a brown and a gray/beige. Do not be tempted by steel wool; the strands will certainly find their way into the magnets in the motors of the locomotives and will cause a short circuit.

Tree Trunks

The trunks and major branches of trees and large bushes can be made from a wide variety of weeds and even the twigs of small

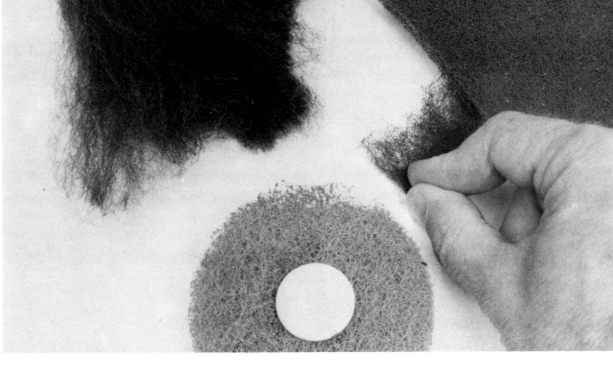

Fig. 13–8. Bulk macramé rope, before weaving (upper left) and plastic scouring pads are some materials to use for the small twig structures of trees.

Fig. 13–9. Dip the largest pieces of plastic "wool" or macramé fiber in white glue before placing them in the ravines of the scenery.

Fig. 13–10. Carefully select weeds and small twigs, which can be used to simulate tree trunks, using ground foam rubber, dyed green, for the foliage.

bushes or trees. If you cannot find sizes and shapes that suit the types of trees in the geographic area of your model railroad, then make your own. Stranded steel clothesline can be cut into four to eight-inch lengths with diagonal cutters. Unwrap the individual strands for about half the length of the piece of wire and bend them into the shape of branches. Bend out all but two of the strands at the bottom of each piece to form roots. The two remaining strands will be pushed into the plaster to support the tree. Use the putty-style two-part epoxy and catalyst to make the trunk texture for each tree, and paint the trunks with brown, gray, and beige acrylics to simulate bark.

The unwoven macramé fiber or Woodland Scenics' Poly Fiber can be applied in two different ways to simulate two different types of branch structures: The material can be cut and wrapped into a very loose ball or "cloud" and then glued to the tree-trunk structure, or

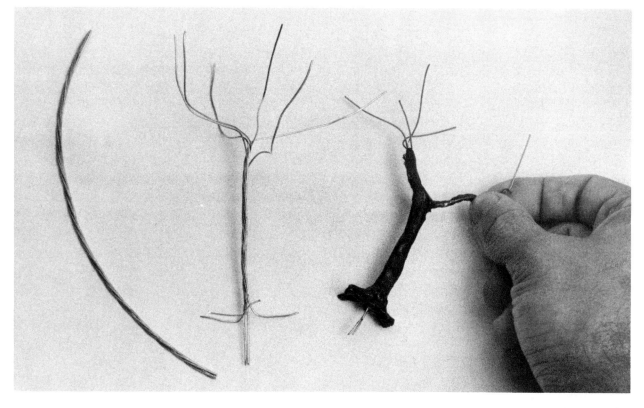

Fig. 13–11. Shape the basic tree trunk from pieces of wire clothesline and cover them with putty-type epoxy and catalyst (right) to simulate the thicker tree-trunk area and bark.

the macramé material can be cut into short lengths and fanned out before being glued to the trunk structure.

Leaves

The final step in making the tree is to spray the "twig" portion with a fifty-fifty mixture of

Fig. 13–12. Woodland Scenics' Poly Fiber is one of the better materials to use in creating the "twig" structures of trees or bushes.

white glue and water. Let the glue dry until it is just becoming tacky, then dip the tree into a box of dyed ground foam rubber or sawdust. This creates the individual "leaves," as shown in Figure 13–14. Drill or punch a hole for the tree in the plaster or Homosote and dab on a bit of precolored plaster to be worked in around the roots system. Finally, glue a bit of ground cover around the base of the tree. Pay attention to nature's examples when you "plant" the trees on your model railroad. Most trees grow in small valleys or hollows, and they are often clustered in groups of three or more. Use some of the gray-colored "twig" and "trunk" trees without the application of "leaves" to simulate an occasional dead tree in a small grove of living trees. Now your layout has really come alive!

Commercial Trees

The trees featured up until now were made with either real twigs or the dried roots of

Fig. 13–13. The unbraided macramé rope can be puffed into rounded shapes (top) or cut and spread into fanlike shapes (bottom) to simulate different types of tree structures.

Fig. 13–14. Spray the tree with white glue and water, and, when it's tacky, dip it into a box of ground foam rubber or sawdust to simulate leaves.

Fig. 13–15. Woodland Scenics' Foliage Material is essentially Poly Fiber with ground foam already glued in place. Stretch the material as thin as possible for maximum realism.

Fig. 13–16. These models were built from AMSI (left), Woodland Scenics metal (center) and Woodland Scenics plastic tree kits. The AMSI Plastruct and Woodland Scenics kits are available with metal trunks and Woodland Scenics offers some bendable plastic trunks in some tree kits.

weeds covered with macramé mesh and ground foam. Woodland Scenics offers a Poly Fiber material that is similar to the macrame mesh we used for these trees. Woodland Scenics has a similar material in their tree kits, but the ground foam is already glued to the mesh to save you a step in the construction of the tree or bush. Hobby shops also carry at least one brand of packaged, dyed and treated Norwegian lichen moss (usually called, simply, "lichen") that can be used in place of the macrame mesh. Some modelers use the lichen as-is for trees and bushes and it is part of some of the ready-made trees from firms like Bachmann, Life-Like, and Model Power. The lichen looks far more realistic, however, if it, too, is covered with a bit of ground foam to disguise the lichen tip texture.

Most of the ready-made trees have a wire core with bristle "limbs" similar to a baby bottle brush. These trees can be made more realistic by trimming their shapes with scissors to create a rougher, more natural form and by covering them with ground foam for a more random texture.

PART V

Miniature Empires in Action

CHAPTER 14

Automatic Coupling and Switching

THE REAL EXCITEMENT that model rail-roading offers is not only running the trains but the actual coupling, uncoupling, and switching, just as real railroads do each day. Some model railroaders place a string of cars and a locomotive and caboose on the track and never uncouple a car until they take that train off the layout to replace it with another. Of course it is exciting to watch any train move around a model railroad layout, partic-ularly one that has some buildings and sce-nery for that train to pass. This makes it seem like it's really going somewhere. But there is much more to a realistic model railroad than that.

If you are one of the many model railroad-ers who consider "switching" to be nothing more than simply running a train forward, backward, and forward again, I think you are missing one of the more fascinating aspects of the hobby. The real excitement of switch-ing comes from the duplication of *all* the movements of the real trains—and for pre-cisely the same reasons. If you want your model railroad to be authentic, you will want to switch that train back and forth.

The "Hands-Near" Approach

One of the many differences between a toy-train operator and one who is running a real railroad in miniature is a "hands-off" approach. That's why those endless laps around the layout with the same old trains become boring. There's a thrill in sitting or standing at a control panel while you flip levers to switch trains in and out of sidings or stop one train while you start another. The "towerman's" job is always going to be a part of both real and model railroading. Please don't let that be the only part of the hobby for you though. Step down from that tower (here is where walk-around control is a big help) and try the "engineer's" or "brakeman's" jobs for a while. You still won't have to destroy the illusion that yours is a real railroad by actually touching the miniature trains. The true model railroader is the person who prac-tices a "hands-near" approach, which means that he or she remains close enough to the moving train to be a participant rather than being only a spectator at a control panel.

Couplers

The couplers on your HO-scale cars and locomotives will couple together just about

Fig. 14–1. The wires on the uncoupling ramps force the couplers apart.

anywhere, except on a curve or a downgrade. Coupling, then, can always be a hands-off operation as long as the couplers are working properly. Uncoupling is a bit tricky to do from a distant control panel because you have to be able to judge exactly where the couplers and the cars are. The couplers on your HO-scale models will only uncouple "by remote control" when they are directly over the wire and plastic uncoupling ramps made by the various r-t-r companies. The two wires force the pins on the bottom toward the rails and that opens the coupler. When you pull the train away, the uncoupled car or that portion of the train will stay at the uncoupling ramp. You must perform a quick succession of moves for reliable uncoupling. Stop at the ramp, back up just a fraction of an inch, then pull forward immediately. You can put the wire and plastic ramps on any six-inch or longer piece of straight track.

Manual Coupling

There's a better way of uncoupling that will let you get even more involved with the operation of your trains. Simply use a small screwdriver, an ice pick, or an awl to operate the couplers. You're still not actually touching the models but you *are* performing the function of the brakeman, in addition to your other duties as towerman (or dispatcher) and engineer. This may sound simple, but don't laugh until you've tried it for several operating sessions.

You don't have to put your miniature railroad equipment through those toy train gyrations of lurching backward and forward to get the couplers to open, and you don't have to try to figure out how to place an uncoupling ramp every place you want or need one. You really should use the uncoupling tool in conjunction with the walk-around throttle (in Chapter 7), so you can use the throttle to set the locomotive in motion when you have the couplers open. It will take some practice to determine the best ways to use the screwdriver or ice pick. The trick is to push the point straight down to get it just into the gap between the couplers, then twist or lean the tool slightly to pry the couplers apart. The movement should be very delicate.

Coupler Maintenance

The couplers are the most vulnerable parts of your models, and it's easy for them to be knocked out of alignment. You should check every coupler on every piece of equipment you own, and make it a habit to check the couplers whenever you put a new piece of equipment into operation. Be sure the coupler is free to pivot from side to side without any binds or jerks. Try coupling it to a coupler on another car by pushing the two cars together on the track, by hand, so you can feel if it takes too much pressure to get the two to couple. Sometimes small wisps of plastic or

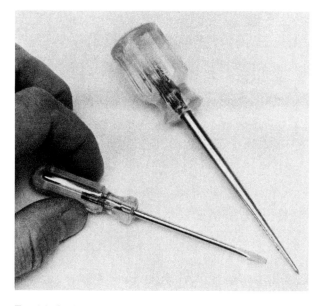

Fig. 14–2. A small screwdriver or an awl (right) can be used to operate the couplers by hand.

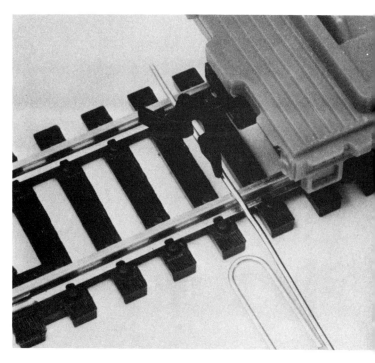

Fig. 14–4. Each coupler must be adjusted so the bottom of the pin clears a partially straightened paperclip placed temporarily across a test track.

Fig. 14–3. Insert the screwdriver between the coupler faces and twist it to force the couplers apart.

small ridges of "flash" must be sliced off cleanly with a sharp hobby knife in order to get the coupler to work properly.

The couplers, like the trucks beneath freight and passenger cars, are self-lubricating, so if someone has applied any oil or grease, it should be cleaned away before it has a chance to attract dust and lint. A medium-size paperclip can be used as a coupler gauge; if the coupler pin just clears the paperclip, it means the coupler is in the correct position. If the coupler hits the paperclip or clears it by more than $\frac{1}{64}$-inch, the coupler must be adjusted. Pull the truck and coupler off the bottom of the car (the trucks are a snap-fit on all but the locomotive tenders). Bend the coupler bracket (but not the coupler itself) up or down enough so it will stay in the proper position. If you find a broken coupler, you can purchase a replacement coupler—or a complete truck. The couplers on most cars can be removed or installed by

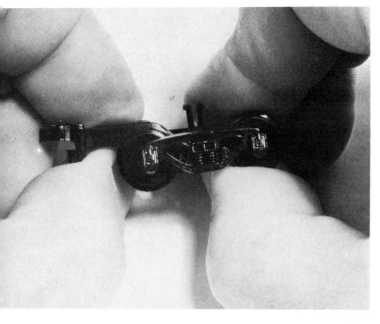

Fig. 14–5. Bend the coupler mounting bracket (pocket) up or down by hand to correct the coupler height.

prying down on the center tab, as shown in Figure 14–6, while you position the coupler over the pivot pin. The couplers on locomotives must be replaced by your dealer when a new screw is needed to replace the broken plastic pivot pin.

Kadee Automatic Couplers

The couplers that are supplied with nearly all ready-to-run equipment and with the inexpensive kits are among the most exasperating items with which you'll need to work

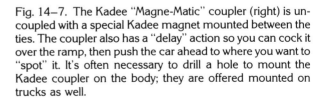

Fig. 14–7. The Kadee "Magne-Matic" coupler (right) is uncoupled with a special Kadee magnet mounted between the ties. The coupler also has a "delay" action so you can cock it over the ramp, then push the car ahead to where you want to "spot" it. It's often necessary to drill a hole to mount the Kadee coupler on the body; they are offered mounted on trucks as well.

Fig. 14–6. If you must replace a broken coupler, pry down on this center tab to remove or replace the coupler.

in the hobby. These strange-shaped couplers are referred to as "horn-hook" couplers because that is a close description of their appearance. The only thing these couplers will do reliably is couple—and then only if the locomotive slams one car into the next. That excessive force can be reduced somewhat if you use a hobby knife to cut $\frac{1}{16}$-inch from the hairlike spring that is beside the couplers inside the truck. Keep cutting off $\frac{1}{16}$-inch increments until the coupler still centers but only light coupling force is needed. It's also possible to uncouple these couplers with a screwdriver as outlined earlier in this chapter. Rarely, however, will the horn-hook couplers actually uncouple over the wire uncoupling ramps designed for their operations without derailing the train. Besides, they look weird.

The majority of serious model railroaders replace the horn-hook couplers with couplers made by Kadee. These couplers look like real railroad couplers, although they are about 25 percent larger than they should be for truly accurate HO scale couplers. The coupler knuckle actually opens like a real coupler, too. The real magic of Kadee couplers, however, is that they really will couple with a gentle force. The Kadee couplers will uncouple without derailing the train by using a magnetic "ramp" that is buried beneath the track or placed between the rails so it looks like a highway crossing. Just stop the car and locomotive with the couplers over the 2-inch long ramp and the two couplers open to disengage. That leaves a lot of room for error, and the train doesn't have to be spotted very carefully to catch part of the ramp.

The Kadee couplers have another advantage—what Kadee calls a "delay" feature. Stop the train with the couplers over a ramp so the couplers will disengage, and then back up just a fraction of an inch as shown in Figure 14–8. The two couplers are now cocked open and the car (or train) can be pushed for any distance. Stop pushing and reverse the locomotive and the car (or train)

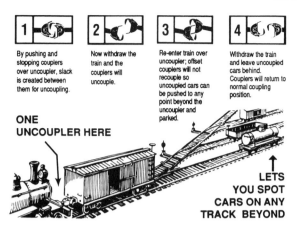

Fig. 14–8. This shows how the Kadee couplers operate over the ramp (1 and 2) and how the delayed-action principle functions (3, 4 and the lower drawing). Courtesy Kadee Quality Products.

will remain behind. You can "spot" a car (or a car and the train behind that car) on any track beyond the ramp. The feature allows the use of fewer ramps. The one disadvantage is that odd back-up movement to cock the couplers.

The Kadee couplers have a small bent wire that hangs below the coupler. This uncoupling pin is repelled by the magnetic ramp and that action is what pivots the coupler knuckle open to uncouple. The wires vaguely resemble the air hoses that hang beside the couplers on real trains, but honestly, the uncoupling pin does not look realistic when a single car is seen from the end. Still, the appearance is vastly more realistic than that of the horn-hook couplers. A few modelers who don't like the appearance of the uncoupling pin simply cut the pin off with wire cutters. The couplers still couple automatically anywhere on the track. To uncouple them, simply insert a screwdriver between the coupler knuckles (as suggested earlier to uncouple with horn-hook couplers). Twist the screwdriver and the couplers will uncouple.

Kadee offers three styles of uncoupling ramps: one that is placed between the rails after the ties have been cut away with a razor saw, another that is buried in a 3-×-3-inch cavity cut about $\frac{1}{8}$-inch deep in the roadbed (before the track is laid), and an electromagnetic ramp that is mounted in a $\frac{1}{2}$- × -3-inch slot cut through the roadbed and tabletop. The first two ramps are permanent magnets. The third is actuated electrically with a small pushbutton. The ramps include instructions on their installation and suggestions on where to place them.

Kadee manufactures approximately one dozen different coupler mounting designs, including Numbers 26, 27 and 28 designed to be mounted on the trucks of inexpensive ready-to-run rolling stock (and locomotives) from Tyco, Bachmann, Life-Like and Model Power. The couplers require some slight trimming on the stock trucks for some applications and they are furnished with complete instructions. I suggest you buy all three so you'll have a proper coupler for any truck-mounted coupler pocket design.

Most modelers, however, prefer the more realistic coupler mounting on the bottom of the car. All of the plastic car kits have coupler pockets designed to accept a Kadee Number 5 coupler. If you are fitting the Kadee Number 5 to a car that has its couplers mounted on the trucks, you will have to cut the original coupler and pocket from each truck with a

Fig. 14–10. Use a hobby knife to remove the small peg from inside any Athearn freight or passenger car coupler pocket before installing the Kadee number 5 coupler and spring.

Fig. 14–9. The number 5 Kadee coupler pocket (top and bottom), flat bronze spring and coupler.

razor saw or diagonal cutters. The Kadee Number 5 coupler pocket then can be mounted by drilling a small hole and threading that hole as shown later in this chapter.

Athearn cars have a coupler pocket that will accept the Kadee Number 5 coupler, but there is a small tab inside the pocket that must be cut off with a hobby knife (as shown in Figure 14–10) before using the Kadee coupler and copper spring. Athearn's metal coupler cover is used.

The Kadee Number 5 couplers also will fit the coupler pockets on most Athearn locomotives, but the couplers' performance is often erratic. For reliable Kadee coupler performance, use the Number 5 coupler and

Fig. 14–11. Kadee number 5 couplers (and springs) installed in an Athearn boxcar (left) and MDC Roundhouse boxcar (right).

coupler pocket on Athearn locomotives. Use an electric drill with a Number 50 (size) drill bit to drill a hole in the round recess in the Athearn coupler pocket. Thread the hole with a Number 2-56 tap held in a pin vise. The Kadee Number 5 coupler, spring and pocket are then installed with a $\frac{1}{4}$-inch-long 2-56 screw. The Number 50 drill bit, the 2-56 tap and the $\frac{1}{4}$-$\times$-2-56 screw are available from hobby shops and larger hardware stores.

Kadee sells a special coupler height gauge (the Number 205) that is an essential tool for reliable coupler operation. The gauge is a cast metal device that holds a coupler and rests on the track. Some modelers glue a 12-inch-long piece of track to a board and mount the Kadee Number 205 gauge permanently to the track as a test track. Place the car or locomotive with the new Kadee cou-

Fig. 14–12. Use a number 50 bit in an electric drill to make the hole in the Athearn coupler-mounting pad.

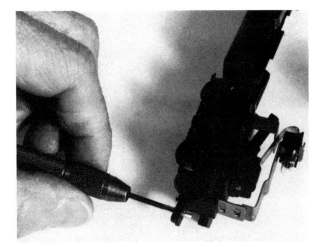

Fig. 14–13. Hold a number 2-56 tap in a pin vise to cut the threads in that number 50-size hole in the Athearn coupler mounting pad.

Fig. 14–15. Use a $\frac{1}{4} \times$ 2-56 flat head screw to mount the Kadee number 5 coupler on the Athearn coupler mounting pad.

Fig. 14–14. Use a razor saw to remove the back $\frac{1}{8}$-inch of the Kadee number 5 coupler pocket to mount the number 5 coupler and spring on the Athearn coupler mounting pad.

Fig. 14–16. Use the Kadee number 205 Coupler Height Gauge to check the height of the coupler and the pins on every Kadee coupler.

plers installed on the track and roll the coupler up to the gauge. The height of the coupler and the height of the uncoupling pin must match the gauge. If the pin or coupler is too high, the couplers won't operate properly. If the pin is too low it can catch on the turnouts and cause derailments. To lower the coupler, install some thin plastic or cardboard shims between the coupler pocket and the bottom of the car. On some Athearn locomotives, the coupler can be lowered by filing

the top of the coupler-mounting pad as shown in Figure 14–17. To raise the coupler, add washers between the trucks and the underframe on rolling stock. On some locomotives the frame can be filed; Kadee also makes offset couplers that can be used to raise the coupler about $\frac{1}{16}$-inch. Kadee includes lubrication and installation instructions with each package of couplers.

Fig. 14–17. If the coupler is too high, remove it and file the top of the Athearn mounting pad to remove the necessary metal to lower the coupler.

Trailing Switch Maneuvers

Once you understand how to perform switching maneuvers, you'll discover why those freight trains make so many back and forth movements. And once you know the reasons for them, you'll realize that it can be an important part of your model railroad operations. When you've learned how to perform switching movements, you may find you like that kind of action far more than just running trains. When you learn how to operate the "Waybill" switching system (discussed in Chapter 15), you may want to spend most of the time at any operating session just switching cars in and out of trains. Even without the "Waybill" system, though, you'll need to learn the basic switching moves. Then you can make-up trains and break them down, using a locomotive, rather than your hands, as a switch engine.

There are really only three basic switching moves, the "trailing-point" move, the "facing-point" or "run-around" move, and the "reverse" move, which reverses a train through a wye. Since most track plans group these

three, there are endless combinations. These are the only ways to move railroad cars on railroad track by pushing or pulling them with locomotives. When you get really good at switching, you may want to duplicate at least the "Timesaver" portion of the 10 × 10-foot track plan in Chapter 16. The three-track "Timesaver" is a 10- × 68-inch track arrangement that has been developed over the years for use in switching contests, so it's deliberately challenging.

"Trailing-Point" Moves

The "trailing point" simply describes the direction of the switch points of the siding relative to the direction of the train on the main line. If the siding (and the switch points) trails off behind the train as the train passes it, it is considered a "trailing-point" siding. The

Fig. 14–18. The locomotive and stock car uncouple from the train at this point.

direction of the train determines the type of maneuver; if the train were traveling in the opposite direction (counterclockwise in the illustrations), the siding and the switch points would be facing the train. This would become a "facing-point" switch. However, the moves necessary to get a car in or out of a siding that is a "facing point" are much more complicated than the moves needed to switch a car in or out of a "trailing-point" siding. Figures 14–18 through 14–21 illustrate where the locomotive is uncoupled and switched. The locomotive stops its train so it can uncouple however much of the train is behind the car that is to go onto the trailing-point siding (Figure 14–18). The car happens to be next to the locomotive in the illustrations, but there could just as well be one or two or more cars between the locomotive and the car that is to be switched or "spotted" on the siding. The locomotive then moves forward with the car to be spotted on the siding until the wheels of the car clear the points of the switch (Figure 14–19). The locomotive stops while the brakeman throws the switch from the main line to the siding. The locomotive then reverses to shove the car into the siding and stops while the car is uncoupled (Figure 14–20). The locomotive pulls forward again until it (or the last car) clears the switch points, where it will stop, while the brakeman moves the switch from the siding position to the main-line alignment. The locomotive reverses until it gently couples back to the remainder of the train (Figure 14–21). Then it stops while the brakeman sets the couplers and connects the air hoses. The train then moves forward to its next destination. Each time the train starts and stops is counted as a "move"; the fewer moves, in a complex switching situation, the quicker the time. There is no way to complete this maneuver with any fewer moves.

Most of the sequence for switching the car into the siding would, of course, be reversed if

Fig. 14–19. The stock car is pulled forward just enough to clear the switch points.

a car was already on the siding waiting to be added to the train. When you become proficient at switching maneuvers, you may want to set up situations where two or three cars need to be moved in or out of any given siding. For instance, imagine how many moves it would take if that empty log-dumping car at the Lumber Supply Company's log pond was supposed to be picked up by the same train that spotted that stock car at the

Fig. 14–20. The stock car is backed into the siding and uncoupled.

Fig. 14–21. The locomotive pulls forward to clear the switch and then backs up to couple to the remainder of the train.

cattle pens. The loaded car of lumber wasn't quite ready for pickup, of course, so it would have to be put back where it is before the train could proceed. It can be done in eleven "moves" or less, including the single "move" of stopping and starting the train for the beginning and end of the maneuver. Here's a hint: pick up the flat car and the log car at the same time (two "moves"). Remember, you want to leave here with the log car in the train,

and the flat car loaded with lumber at the sawmill, and the stock car at the cattle pens.

"Run-Around" or "Facing-Point" Moves

The switching moves are more complex when the siding is facing the direction in which the train is traveling. In the old days, the train crews would make such a move with a

Fig. 14–22. The lone hopper car full of coke is waiting for pickup.

Fig. 14–23. The locomotive uncouples from the train, pulls forward to clear the switch, then backs up and moves on across the distant bridge.

Fig. 14–24. The locomotive pulls forward, couples to the train, backs up until the first car clears the switch just in front of the bridge, then pushes the train forward.

"flying switch." This means running the locomotive forward past the switch, throwing the switch just as the locomotive clears it (but while the train is still moving), and uncoupling the car so it will roll on into the siding. That's no longer "legal" on real railroads, and it's impossible to do on a model railroad because there's no way to uncouple while the train is still in motion. The only way to get that car into or out of a "facing-point siding" is to "run around" the car at the nearest passing siding. A passing siding is generally considered to be a siding that has a switch at both ends, although a train can back into a stub-ended siding (and they often do) to wait while another train passes by. The siding with a switch at both ends is needed so the locomotive can literally run around its train to couple onto the back of it.

The sequence of the "run-around" moves in Figures 14–22 through 14–26 shows the

Fig. 14–25. The locomotive uses the train to pick up the single loaded car; then it uncouples from the train on the passing siding.

Fig. 14–26. The locomotive backs up to the bridge, then heads forward and on past the train to the right of the passing siding's switch.

Fig. 14–27. The locomotive couples back onto the train to complete the move.

essential moves that are used to pick up the loaded hopper and to place it in the train. The illustrations skip one or two of the obvious start-stop moves. You can understand, from studying these moves and from trying them on a section of your own railroad, how complicated even this basic switching situation can be.

You will notice that there is at least one passing siding on every layout plan in this book, as well as one or two stub-ended sidings. Both types of track configurations are needed if you want to operate your layout like the real thing. That's why I suggested in Chapter 1 that you consider the purchase of a pair of switches to be more important to the enjoyment of the hobby than having another locomotive. Even the simplest of layouts should have at least four switches to provide a passing siding and two stub-end sidings. Position those switches for the stub-end sidings so that one will be a "facing point" when the other is a "trailing point." This will provide the maximum amount of operating action.

The "facing-point" or "run-around" sequence can be completed in a total of eleven "moves" if done in the manner shown in the illustrations. It would also be possible to use one of several alternate methods, such as leaving the remainder of the train back on the main line behind the bridge. The moves shown are typical of those used by the real railroads' switch crews, who must leave the main line clear for as long as possible.

Wye-Switching Operations

The wye that is shared by switch crews in "Alliance" and for reversing trains for hold-over at "Points East" on the 9 × 9-foot Burlington Northern layout in Chapter 16 is an example of the type of double-duty that track-work must do on a typical model railroad. The situation is often seen in the tight track-age in older industrial areas and yards on the real railroads, so the problems are as real as

any you'll duplicate on your model railroad. The reversing sequence for turning trains (or just for turning locomotives and cabooses when the stub end of the wye is short) is simple enough. The train moves forward along the "main-line" leg of the wye (Figure 14–28), backs up the stub end through the far switch until the stub-end switch is cleared (Figure 14–29), then moves forward down the near leg of the wye and back out to the main line (Figure 14–30), traveling in the opposite direction from the way it entered the wye.

This wye at "Alliance," although it does have a stub end, actually functions like the main/branch-style wye in Figure 7–11 in Chapter 7. The "straight" portion of the wye is the main line out of "Alliance," and the leg of the wye that curves from "Emmett" toward "Corning" is the branch line (actually the main line again). You'll see that the wye is wired so that the short, curved portion with the Tyco Number 931 Freight Unloading Depot ("F. C. Rode & Co." concrete pipe; see Figure 16–4) is the electrically isolated "reversing section." When trains arrive at the wye from "Emmett," they take the left leg past "F. C. Rode & Co." so they can be turned to back into the holding track called "Points East" (the track with the "f" block on the plans and control panels), to be ready for a later return trip over the layout. There's a deliberate switching problem here because the "main line" beyond the switch points on that leg of the wye is only about 24 inches long which is just long enough for a typical four-car train but not enough for its locomotive. There would be room for another car or for the locomotive if the "Alliance Freight Station" were not where it is, but that's the "easy" solution to the problem. You'll enjoy this layout more because it does have a few "problems" incorporated into the design. If you get tired of switching every train at the wye, just add another length of track to the stub end of the wye at "Alliance" and put the freight station somewhere else.

Fig. 14–28. The train pulls to the left leg of the "Alliance" wye.

Fig. 14–29. The locomotive can back its train down the straight side of the wye to clear the far switch.

Fig. 14–30. The train now pulls forward to complete the reversing wye moves.

CHAPTER 15

Trains in Action

THE MOVEMENTS of the train are what make any model railroad a truly "living" replica of real railroading. You have nothing more than a three-dimensional sculpture until you add the action of the trains. Your railroad will revert back to that toylike state if the action doesn't at least represent the way real trains move. That's what this chapter is all about.

There's also an "almost-magic" method of installing four switches and some track so you can switch loaded cars into an industry and pull unloaded ones out (or vice versa). This is called "Loads-In Empties-Out."

Achieving Authenticity

One of the problems that a model railroader must face is a lack of credibility. We have to keep reminding ourselves that our miniatures often aren't real enough, and we don't need some glaring toylike sight to make it more difficult for our imaginations to work. The switching suggestions you'll find here in the "Waybill" system will allow you to move freight cars into and out of industrial sidings

almost exactly as though those cars were indeed carrying freight. That scene will be silly, though, if you try to imagine that an empty flatcar really does have a load after it leaves the factory that was supposed to have "loaded" it. The "Loads-In Empties-Out" system is one way around the problem because it will really put "loads" in those cars.

There are easier ways of doing almost as good a job of tricking even your own imagination. First, try to include as many industries as you can that would ship and receive something in the same kind of car. A furniture factory might receive fine hardwood in a boxcar and ship furniture out in the same car. A sawmill might receive rough-cut lumber and ship finished lumber on the same flatcar. A coke oven might receive hopper carloads of coal and ship almost identical-appearing carloads of coke. A Trailer Train terminal is just as likely to receive flat carloads of full trailers as it is to ship similar loads. Second, try to "load" flatcars and gondolas with only a $\frac{1}{2}$ to $\frac{2}{3}$ load so they can be considered *either* "empty" or "full." Load a few of those Trailer Train "Piggyback"-style flatcars with just one trailer. Both methods will add to the "power of suggestion."

The Waybill System

Each shipment made by rail is the result of dozens of papers that order the shipment and

the car that will hold it and route that car to the customer. Paperwork is seldom enjoyable enough to become a hobby, and we certainly don't need it to operate a model railroad. But you should have some system of directing the flow of each and every car over your railroad so that your line will have the appearance of really moving goods, not just freight cars.

The waybill system will make every car have a definite purpose as it moves empty or loaded with a specific commodity bound for a specific destination. The system requires only a $2\frac{1}{4} \times 3\frac{1}{2}$-inch clear plastic envelope (billfold photo-carriers will do) for each and every freight car you operate. A self-adhesive white sticker is applied to the upper-left corner of each of the clear plastic envelopes and shows the car's railroad initials and the car number. The envelope then "follows" that car wherever it goes on your layout. A small box can be glued to the side of the table near every town to hold the envelopes for any cars that may be sitting in that town. The enve-

Fig. 15–1. The waybill tells the engineer where that car should go.

Fig. 15–2. The materials for the waybill system are available at any stationery store.

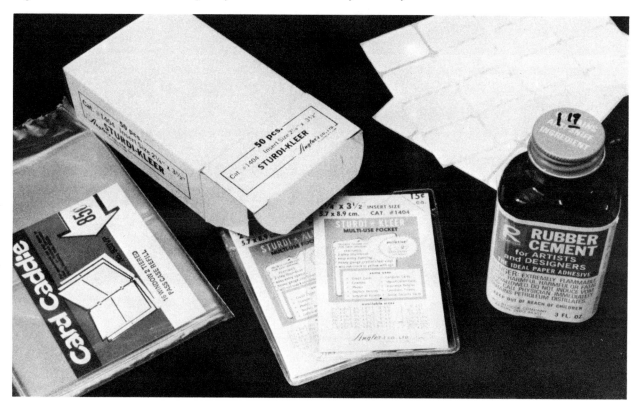

CUT
↘

CUT
↘

CUT →

When delivery is made, separate card from packet. Place empty packet in "Town" set-out box. Place card in "Yard" file.

When delivery is *made,* turn over way-bill and file waybill and packet in "Town" set-out box.

CUT →

When delivery is made, separate card from packet. Place empty packet in "Town" set-out box. Place card in "Yard" file.

When delivery is *made,* turn over way-bill and file waybill and packet in "Town" set-out box.

CUT →

When delivery is made, separate card from packet. Place empty packet in "Town" set-out box. Place card in "Yard" file.

When delivery is *made,* turn over way-bill and file waybill and packet in "Town" set-out box.

CUT →

When delivery is made, separate card from packet. Place empty packet in "Town" set-out box. Place card in "Yard" file.

When delivery is *made,* turn over way-bill and file waybill and packet in "Town" set-out box.

CUT →

Fig. 15–3. Four waybills that can be photocopied and cut apart.

lopes for cars in trains are simply carried by the engineer along with the walk-around throttle.

Place a larger file box near whatever area you consider to be your main yard to hold the cars stored there. Put some dividers in the box for stock, refrigerator (reefer), tank, flat, box, gondola, hopper, and covered hopper cars to make it easier to find them when you need a specific car and its matching card. That main yard may well be the shelf or box where you store the cars that you don't have room for on the layout!

Waybills

The second part of the system is the waybills themselves. These are patterned after the waybills the real railroads use with most shipments, but they are somewhat simpler and are much more "powerful" and versatile in directing the railroad crew's actions. Four blank waybills are included in Figure 15–3. Have photocopies made of that page so you will have about four times as many waybills as you do freight cars. Because waybills are supposed to be folded in half, you need only one-sided copies. You can then cut the waybills apart, apply some rubber cement to the backside, and fold them to give a two-ply piece of paper that is about as stiff as cardboard. You might want to spray them with clear paint (the same kind you use on your models after decal applications) so they will last "forever" without any fingerprint-grease smudges. Save the clear coat, though, until you've used the waybills for a week or so and you know the information on them is the information you need. Each of the waybills must be filled out to indicate how its particular commodity should be transported.

Shipping and Receiving

You will use the waybills to decide which cars to move and where to move them. The first consideration, when creating the way-

Fig. 15–4. Cut apart the photocopies of the waybills; then fold them as shown and glue the backs together with rubber cement.

bills, however, will be the industries and other "sources" of freight on your own railroad. On a pad of paper, list each of the industries you plan to locate on the sidings of your layout. The industries don't have to be there yet, but the sidings must be, so you'll have a place to spot that freight car. The copy-and-cutout station and industrial signs in Chapter 11 will give you an idea of the different types of industry you might choose, and there are others indicated on the key (Figure 16–4) to the 9 × 9-foot Burlington Northern layout in Chapter 16.

Write down the goods or commodities that might be received by each industry under an "IN" column and the goods or commodities it might ship under an "OUT" column. There is no reason why any industry would ship or receive everything by rail, however. A power plant, for instance, would receive coal, but it would "ship" electrical power over wires rather than over rails. You'll need to do this paperwork only once; when it and the waybills are completed, operations will only involve placing cards in the clear plastic "car" enve-

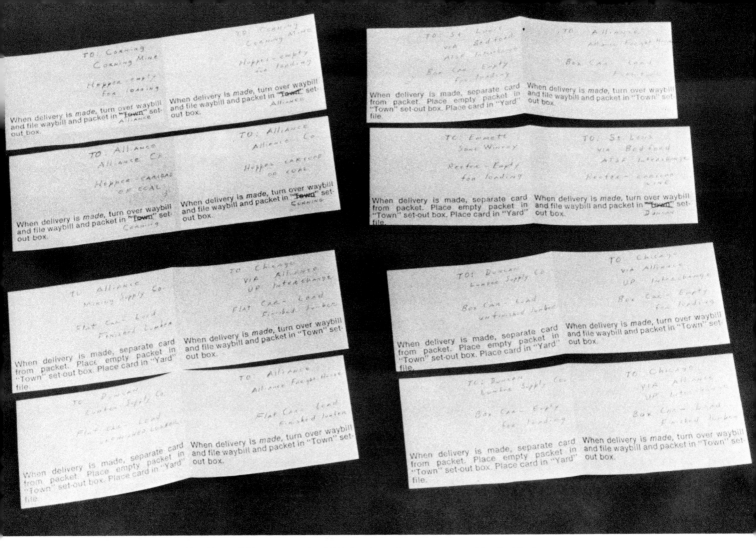

Fig. 15–5. Samples of eight waybill variations (unfolded only so that you can read both sides).

lopes. You can also add additional goods or commodities to the list to make more waybills after you have used the system for a few months and you are more familiar with the kind of freight traffic your railroad needs.

Add two more columns beside each of those industries for "TO" and "FROM." List all of the places that each industry might ship those commodities to in the "OUT" column and the places where it might get the stuff from in the "IN" column. Those places can be other industries on your own railroad. A fuel dealer for instance, might receive its coal from the coal mine on your layout. About half of the places should be "off" your layout because that's a bit more like real life; few rail-

roads are lucky enough to have both the shipper and the receiver.

Interchanges

It is most common for a shipment to be loaded on one railroad and transferred (railroads use the word "interchanged") with three or four or more other railroads before it reaches its final destination. For our purposes, the "off-line" places can be marked simply "interchange," and one end of a stub-end siding can be designated as the "industry interchange."

I suggest that you put a rerailer track section at the end of that siding so your "interchange" area can be the box or shelf where you store extra cars. That way, cars destined for interchange really do travel off the layout. The interchange track may also be a simple tunnel, such as track "j" (the interchange with the Union Pacific Railroad) on the Burlington Northern layout in Chapter 16. You can use a passing siding (such as the track "i," the AT&SF RR interchange) on the Burlington Northern layout. Designate one end as "IN" (it's at "Bedford" on the Burlington Northern layout), so you can just keep adding cars until they appear for "pickup" at the other end of the siding (at "Duncan" on the Burlington Northern layout).

Filling Out the Waybill

You can now use your list of industries and their shipments to fill in both sides of the waybills. Begin on the side of each waybill that ends with the sentence "Place card in 'Yard' file." Then, follow these steps:

1. Write "TO:" and list the name of the town where the industry is located, followed by the name of the industry.

2. List the type of car that would be used for the commodity that that industry "receives." (This is the "IN" commodity from your list.) Then write "Empty—For Loading."

3. Turn the card over, and write "TO:" and the destination for that industry's products. The destination can be a bit tricky, but it's logical if you think it out: List the name of any city (say, Chicago) as the destination, write "VIA" (meaning "through"), the name of the town on your layout, and the interchange track in that town (write "Interchange").

4. Note the type of car, just as you did on the opposite side of the waybill, but here add the words "Carload" (or "Loaded") and the commodity the car will actually carry.

That completes the standard waybill. A variation would be simply to list the town and industry name for a "receiver" industry that is actually on your layout. Make about four cards, each with a different destination, for each industry on your layout.

You will also want to make some variations on those "standard" cards to suit particular industries and track situations. If the car is a flat car or a gondola, try to list a "load" on both sides of the waybill so there will be no "Empty—For Loading," just two different loads. You can do the same thing for any type of car that might appear on both the "IN" and "OUT" lists for a specific industry.

"Empty—For Loading"

If you do add a pair of passing sidings for the "Loads-In Empties-Out" operations, you'll need a special card for the cars that are always empty. It should read: "Empty—For Loading" on both sides. That lists the town the "empty" is *picked up* from in place of the preprinted word "Yard" on both sides of the card. Cross out the sentence "Place card in Yard file" because the car (and the card) will never get back to the yard. Make another type of card for the cars that are always loaded, which reads: "Carload of Coal" (or whatever the commodity) on both sides of the card. Cross out the word "Yard" on both sides of this card and list the name of the town that *ships* that load. Cross out the sentence "Place card in Yard file" on these cards too. The cars that have these special cards will be cycled back and forth through "their" industry until you decide to pull the cards and insert them in some other cars' clear plastic envelopes. The cards in Figure 15–5 that read "TO: Corning . . ." on both sides and "TO: Alliance . . ." on both sides are examples of the "Loads-In, Empties-Out" cards.

The "Yard" File

The waybill system of operation begins when you pick some of the waybills at ran-

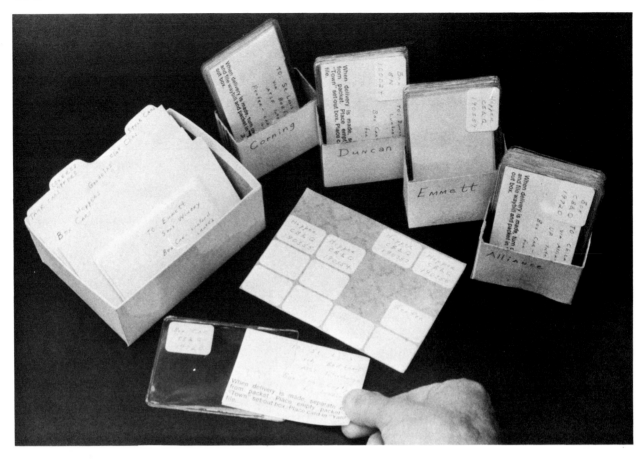

Fig. 15–6. A waybill file box is needed for each town, plus a master or "yard" file for the waybills themselves and for "empty"-car envelopes.

dom that match the types of cars in your "yard" area. Follow the directions on those cards to switch the now-loaded cars onto the appropriate sidings. From that point on the system is self-perpetuating, so long as you follow the instructions on the waybills. Keep the extra waybills in that "yard" file and return the "used" waybills to the rear of the pack of waybills. Draw fresh ones each time you're ready to operate a train. Figure 15–7 shows how the car (and its clear plastic envelope) originates in the "yard" where the waybill is inserted. The waybill is then turned over (according to its own printed instructions), and that car is ready to be picked up by the next train through town. In some cases, the car may go directly back to the yard, or, in the case of "Loads-In, Empties-Out," the car may never go back to the yard. If you want the

car to sit on the siding for awhile, add another "hold" card with a note stating it is to be picked up after one or more passes ("days" or "weeks") by the freight trains through town.

Loads-In, Empties-Out

Most of the commodities that are loaded into hoppers or gondolas are raw materials that are used by another industry, so the flow of traffic is mostly a repetitive pattern of loaded cars traveling to the industry and empty cars traveling back to the commodity source for reloading. Hoppers loaded with coal for a power plant or to be dumped into ships, gravel traveling from a quarry to a cement plant, iron ore traveling to a steel mill or to be dumped into ships, and logs traveling

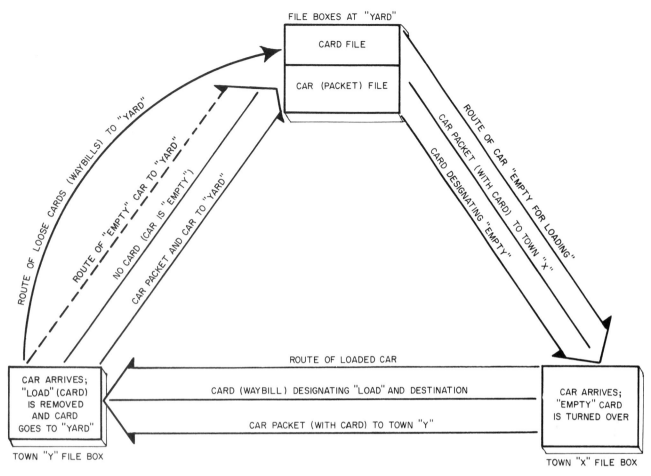

FILE BOXES AT "YARD"

CARD FILE

CAR (PACKET) FILE

ROUTE OF LOOSE CARDS (WAYBILLS) TO "YARD"

ROUTE OF "EMPTY" CAR TO "YARD"

NO CARD (CAR IS "EMPTY")

CAR PACKET AND CAR TO "YARD"

ROUTE OF CAR "EMPTY FOR LOADING"

CAR PACKET (WITH CARD) TO TOWN "X"

CARD DESIGNATING "EMPTY"

ROUTE OF LOADED CAR

CARD (WAYBILL) DESIGNATING "LOAD" AND DESTINATION

CAR PACKET (WITH CARD) TO TOWN "Y"

CAR ARRIVES;
"LOAD" (CARD)
IS REMOVED
AND CARD
GOES TO "YARD"

TOWN "Y" FILE BOX

CAR ARRIVES;
"EMPTY" CARD
IS TURNED OVER

TOWN "X" FILE BOX

Fig. 15–7. The "cycle" for each standard type of waybill and plastic envelope for each car follows this pattern.

from the mountains to the sawmill are other examples of heavy traffic flow that are popular prototypes for model railroaders.

All of these involve the use of cars that are most obviously loaded in one direction and unloaded in the opposite direction—a difficult challenge for the modeler, because even the operating type of cars would be too time-consuming to load or unload three or four or more at a time. The answer to this is the concept known as "Loads-In, Empties-Out."

"Loads-In, Empties-Out" concept requires a model of both the shipping industry (a coal mine, for example) and the primary receiving industry (say, a power plant). Either industry

Fig. 15–8. Use a larger clear plastic envelope to hold the waybills for the entire train.

Fig. 15–9. The "Alliance Company" (far left) and the "Corning Mine" are served by the same sidings, which connect inside the mountain.

may also use cars from or to other sources, but the majority of the traffic is between the two. The "unit trains" that carry a hundred carloads of coal, and that never uncouple as they cycle from Colorado mines to Illinois power plants, are a modern example of such traffic.

Each industry must have two tracks of its own, and the two must be located near each other on your layout. They could be separated visually by a mountain, a painted sky backdrop, or some other feature that breaks any visual connection between the two industries. The two sidings appear to be stubended at each industry, but, in fact, they connect inside a tunnel between the two industries. The two tracks that lead into the "Corning Mine" on the Burlington Northern layout in Chapter 16 are actually the same

two tracks that lead into the "Alliance Company."

You can see the two tracks in the "satellite" view in Figure 16–4, but the mountain effectively blocks any connection between the two from normal viewing angles. It helps the illusion if the tracks enter each industry from slightly different directions. The right-hand track into the mine receives *only* empty hoppers; and loaded hoppers are picked up *only* on the left-hand track at the mine. Those "loaded" cars are actually shoved through the mountain by other loaded cars being delivered to the power plant. The empty hoppers that are pushed into the mine will eventually be pushed out from the power plant as empties. It takes about nine cars to fill each track, in this example, so the ninth car into the mine will always push the first car out the

Fig. 15–10. The coke ovens at Cardiff, Colorado, about 1900. Coal is dumped into the top and super-heated to make coke, which is then loaded into boxcars or hoppers. (Photo courtesy Library, State Historical Society of Colorado.)

Fig. 15–11. The r-t-r "action" ore-dumping car ramp was elevated to simulate a coke oven, where coal is baked into coke for steel-making.

power plant's end. The system provides an endless supply of loaded hoppers at the mine and an endless supply of empty hoppers at the power plant.

The "Loads-In, Empties-Out" system does exactly what its name implies. It allows you to have extremely realistic operations, which includes empty cars traveling toward a mine and carloads of coal traveling toward the power plant. Notice that no locomotive actually travels through the tunnel that connects the mine and the power plant. The cars alone are pushed, by other cars, through the tunnel.

If you want to simulate the operation of modern unit trains, you could just as well

Fig. 15–12. For more credibility, load flatcars (like Walthers' 75-foot Trailer Train car) with just one trailer. Photo courtesy Wm. K. Walthers, Inc.

operate a single complete train of loaded hoppers with a permanently coupled locomotive and caboose. You would need matching trains with identical car numbers and identical weathering, however. One set of cars would be filled with coal and the other set would be empty. When the train of empty hoppers entered the mine on the right track, you would hold it there and wait a moment before flipping the block switch, which would allow the second train of loaded cars to exit on the left track, thus simulating the loading cycle. The process would be repeated when the loaded train reached the power plant, except that the train of empties would appear after the train of loaded cars disappeared. I prefer the individual-car method over the "unit-train" operation, but you can take your choice with the same trackwork and industries. You would alter only the shape of the industries to duplicate the "Loads-In, Empties-Out" coal-hauling with gravel, ore, or logs.

Timetable Operations

You can establish a timetable just like the real railroads when you establish a point-to-point run, such as that for the layouts in Chapters 3 and 16. Time the amount of sec-

onds it takes for a train to travel from one "town" (siding) to the next and call the seconds "minutes." Duplicate the general format of any real railroad timetable. There is, I feel, a better way to run a railroad in miniature than to spend your leisure hours "watching the clock." Timetable operations really are necessary on some of the gigantic club layouts, where there may be as many as twenty trains on the tracks at the same time. The timetable that helps to keep the real trains from running into each other works on these club layouts as well. Most home layouts, however, are operated by just one person for most of their sessions, and, at most, there may be three operators.

The figure-eight track plan in Chapter 3 and the 9 × 9-foot and 10 × 10-foot plans in Chapter 16 are large enough to keep three operators busy. One person is in the "yards" making up trains, while the other two are operating trains out on the main line. Another blocking switch must be added to allow the yard areas to be operated by a third power pack. There's little need, then, for more than two trains to be out on the main line at any one time.

The "Sequence" Timetable

If you have as many as six trains waiting on the holding tracks or passing sidings, no more than two ever need to be running at one time. With that thought in mind, you can stage what I call "sequence" timetable operations. The sequence timetable merely means that you establish an operating pattern for your trains, such as that on the 9 × 9-foot Burlington Northern layout. Those trains originate in "Alliance" and travel over the route described in Chapter 1, to be turned and held on the "Points East" track ("f"), and shown in the schematic diagram (Figure 15–16).

Two additional patterns can be applied to this particular layout. Every fourth or fifth train can be routed into the tunnel at "j," which

Fig. 15–13. Create modern intermodal terminal scenes with containers and cranes like Walthers' Kalmar container crane. Photo courtesy Wm. K. Walthers, Inc.

Fig. 15–14. This well-styled car, from Walthers, is a replica of the cars used to haul containers stacked two-high. Photo courtesy Wm. K. Walthers, Inc.

for an imaginary interchange with the Santa Fe Railroad. The two alternate routes allow you to use locomotives from different railroads to break up the pattern of running Burlington Northern trains alone from "Alliance" to "Points East" and return. The Union Pacific train can be a once-a-day Amtrak passenger train for even greater variety.

A Typical Day

Figure 15–16 shows the locations of five trains on the Burlington Northern plan (in Chapter 16) at purely imaginary times of a 24-hour day. By stipulating that it takes one hour for a train to travel from "Alliance" to "Points East," you can create your own 24-hour day by completing 24 train movements over the railroad. The arrows indicate the direction of travel of trains 5, 6, 7, 8, and 9 at eight random hours during a "typical" day. When any arrow changes direction, that train has been reversed at the "Alliance" wye.

Train 5 would be the best one to pick as that Amtrak streamliner. Train 5 makes an imaginary trip "off" our layout and onto the Sante Fe at 2:00 P.M., to reappear about 7:00 P.M., before heading back to the Union Pacific. Train 8 has a similar route and "timetable." Train 6 is a "through freight" going cross-country over our railroad. Cars would be added or taken off this train only at "Alliance." Train 7 is a "pedlar freight," or "way freight," which means that it makes switching moves at almost every town (where there's a car ready to be picked up or scheduled to be dropped off—all through the "waybill" process). Train 9 can be another pedlar freight.

Fig. 15–15. The brakeman in the doorway of Bachmann's Operating Action Caboose reaches out to pick up his triangle with working orders as the train moves by.

leads to an imaginary interchange with the Union Pacific. The operator in the "Alliance" yard then makes up a new train in the tunnel by hand-carrying cars to and from storage shelves. (The single track qualifies as a "fiddle" yard for just that reason—cars are "fiddled" on and off the layout.) The second path routes trains into the passing siding track "i"

From Imaginary to Real

The waybill system, as well as every operating and construction idea on these pages, is based on the actual operations of the prototype. None of this was created for "toy trains." When you operate with the quick "through-

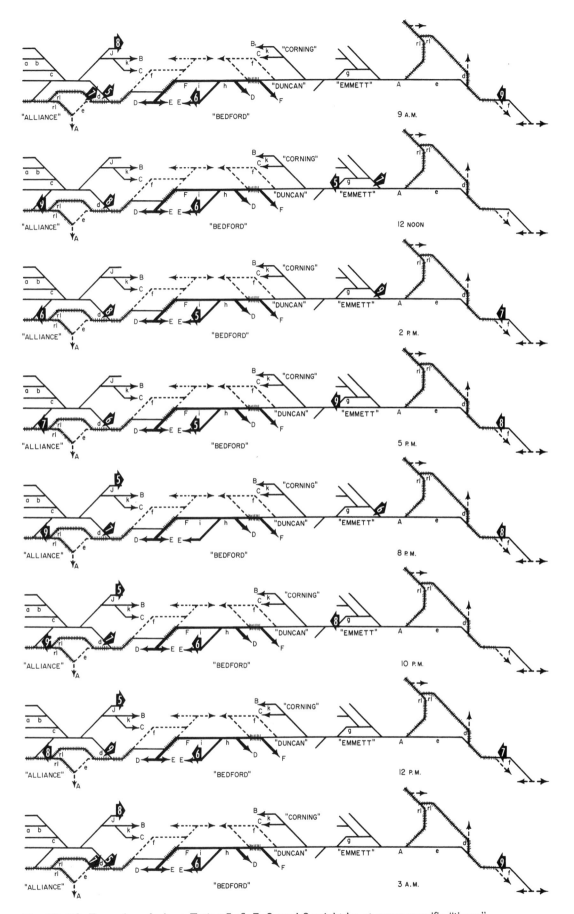

Fig. 15–16. Examples of where Trains 5, 6, 7, 8, and 9 might be at some specific "times" during a "24-hour" operating period with the use of the sequence timetable. This is similar to playing musical chairs but with trains.

•	Apply brakes. Stop.
— —	Release brakes. Proceed.
— — —	Train parted or uncoupled.
• • •	Back-up. Reverse.
— — • —	Approaching highway crossings at grade (track level).
——	(A prolonged whistle.) Approaching railroad stations or railroad crossings with other railroad tracks.
• • • • • • • •	Alarm for persons or livestock on the tracks.
— •	Used when running against the normal flow of traffic to warn approaching trains and stations.

Fig. 15–17. Whistle signal codes. The signals used by steam-locomotive whistles and diesel horns on the real locomotives always mean something. The whistle code used by many full-size railroads is shown here with dots (·) to indicate short notes and dashes (—) to indicate long notes.

freight" system of endless oval operations to simulate cross-country trains, when you make up trains using a switch engine in the yards, when you move every freight car with the waybill system, and when you operate with a sequence timetable, you are running a real railroad in miniature. Combine all these types of operation with, perhaps, one of those Santa Fe interchange freight trains or an Amtrak passenger train added to the sequence timetable and you can plan to keep yourself busy for years before you even think about building another railroad.

CHAPTER 16

Miniature Empires

THIS IS THE PLACE where you might just bring some of those dreams of real railroading in miniature to life. The layout you see in this chapter is an "attainable" goal for anyone who has successfully completed and operated that "first" 4 × 8-foot tabletop model railroad. You can build this model railroad empire in two ways: either as a freestanding layout, such as that in Figures 16–3 and 16–4, or as an around-the-wall version, shown in Figure 16–5.

The freestanding layout is designed so that only the nine-foot edge behind the town of "Alliance" and the "Corning Mine" (the top of the plan) and the short two-foot edge to the left of "Alliance" will be against the wall. You must have at least two feet of aisle space, so this layout will fit in any room that is 11 × 11 feet or larger.

The around-the-wall version in Figure 16–5 is designed for an 8 × 10-foot corner of any room, but it can be extended into a 10 × 10-foot "C" shape by adding the "Alliance" and "Corning" portion of the layout in Figure 16–3. The around-the-wall layout can be extended in any direction, at the points shown on the plan, to fill, for example, the

walls in a 12 × 15-foot room. The plan can also be reversed or "mirrored" to relocate the entryway to suit an existing doorway.

Each of these layouts should be assembled in "modules" of open-grid benchwork (such as that discussed in Chapter 4) no larger than 30 × 60 inches. Figure 16–1 shows how to cut the $\frac{1}{2}$-inch Homosote roadbed and $\frac{1}{2}$-inch plywood tabletops for a 5 × 9-foot layout from 4 × 8-foot sheets of both materials. You'll need both Homosote and plywood in the shapes and sizes "A" through "G" to duplicate the 9 × 9-foot layout. The around-the-wall layout can be cut from a single sheet each of Homosote and plywood by just cutting them into 2 × 4-foot panels and arranging them in the L-shape of the plan. The open-grid benchwork for any of these layouts should be assembled in "modules" to match the sizes of the Homosote and plywood pieces. The 30 × 60-inch maximum is just small enough to fit through any door, even with mountains of scenery. You will probably want to move the layout some day, and the planning stage is the time to prepare for it.

The Burlington Northern in Stages

The Burlington Northern "empire" has just about everything you could want in a model

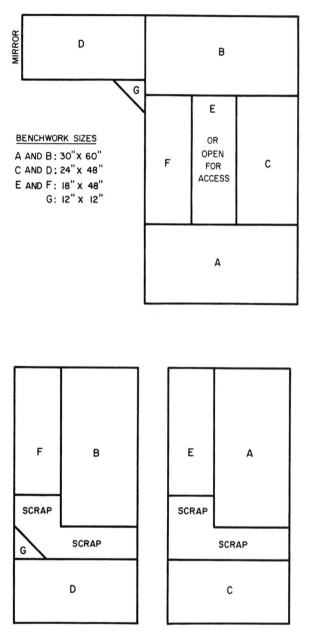

BENCHWORK SIZES

A AND B: 30"x 60"
C AND D: 24"x 48"
E AND F: 18"x 48"
G: 12"x 12"

Fig. 16–1. Method for cutting two 4 × 8-foot panels for a 9 × 9-foot layout.

railroad, from walk-around control to most of the industries served by the real railroads to scenery. Its greatest asset, though, is the track plan. Larry Larson built the layout and detailed it using the techniques you see in each chapter of this book. There are a large number of small sections of track because the operating concept of the layout was developed first, and the track was then fitted into that concept. If Larry were to do it again, he

would use pencil lines to locate most of the track centers with flexible track sections rather than the dozens of sectional-track pieces. The sectional track, however, does allow you to add just a little bit at a time as your funds allow.

The layout can begin as a simple oval with the "minimum-switch allotment" (Fig. 16–2). I recommend to allow a passing siding or "runaround" track and both a "facing-point" and a "trailing-point" stub-end siding. If you want an unusual effect during this early stage, leave the center 2 × 4-foot panel "E" off the benchwork and operate the layout from a central pit. You'll soon discover why no one makes "duck-under" layout plans anymore; all that ducking and stooping is tiring. This layout is really designed to be operated from three of the outside edges.

You can expand outward from the oval in Figure 16–2 in almost any direction, working toward the final plan in Figure 16–3. The final plan will provide just about every type of real railroad operation you could desire, including:

1. Trains can operate in the "orbiting" style so popular in Europe and in toy departments, with two trains circulating endlessly on the inner and outer ovals.

2. A single train can operate over a rather lengthy route using both the inner and outer oval for a two-lap trip around the layout. That same route can add extra miles to any type of train operation you choose.

3. The railroad can be operated as a point-to-point line (as illustrated in Chapter 2 and in the color section) to run trains from "Alliance" to the holding siding "F" called "Points East," and back again.

4. The layout can be operated as an out-and-back plan from "Alliance" to "Bed-
(Text continued on page 216)

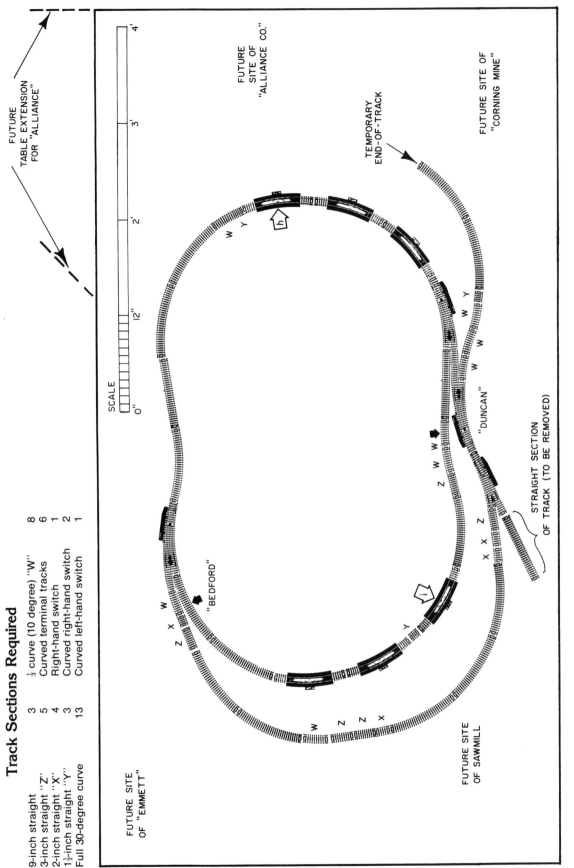

Track Sections Required

9-inch straight	3
3-inch straight "Z"	5
2-inch straight "X"	4
1½-inch straight "Y"	3
Full 30-degree curve	13
⅓ curve (10 degree) "W"	8
Curved terminal tracks	6
Right-hand switch	1
Curved right-hand switch	2
Curved left-hand switch	1

FUTURE
TABLE EXTENSION
FOR "ALLIANCE"

FUTURE
SITE OF
"ALLIANCE CO."

TEMPORARY
END-OF-TRACK

FUTURE SITE OF
"CORNING MINE"

SCALE

"BEDFORD"

"DUNCAN"

STRAIGHT SECTION
OF TRACK (TO BE REMOVED)

FUTURE SITE
OF "EMMETT"

FUTURE SITE
OF SAWMILL

Fig. 16–2. The "inner oval" can be the first stage in building the Burlington Northern layout in Figure 16–3. (See Figure 7–9 for the key to track symbols.)

209

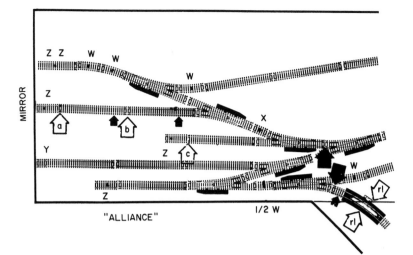

Track Sections Required

9-inch straight	32
3-inch straight "Z"	29
2-inch straight "X"	10
1½-inch straight "Y"	10
* ¾-inch straight "½Y"	1
9-inch rerailer straight	4
Full 30-degree curve	24
⅓ curve (10 degree) "W"	30
* ⅙ curve (hand-cut 10-degree curve) "½W"	1
Curved terminal tracks	15
Right-hand switch	9
Left-hand switch	10
Curved right-hand switch	3
Curved left-hand switch	1
Wye switch	2

* These sections must be cut from
longer track sections, as shown
in Chapter 5.

Fig. 16–3. The track plan with wiring connections and gaps
for the 9 × 9-foot Burlington Northern layout. (See Figure
7–9 for the key to track symbols.)

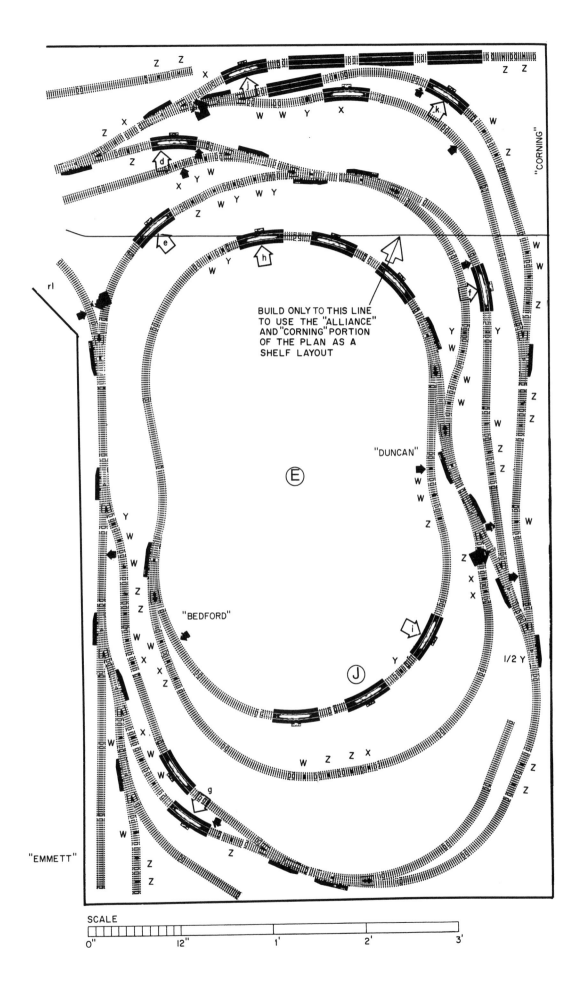

"CORNING"

Z   Z
Z   Z
X
j
A
X
X
W   W   Y   X
Z
d
k
W
Z
W   Y
X
Y
W   Y   W   Y
Z
e
h
W   Y
W
W
f
rl

BUILD ONLY TO THIS LINE
TO USE THE "ALLIANCE"
AND "CORNING" PORTION
OF THE PLAN AS A
SHELF LAYOUT

Y
W
W
"DUNCAN"
W
W
W
W
E
W
Z
Z
Y
W
W
Z
Z
Z
"BEDFORD"
W
W
W
X
X
Z
i
Z
J
Y
1/2 Y
X
X
X
W
X
W
Z
W
X
Z
Z
W
g
W
Z   Z   X
Z
Z
"EMMETT"
W
Z
Z

SCALE

0"   12"   1'   2'   3'

Key to Industries and Features
on the Burlington Northern Layout

AA   Ford & Sons Ice Co.: meat and other food (reefers) *IN;* ice (reefers) *OUT*

AB   Mining Supply Co.: timber and hardware (flatcars and boxcars) *IN* and *OUT*

AC   Farming Tools, Inc.: hardware, tools, and tractors (flatcars and boxcars) *IN;* empties *OUT*

AD   Company Furniture Co.: lumber and hardware (flatcars and boxcars) *IN;* furniture (boxcars) *OUT*

AE   Alliance Coal & Fuel: coal and coke (hoppers) *IN;* empties *OUT*

AF   American Express Co.: paper and cartons (boxcar) *IN* and *OUT*

AX   Alliance Co.: coal (hoppers) *IN;* empties *OUT*

C   Cattle pens (railroad-owned): empties (stock) *IN;* cattle *OUT*

CD   Coke ovens: coal (hopper or ore) *IN,* coke (hopper) and empties *OUT*

D   Dwelling or boarding house owned by railroad

DF   Duncan Feed & Fuel: seed and coal (boxcar and hopper) *IN;* grain (boxcar, C.F. hopper, and covered hopper) *OUT*

DM   Dwellings owned by Corning Mining

DT   Duncan Signal Tower for Atchison, Topeka & Santa Fe Railroad interchange

E   Engine House

ET   Engine, Tool & Supply Co.: engines and tools (boxcar) *IN;* empties *OUT*

FC   F. C. Rode & Co.: concrete and steel pipe (flatcars) *IN;* empties *OUT*

FT   Alliance Freight House (Tyco or ConCor Freight Station and modified): lcl merchandise (boxcar) *IN* and *OUT*

G   Grade crossing

GG   Grade crossing

ISF   Interchange track with Atchison, Topeka & Santa Fe Railroad (every type of car *IN* and *OUT,* empty or loaded)

IUP   Interchange track with Union Pacific Railroad (every type of car *IN* and *OUT,* empty or loaded)

L   Lumber Supply Co.: empties (boxcar) *IN;* finished lumber *OUT*

LS   Log dump for Lumber Supply Co.: logs (log cars) *IN;* empties *OUT*

MX   Corning Mining Co.: timber, tools, and empties (flatcar, boxcar, and hopper) *IN;* coal and empties *OUT*

O   Diesel fuel-oil storage and refueling: oil (tank) *IN;* empties *OUT*

PE   Trailer Train loading dock (Piggyback Flatcar set): lcl merchandise (trailers on flatcars and boxcars) *IN* and *OUT*

PL   Trailer Train terminal: lcl merchandise (trailers on flatcars) *IN* and *OUT*

PT   Trailer Train terminal: lcl merchandise (trailers on flatcars) *IN* and *OUT*

SA   Passenger station at Alliance

SB   Passenger station at Bedford (AT&SF interchange *IN*)

SD   Passenger station at Duncan

SE   Passenger station at Emmett

ST   Sand house, tower, and bins: sand (gondola) *IN;* empties *OUT*

SW   Sons Winery: crates (boxcar) and empties (boxcar and reefers) *IN;* empties (boxcar) and wine (boxcar and reefers) *OUT*

W   Water tower

WW   Billboard

NOTE   The types of cars in parentheses, near the *IN* or *OUT* traffic pattern of each industry, are the types of cars the industry uses to carry the commodities it receives (*IN*) or ships (*OUT*).

212

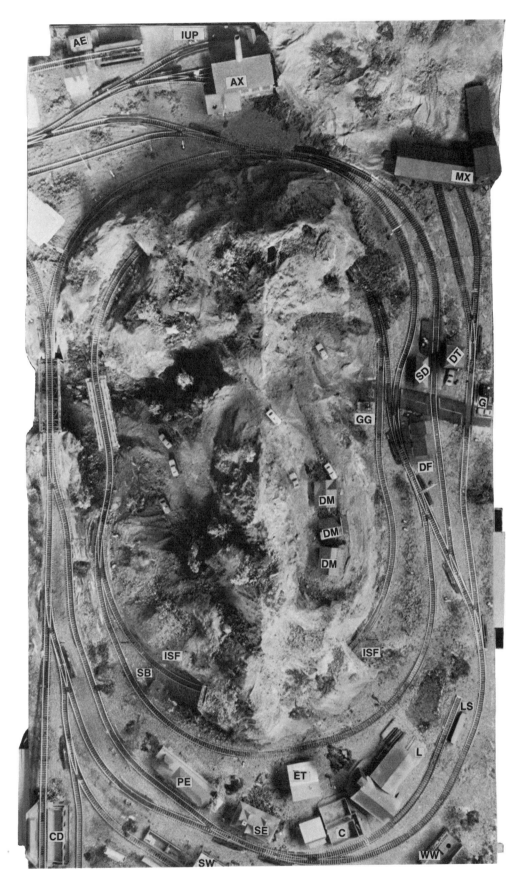

Fig. 16–4. A "satellite" view of the Burlington Northern HO-scale layout.

213

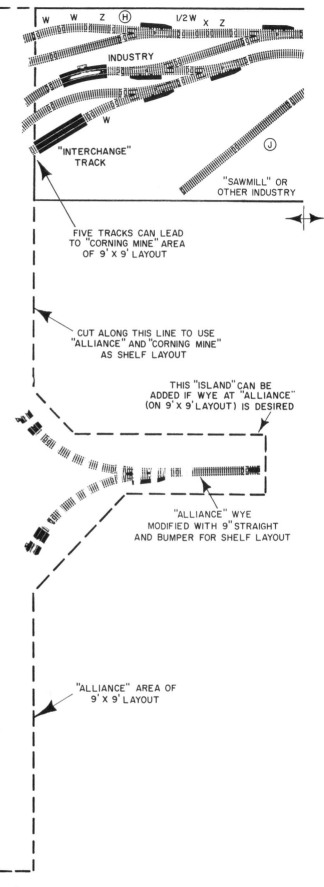

FIVE TRACKS CAN LEAD
TO "CORNING MINE" AREA
OF 9' X 9' LAYOUT

CUT ALONG THIS LINE TO USE
"ALLIANCE" AND "CORNING MINE"
AS SHELF LAYOUT

THIS "ISLAND" CAN BE
ADDED IF WYE AT "ALLIANCE"
(ON 9' X 9' LAYOUT) IS DESIRED

"ALLIANCE" WYE
MODIFIED WITH 9" STRAIGHT
AND BUMPER FOR SHELF LAYOUT

"ALLIANCE" AREA OF
9' X 9' LAYOUT

Track Sections Required

9-inch straight	39
3-inch straight "Z"	17
2-inch straight "X"	13
1½-inch straight "Y"	2
9-inch rerailer straight	1
Bumper track	6
Full 30-degree curve	11
⅓ curve (10 degree) "W"	13
* ⅙ curve (hand-cut 10-degree curve) "½W"	1
Curved terminal tracks	5
Right-hand switch	10
Left-hand switch	11
Wye switch	3

* These sections must be cut from
longer track sections, as shown
in Chapter 5.

Fig. 16–5. An around-the-wall plan for a minimum 8 ×
10-foot or 10 × 10-foot area. (See Fig. 7–9 for key to track
symbols.)

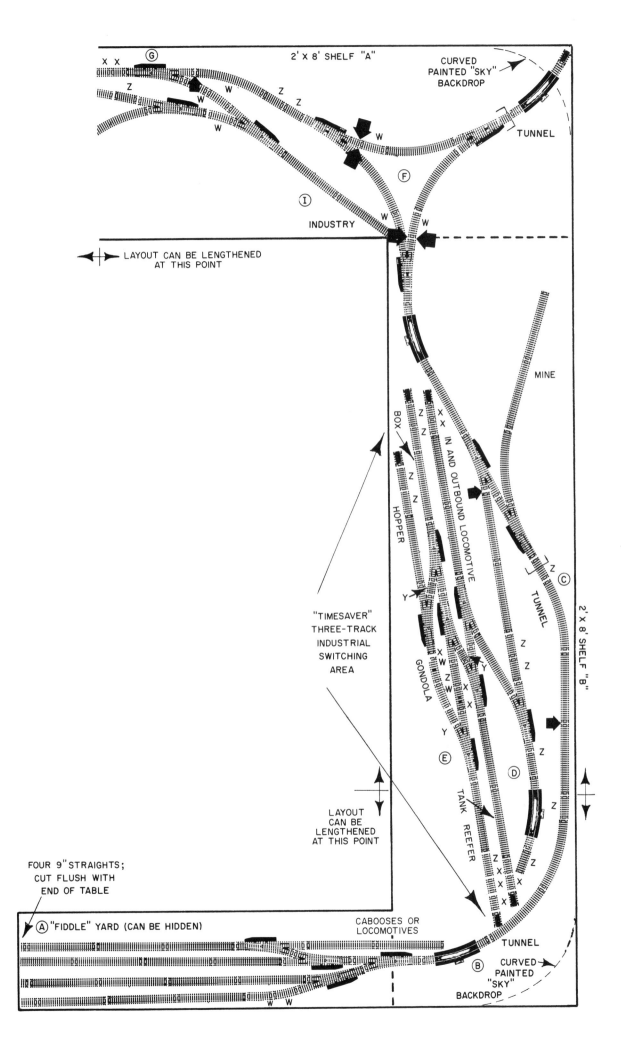

2' X 8' SHELF "A"

CURVED PAINTED "SKY" BACKDROP

TUNNEL

X X

G

Z

W

Z Z

W

W

F

I

INDUSTRY

W W

LAYOUT CAN BE LENGTHENED AT THIS POINT

MINE

BOX

Z
X X

Z

HOPPER

Z

Z

IN AND OUTBOUND LOCOMOTIVE

TUNNEL

Z

C

"TIMESAVER" THREE-TRACK INDUSTRIAL SWITCHING AREA

Y

Z

Z

GONDOLA

X W

Z W X
Y

X

Y

E

Z

D

Z

2' X 8' SHELF "B"

LAYOUT CAN BE LENGTHENED AT THIS POINT

TANK

REEFER

Z

Z

X X

X

FOUR 9" STRAIGHTS; CUT FLUSH WITH END OF TABLE

CABOOSES OR LOCOMOTIVES

A "FIDDLE" YARD (CAN BE HIDDEN)

TUNNEL

B

CURVED PAINTED "SKY" BACKDROP

W W

ford" to "Emmett" and back to "Alliance" using the left leg of the "Alliance" wye.

5. The "Loads-In, Empties-Out" trackage can be used through the "Corning Mine" and the "Alliance Co." for switching individual cars, as described in Chapter 15 or for complete "unit trains."

6. The hidden siding "J" (the interchange with the Union Pacific) can be operated as a one-track "fiddle" yard, where cars and locomotives are hand-carried to and from the layout.

7. The switching operations of the Pedlar Freight or Way Freight can be duplicated (with or without the system of waybills in Chapter 15) thanks to numerous industrial sidings.

8. The tracks near the "Alliance Station" can be used by a locomotive to perform the typical "yard" operations of making up and breaking down trains. Frankly, the "Fiddle Yard" area of Figure 16–5 is better for that type of yard work, and you'll probably enjoy operating this layout (Figure 16–3) more by just "fiddling" new trains on and off the layout by hand on the hidden track "J".

The track plans on these pages are "wired" for two-train operation based on the principles of "common-rail" wiring and blocks in Chapter 7. However, a lot more terminal tracks would be needed in some areas, and no terminal tracks would be necessary at all in other areas (such as the "Alliance Engine-House" track). Most of those terminal tracks are there to provide an automatic car-rerailer inside tunnels. That's why there's a string of straight rerailers inside the tunnel at track "J"; that's a fiddle track where you'll be taking cars on and off the layout, and the rerailers will make the job much easier. One of the rail

joiners with a wire soldered to it (as described in Chapter 7) must be used wherever an electrical connection is indicated on these plans but where no terminal track is present. Almost all of the buildings are modified with at least a different shade of paint, but they are all kits or "lighted" ready-builts. The major building modifications or conversions are described in Chapter 11.

Around-the-Wall Layout Plan

The around-the-wall type of layout plan offers the greatest possible degree of realism but the least degree of flexibility in layout planning. The around-the-wall plans are only for really experienced model railroaders who know what type of operation and construction they prefer. It is difficult to provide any type of oval or distorted oval for continuous operation on an around-the-wall layout because the shelf for the layout can't be much more than 24-inches wide or you won't be able to reach the tracks near the rear. Ways around the problem would include ideas such as extending the 9 × 9-foot layout in Figure 16–3 to the left from the town of "Alliance" around a room. If you have the space, that's one of the ways that any layout plan can grow in the years to come. The general areas and track arrangements in Figure 16–5 could be used to extend any layout into an around-the-wall configuration.

The plan in Figure 16–5 is really three shelf-style layouts combined into one. You could decide to build either one of the 2 × 8-foot portions with or without the 9 × 68-inch "Fiddle Yard." The wye in the corner could be used by either plan with a two-foot extension beyond the 2 × 8-foot "limit." One other source of a 2 × 9-foot "shelf" layout is included: Use *only* the upper two feet of the plan in Figure 16–3, and eliminate any trace of the inner oval. The five tracks on the upper left of the around-the-wall plan are designed to connect to those at the "Corning Mine," and the "Alliance" wye is extended (with dashed lines) directly out into the center of the room. The resulting layout would fill a 10 × 10-foot area with a two-foot space in the lower left corner for a doorway or entrance to the layout. Steep mountain scenery and tunnels would be most effective on the 2 × 8-foot portion of the layout that includes the wye. The other 2 × 8-foot area could just as well be designed with large industrial buildings. The tunnel leading to the "Fiddle Yard" could really be a tunnel through plastic buildings to reach the fiddle yard inside a closet.

The Timesaver Layout Module

You can consider any of the three portions of the around-the-wall layout in Figure 16–5 to be a "module" that can be combined with any other layout. These plans are primarily for those who enjoy the Way Freight or Pedlar Freight switching action, so these can be self-contained layouts of their own. The three parallel tracks on the "Timesaver" portion of the layout are a duplicate of a track plan developed years ago by those who enjoy switching contests.

Switching Contest

The switching contest that was developed around the compact Timesaver area begins with two empty cars sitting on the track marked "Inbound/Outbound" and a locomotive sitting where it says "Locomotive." Three more loaded cars rest at any three of the locations that would match the cars' style.

Let's say that a tank car, a boxcar and a reefer (refrigerator) car are sitting on their appropriate tracks. If that's the case, then the two empty cars would be a hopper car and a gondola car. Two of the three loaded cars are picked as "ready to be shipped." The engineer then has the "switching problem" of delivering those two empty cars to their appropriate spots and picking up the two loaded cars so they end up on the "Inbound/Outbound" track with the locomotive, where they belong.

The game is run against a clock with the throttle preset to the slowest possible speed so that moves can be made with the directional switch. The switching "moves" needed to do the job are described in Chapter 14, but, in this game, the number of moves are less important than the time it takes to make them all. A different pair of cars would be designated as "ready for pickup" for the next player/engineer, so he or she would not benefit from the experience of the first engineer. The two cars on the "Inbound/Outbound" track can always be designated empty for the next game. The cars must all be a scale 40-feet or shorter, and the locomotive must be a small one, such as the GP–20.

The game can be made more complicated by adding up to four more cars once you've mastered the moves for five. You'll find that switching will be far more enjoyable once you've developed the skill of moving the cars more efficiently by playing the "Timesaver" game. When the Timesaver is incorporated into a layout, as it is here, it can also be used for normal switching if each of those sidings serves a structure that would normally use the type of car intended for that spot in the game.

Glossary

AAR: The full-size railroad's trade group, the Association of American Railroads, that establishes their standards for equipment and safety.

Articulated: A steam locomotive with two separate sets of drivers, rods, and cylinders beneath a single boiler. Usually one set of drivers, rods, and cylinders is pivoted so it can swing from side-to-side around curves while the boiler remains rigidly attached to the rear set of drivers, rods, and cylinders.

Bad order: The term the real railroads use to describe a malfunctioning part.

Big Hook: The wrecking crane.

Block: A section of track that is electrically isolated from the adjoining sections for multiple-train operation or to prevent short circuits.

Bolster: The portion of a railroad freight or passenger car that runs across the underbody of the car to connect the trucks' pivot points to the body of the car. Sometimes used to describe all the cross members, including the ends, of a car's underframe.

Branch: A portion of a real railroad that branches off from the main line to reach a town or industry or to connect with another railroad.

Bumper: A device placed at the stub end of a track siding so cars or locomotives do not derail.

Caboose: The rolling office and living quarters for the crew of a freight train. Usually identifiable by a small box with windows on the roof (called a cupola) or one on each side (called bay windows) so the crew can see the length of the train from inside. Sometimes called crummy, bobber, or way car.

Catenary: Overhead trolley wires, usually used by prototype interurbans (electric-powered locomotives and self-propelled cars) with diamond-shaped current pick up devices on the roofs called pantographs.

Coaling station: Any building where coal for steam locomotives is stored and shoveled or dumped through chutes into the locomotives' tenders. When the storage bins are elevated and the coal hoisted by conveyor belts or buckets, the structure is usually called a coaling tower. When the elevated storage bins are reached by a trestle so the coal can be dumped from the cars or shoveled right into the storage bins, the structure is usually called a coaling trestle.

Crossing: When two tracks cross each other, as in the center of a one-level figure-eight-style model railroad.

Crossover: The pair of turnouts that allows trains to travel from one parallel track to the adjacent one on double-track systems.

Cut: When the railroad has to dig or blast through a hill or mountain to maintain a level roadbed. Also, a few cars coupled together.

D.P.D.T.: An electrical slide or toggle-type switch that is used for reversing the flow of current to the tracks by wiring across the back of the switch. Some types have an "off" position midway in their throw and these "Center-off D.P.D.T." switches are often used for wiring model railroads to allow two-train and two-throttle operation.

Draft gear: The box under the ends of a prototype car or locomotive (and on most models) where the coupler is spring-mounted to center it and to help absorb shocks and bumps.

Fiddle yard: A hidden track or series of tracks used by modelers to make up or break down trains, lifting the equipment by hand.

Fill: When the prototype railroad has to haul dirt to fill in a valley to bring the roadbed level up to that of the nearest trackage.

Flange: The portion of any railroad wheel that guides that wheel down the rails. The flange extends around the circumference of each railroad wheel as its largest diameter.

Frog: The point where the track rails actually cross at every turnout and rail/rail crossing.

Gap: A break in the rails to electrically isolate some portion of the track from another to prevent short circuits or to allow for multiple-train operation on the same stretch of track.

Gauge: The spacing of the rails as measured from the inside of one rail head to the next. The "standard gauge" for most American railroads is 4 feet $8\frac{1}{2}$ inches; this distance was also once the standard center-to-center spacing for wagon wheels.

Grade: The angled rise or fall of the track so it can pass over another track or so it can follow the rising or falling contour of the land.

Grab iron: The steel hand rails on the sides, ends, and roofs of rolling stock.

Head-end cars: The cars that are normally coupled to the front of a passenger train, including express refrigerator, express baggage, and mail cars.

Helper: The locomotive that is added to a train to supply extra power that may be needed to surmount a steep grade.

Hostler: Men who service and sometimes move locomotives from one servicing facility to another to prepare the locomotive for the engineer.

Hotbox: A bearing that has become overheated from lack of lubrication.

Interchange: A section of track or several tracks where one railroad connects with another so trains or individual cars can move from one railroad to the next.

Interlocking: A system of mechanical or electrical controls so only one train at a time can move through a junction of two or more tracks like a crossing or yard throat.

Interurban: Prototype railroads and railroad cars that were self-propelled with electrical power pick-up from an overhead wire, catenary, or from a third rail suspended alongside the track. The cars ran from city-to-city as well as inside the city limits and hence the name. (See also trolley and traction.)

Journal: The bearing that supports the load on the end of a railroad car or locomotive axle.

Kingpin: The pivot point for a freight or passenger car truck where it connects to the bolster.

Kitbash: To combine parts from two or more kits to produce a model different from both. Sometimes called cross-kitting, customizing, or converting.

LCL: Less-than-carload lot; freight shipments that are too small to require an entire car.

Main line: The most heavily trafficked routes of the railroad.

Maintenance-of-way: The rolling stock or structures that are directly associated with maintaining the railroad or with repairing and righting wrecked trains.

Narrow gauge: Railroads that were built with their rails spaced closer than the 4-feet 8½-inch standard gauge. Two-foot and three-foot spacings between the rail heads were the most common in this country, particularly in the 1880–1900 period.

Pedlar freight: A freight train that switches cars at most towns along its route from terminal to terminal. Also called a way freight.

Piggyback: The modern railroads' special flatcar service to transport highway trailers. Sometimes called TOFC.

Points: The portions of a turnout that move to change the track's route from the main line to a siding. The point where the rails actually cross is called the "frog" part of the switch.

Prototype: The term used to describe the full-size version that any model is supposed to duplicate.

Pullman: The passenger cars that were owned and operated by the Pullman company, usually sleeping cars, diners, or parlor cars. Sometimes used to describe any sleeping car.

Rail joiner: The pieces of metal that join two lengths of rail together. They slide onto the ends of the rail on a model railroad; they are bolted to the rails on the prototype.

Reefer: The insulated cars, cooled by either ice in bunkers fed through hatches on the roof or, in modern times, by mechanical refrigeration units.

Right of way: The property and the track owned by the railroad.

r-t-r: Abbreviation for ready-to-run that also includes the simple snap-together and glue-together plastic kits. Some of the brands included are: Athearn, Atlas, Bachmann, ConCor, IHC, Life-Like, Mantua, McKean, Model Die Casting, Model Power, Model Rectifier Corp., Pola, Rivarossi, Tyco and Walthers.

Snowshed: The protective buildings that cover the track, usually in mountain areas, so deep snow and drifts won't cover the tracks themselves.

Spot: The switching maneuver whereby a freight or passenger car is moved to the desired position on the track, usually beside some industry's loading platform.

Superelevation: Banking the tracks in a curve so the trains can travel at some designated speed with a minimum of load on the outer wheels and rails and with a minimum of sway.

Switch: Usually used to refer to the portion of the railroad track that allows the trains to change routes, but also used for electrical switches on model railroads, such as D.P.D.T. or S.P.S.T. switches. Track switches are often called "turnouts" to avoid this confusion.

Switch machine: The electrical solenoid-type devices that move the track switch from one route to another to allow remote-controlled operation of trains over diverging trackage.

Switch points: The moving portion of a turnout that changes the route.

Talgo: Model railroad trucks with the couplers mounted to them so the couplers swivel with the trucks to allow operation of longer cars on tighter radius curves. Talgo trucks can, however, cause derailments when pushing or backing a long train.

Tangent: Straight sections of trackage.

Tank engine: A steam locomotive without a tender where the coal or fuel oil is carried in a bunker behind the cab and the water in a tank over the top of the boiler. Often used for switching on the prototype and on model railroads.

Tender: The car just behind most steam locomotives that carries the water, coal, wood, or fuel oil.

Throat: The point where the yard trackage begins to diverge into the multiple tracks for storage and switching.

Timetable: A schedule, usually printed, to tell railroad employees and customers when trains are scheduled to be at certain stations or points on the railroad.

Traction: The term used to describe all pro-

totype locomotives and self-powered cars like trolleys and interurbans that operate by electrical power.

Transistor throttle: An electrical speed control for model railroad layouts that is used in place of the more common wire-bound rheostat to provide infinitely better and smoother slow speed and starting control for locomotives.

Transition curve: A length of track where any curve joins a tangent with gradually diminishing radius to ease the sudden transition of straight-to-curve for smoother operation and to help prevent derailments of extra-length cars that are caused by coupler bind in such areas of trackage. Also called an easement.

Turnout: Where two diverging tracks join; also called a switch.

Trolley: Self-propelled, electric-powered cars that ran almost exclusively in city streets as opposed to the interurbans that ran through the country between cities and towns.

Truck: The sprung frame and four (or more) wheels under each end of most railroad freight and passenger cars.

Turntable: A rotating steel or wooden bridge to turn locomotives or cars and/or to position them to align with the tracks in the engine house or round house.

Vestibule: The enclosed area, usually in both ends of a passenger car, where patrons enter the car from the station platform and where they walk to move from one car to the next.

Way freight: See Pedlar freight.

Wye: A track switch where both diverging routes curve away in opposite directions from the single straight track. Also, the triangular-shaped track (in plan view) where trains can be reversed.

Index